BANKS AND MONEY: INTERNATIONAL AND COMPARATIVE FINANCE IN HISTORY

Banks and Money: International and Comparative Finance in History

Edited by

GEOFFREY JONES

FRANK CASS

First published in 1991 in Great Britain by
FRANK CASS AND COMPANY LIMITED
Gainsborough House, 11 Gainsborough Road,
London E11 1RS

and in the United States of America by
FRANK CASS
c/o International Specialized Book Services, Inc.
5602 N.E. Hassalo Street, Portland,
Oregon 927213–3640

British Library Cataloguing in Publication Data

Banks and money : international and comparative finance in history.
1. Finance, history
I. Jones, Geoffrey *1952–*
332

ISBN 0-7146-3444-1

Library of Congress Cataloging-in-Publication Data

Banks and money : international and comparative finance in history / edited by Geoffrey Jones.
p. cm.
"First appeared in a special issue of Business history, Vol. XXXIII, No. 3 (July 1991)"—T.p. verso.
Includes bibliographical references and index.
ISBN 0-7146-3444-1
1. Banks and banking—History. 2. Banks and banking, International—History. I. Jones, Geoffrey.
HG1569.B36 1991 91-9682
332.1'09—dc20 CIP

This group of studies first appeared in a Special Issue of Business History, Vol. XXXIII, No. 3 (July 1991), [Banks and Money: International and Comparative Finance in History].

Printed in Great Britain by
Antony Rowe Ltd., Chippenham

CONTENTS

ABSTRACTS

Conflicting Views on Fiat Currency: Britain and its North American Colonies in the Eighteenth Century, *by Edwin J. Perkins*

Great Britain and its North American colonies possessed radically different monetary systems in the eighteenth century, particularly in regard to the role of governmental fiat paper. Parliament issued no fiat monies because of the fear of irreversible depreciation. In contrast, colonial legislatures started issuing various forms of paper monies in the 1690s and some persisted through the 1770s. Every colony issued tax anticipation bills. Most colonies also created public loan offices – called land banks by contemporaries – which loaned currency to private individuals, and the interest revenues made substantial contributions to several provincial budgets. Ironically, after the War for Independence, the new US Constitution prohibited fiat issues by the state legislatures, and the nation shifted to a system of chartered institutions issuing banknotes convertible into specie very similar to the system prevailing in Britain.

The Coalescence of a Cluster of Corporate International Banks, 1855–75, *by P.L. Cottrell*

Through reviewing the establishment of British international corporate banks during the mid-nineteenth century, the paper reveals the remarkable, disproportionate role played by a promotional group composed of members and associates of the London private bank Glyn, Mills. However, despite the banking and merchanting backgrounds of this group, the successful creation of these international banks involved the resolution of substantial difficulties, arising from competition for the necessary concessions, problems in composing suitable boards of directors, and both economic and political instability. This is shown through an examination in particular of the founding of the Imperial Ottoman Bank, the London & Brazilian Bank and the Anglo-Italian Bank. Lastly, an analysis of the subscribers to the banks' shares reveals that, more widely, they were largely backed financially by the banking and mercantile milieu of the metropolis, but also with a significant capital involvement of a European cosmopolitan bourgeoisie.

Financial Elites in Three European Centres: London, Paris, Berlin, 1880s–1930s, ***by Youssef Cassis***

Bankers and financiers have rarely been included in the discussions on entrepreneurs, or on the relationship between banking and economic development. This article compares London, Paris and Berlin as financial centres between the 1880s and the 1930s. It then considers the socio-professional position of bankers and financiers in these three centres, and shows that London offered greater opportunities than Berlin for the operations of individual financiers, as well as for the survival of a banking aristocracy, Paris being somewhat in between. On the other hand, German professional bankers were integrated earlier into the financial elite than their English and French counterparts. However, these differences appear to have had a limited impact on the shaping of the banking systems of the three countries.

British Investment Banking and Industrial Decline before the Great War: A Case Study of Capital Outflow to Canadian Industry, ***by Gregory P. Marchildon***

The alleged anti-industrial bias of 'the City' is examined through a case study of a constellation of financial intermediaries that raised investment capital on the London market for Canadian manufacturing industry in the decade preceding the Great War. Reflecting the considerable institutional flexibility of the pre-war British capital market, these 'investment banks' ranged from established merchant banks to issue houses of recent origin as well as a few stockbroking firms and trust companies. All were eager to issue the securities of Canadian manufacturing enterprises despite the substantial risk associated with such business. Moreover, they were willing to take their profit in the common shares of such enterprises rather than cash commissions; although this increased the potential profit for servicing an industrial issue, it also escalated substantially the risk assumed in any single flotation, thus belying the image of British investment banks as tradition-bound and risk-adverse.

'No Arbitrary Discretion': Specialisation in Short-Term Commercial Lending by Banks in Late Nineteenth-Century New England, ***by Naomi Lamoreaux***

In the late nineteenth century banks in New England embraced an increasingly specialised role in the economy, focusing on the provision of short-term loans to commercial borrowers and eschewing long-term relations with industrial enterprises. This drive to specialise resulted from a particular combination of circumstances: a tremendous expansion in the number of banks, and an equally dramatic rise in deposits as a source of lendable funds. The latter development increased the interdependence of the banking system, making each institution vulnerable to runs provoked by the unsound practices of its competitors. The former made it difficult to regulate the lending practices of individual banks. By promoting strict standards for short-term commercial loans, bank reformers sought to increase the ability of directors and stockholders to monitor the decisions of their banks' managers and, at the same time, to limit the damage to the system that unscrupulous bankers could inflict. Similar problems of control arose in the British banking system in the last few decades of the century, and may explain the simultaneous shift toward short-term commercial loans that occurred in that nation. By contrast, large German banks were able to limit the independence of their smaller competitors and hence the threat to the security of the banking system that they posed.

Long-Term Contracts in the Swedish Bank-Orientated Financial System during the Inter-War Period, *by Hans Sjögren*

The fact that Sweden had the highest growth rate of per capita GNP of any European country between 1870 and 1914 has very often been explained by the existence of a well functioning financial system, with commercial banks as efficient prime movers. In this essay various characteristic features are presented to shed some light on the financial system during the next period in Swedish economic history – the turbulent inter-war period. Financial systems in capitalist countries can be classified either as market-orientated or bank-orientated. In a bank-orientated system the banks take more responsibility for corporate financing than in a market-orientated one. Therefore, bank–industry relations, especially credit and owner connections, are much longer and more concentrated than in the latter. It is also significant for a bank-orientated system that banks in times of distress increase both the credit granted and their shareholding. This was certainly the case of Sweden. Another 'analytical tool' for the characterisation of the Swedish bank–industry relations is the contracting approach. In institutional theory a company's relations to other actors and institutions within a certain financial system are viewed as a set of various contracts. The credit and ownership contracts are two examples. The aim of complementing the broad financial story of Sweden with various case studies on a micro-level is to illustrate how these contracts were developed in a small economy like Sweden. From this part of the study we attain a much deeper understanding of these important, long-term relations.

Banks, Institutional Constraints and the Limits of Central Banking: Monetary Policy in Britain and West Germany, 1950–52, ***by Till Geiger and Duncan M. Ross***

This paper analyses the anti-inflationary policies which were pursued in Britain and West Germany during the Korean War boom. It argues that the institutional relationships between the government, the central bank and the banking system can have considerable impact on the implementation of policy. The war brought a major shift in raw material prices and a consequent rise in bank lending in both countries to finance the increased import bill. The German independent central bank (BdL) used technical measures to restrain short-term lending, but was frustrated by the willingness of the *Landeszentralbanken* (regional central banks) to discount the bills of their local banking system. In addition, the banks themselves, because they operated in a competitive system, sought ways to circumvent the restrictions. The BdL took steps to tighten these loopholes and introduce a much stronger and more well defined policy transmission mechanism. Shifts in the terms of trade reduced inflationary pressure but the BdL retained tighter control over the banking system.

In Britain, the Bank of England was nominally controlled by the government, although it was able to exercise a degree of independence. Both parties had clear ideas of how inflationary pressure could be controlled in the economy; but these ideas differed significantly and neither one was able to impose their preferred option on the other. The result was a mixture of quantitative restrictions on the banks' balance sheets and qualitative guidelines to the banking system on the nature and extent of lending. The shift in raw material prices in 1952 largely solved the problem which it had created in 1951. The authorities, however, felt that their policies had been successful in constraining inflation and they failed to improve the monetary policy transmission mechanism as the Germans had done.

The British Overseas Banks and Development Finance in Africa after 1945, ***by Frances Bostock***

The role of the British overseas banks in the provision of medium- and long-term finance in British colonial Africa is examined, with special reference to the establishment of the bank development corporations after the Second World War. The origins of the banks' involvement in development financing are traced, and in particular those of the Barclays Overseas Development Corporation, the first in the field. It is argued that, although their performance was modest, at least it was not as disastrous as the initial performance of the public sector Colonial

Development Corporation. The three bank development corporations, and the medium- and long-term lending undertaken by the fourth British bank operating in British colonial Africa, filled a necessary gap in the financial structure of these territories at a time when the British banks were often the only commercial banks in existence.

The House of Morgan Redivivus? The Abortive Morgan International, 1972–73, ***by Kathleen Burk***

The House of Morgan, the most powerful international banking house in the first decades of the twentieth century, had been forced to split up into constituent parts by the American Banking Act of 1933. In the 1960s and 1970s, in response to the growth of international business opportunities, Morgan Guaranty, Morgan Stanley and Morgan Grenfell made several attempts to work together. The most significant of these attempts took place in 1972–73, with negotiations over the establishing of a 'Morgan International', in effect the merging of their non-domestic business. But conflicts of interest, nationalism, cultural incompatibility, and the opposition of the Bank of England doomed the attempt, and the three banks continued on their separate ways.

Introduction

GEOFFREY JONES
University of Reading

Banking and financial history has always been a subject for the devoted few. There are a number of reasons for this comparative lack of interest. Financial archives are often harder to access than those of manufacturing industry. Some issues in banking and financial history call for special technical expertise which is time-consuming to acquire. Moreover, it is hard to escape the feeling that banking history is often regarded as rather a dull subject; a bore to read, let alone research. One negative consequence of comparative neglect has been a tendency for stereotypes and over-generalisations to linger longer than in other parts of business history. The oft-repeated argument that British banks and the City of London have 'failed' British industry over the last hundred years, especially compared to the situation in Germany, is one striking example.

In a subject where quality literature can be scarce, the essays in this collection represent a mine of new data and insights. They are based for the most part on extensive archival research but, more importantly, they demonstrate new ways of looking at old topics, especially by placing them in an international and comparative context. No global re-interpretation of banking and financial history emerges from these pages, for the topics and time periods discussed are wide-ranging, but it is hoped that the originality and freshness of the essays will at least encourage a wider interest in this area of business history.

The essays fall into two distinct but related groups. The majority is concerned with financial systems; a smaller group focus more sharply on international banking. The essay by Perkins begins the first category. Perkins compares the different monetary systems in operation in eighteenth-century Britain and her North American colonies. While the British opposed fiat money because of the threat of currency depreciation, the colonial administrations took a more sympathetic view and the issue of fiat currency became widespread. The disagreements between British and American policy-makers were not confined to discussions about abstract theory, but became one of the major tensions which eventually caused the American revolution. Perkins' comparative study is an original contribution to a subject where the literature has been particularly sparse.

Marchildon, Lamoreaux and Cassis take the discussion of financial systems into the late nineteenth century and beyond. Marchildon is concerned with the vexed question of the alleged anti-industrial bias of the City of London. He argues that, contrary to the conservative and risk-averse image of the British financial system before 1914 suggested by W.P. Kennedy and others,[1] the financial intermediaries active in the City showed considerable flexibility and entrepreneurial ability. The two leading merchant banks, Barings and Rothschilds, may have had an anti-industry bias, but less prominent British institutions were willing to channel long-term capital into Canadian manufacturing industry, sometimes taking part of the equity of Canadian enterprises. If there was a problem in the relationship between banks and industry in pre-1914 Britain, Marchildon argues, it was in the area of demand for, rather than the supply of, capital. British industrial companies were less optimistic about their future earnings potential than their Canadian or American counterparts. As a result, they preferred to rely on capital plough-back and short-term bank finance rather than distribute shares to financiers. This policy reduced the attractiveness of domestic British industrial issues to British investment banks. Marchildon's article represents a substantial re-inforcement to those scholars who have argued that demand rather than supply factors explain any lack of involvement by British financial institutions in domestic industry.[2] The issues are complex, but the Marchildon view of the pre-1914 City as a cluster of innovative and flexible business institutions carries conviction, and is supported by other more recent research.[3]

Lamoreaux provides another transatlantic insight on a traditional area of criticism of the British financial system: the short-term lending policies of British banks. The focus of her article is the shift towards short-term lending to commercial borrowers and the trend away from the long-term relations with industrial enterprises which became pronounced in late nineteenth-century New England banking. Lamoreaux offers a new interpretation. A growth in the number of banks and a rise in deposits increased the interdependence of the banking system and made each institution vulnerable to runs provoked by imprudent policies pursued by competitors. The pressure for short-term loans came from bank reformers trying to increase the ability of bank boards to control the lending decisions of their managers, and so prevent imprudent banking. There are, Lamoreaux speculates, important comparative lessons in the New England story for British and German banking. In Britain an expansion in the number of banks in the second half of the nineteenth century also caused instability, and the observed shift into short-term lending in this period may have been a response, designed to restore prudential standards. In contrast, the more concentrated German banking system felt little pressure to focus on short-term lending to prevent dangerous behaviour by individual institutions.

The focus of Cassis' contribution to this collection is the bankers and financiers themselves. During the last decade Cassis has written a series of studies on the financial elites of Britain, and more recently, Switzerland.[4] In this new study he offers a comparative analysis of the financial elites of three European financial centres – London, Paris and Berlin – between the 1880s and the 1930s. Cassis begins by rehearsing the differences and similarities between these centres. The City of London is cast, as in the Marchildon article, as a particularly flexible centre before 1914, especially in its openness to initiatives by entrepreneurial firms. There were both similarities and differences between the financial elites active in the three cities. Surprisingly, Cassis suggests that the directors of British banks had a higher level of formal education than their German counterparts before 1914, although differences in the organisational structure of British and German banks make exact comparisons difficult. The financial elites in all three countries led a privileged life with close links to their respective political and administrative elites. However the British banking elite had made most progress in being integrated into the aristocracy. In France, bankers laboured under a popular suspicion of their caste and industrialists had more prestige than in England, while in Germany industry carried even more prestige. The fact that Berlin bankers were often Jews was a major obstacle to their integration into the ruling elite.

Swedish economic history since the late nineteenth century is to some extent a mirror image of that of the United Kingdom. Over this period Britain experienced a relative economic decline which, by 1991, had both reduced living standards to below the western European average, and kept an anguished army of historians occupied in seaching for the cause of her national malaise. Sweden, in contrast, experienced long-term economic growth rates above the European average which produced high living standards and a competitive (if far from perfect) economy. While the British 'decline literature' has often focused on that country's dismal educational tradition and the alleged inadequacies of the financial system,[5] Swedish success has often been attributed to a 'universally high level of education',[6] and a financial system which actively promoted industrial development.

Such a picture can fall into the trap of facile over-simplifications, to which Hans Sjögren's essay on the Swedish financial system provides a valuable antidote. Sweden had evolved by the inter-war years a 'bank-orientated' financial system rather than the 'market-orientated' one characteristic of Anglo-Saxon economies, but – Sjögren shows – a proper understanding of bank–industry relations has to reach beyond such general descriptions. Sjögren's uses modern institutional theory to take the analysis of the Swedish situation further. In a bank-orientated system, banks and borrowers make long-term credit contracts which are reinforced by ownership contracts as the bank seek to monitor the behaviour of their customers. In the 1920s Swedish banks, like their British equivalents, found themselves with large loans to companies which could not be repaid. Unlike the British banks operating within a market-orientated system, the Swedish banks placed directors on corporate boards and used their power to enforce desired industrial strategies. In Sweden many contracts were informal or 'gentlemen's agreements', a phenomenon which probably stems at least in part from the high trust levels and 'groupism' observable in Swedish culture.[7]

The final essay on financial systems, by Geiger and Ross, examines how the implementation of monetary policy can be substantially affected by the institutional relationships existing between a government, its central bank and the banking system. Their evidence comes from Britain and the Federal Republic of Germany in the early 1950s. Both countries encountered inflationary problems during the Korean War boom, and both systems found themselves lacking the ideal institutional framework to deal with the situation. The Americans had imposed an independent central banking system on Germany, but the federal central bank had to share its powers with state central banks, and this system and the highly competitive banking structure complicated the monetary policy transmission mechanism. The German federal central bank eventually responded to the problem by introducing measures to enhance its control over policy implementation. In Britain monetary policy was uncomfortably divided between the government and the Bank of England, which retained substantial independence despite nationalisation in 1946. The upshot was serious difficulties in enforcing effective monetary policies. B.W.E. Alford has recently characterised the Bank of England and the British Treasury after 1945 'as the two Ugly Sisters who through their actions succeeded in making the British economy the Cinderella of the industrialised world'.[8] Geiger and Ross, by demonstrating the inability of the 'Sisters' even to agree on a single policy, add a new dimension to such a view.

The articles by Marchildon and Cassis stress the flexibility of dynamism of the nineteenth-century City of London. An illustration of that vigour was that it became the base for a large number of multinational and international banks. Before 1914 Britain was the world's leading multinational banker, with around 30 British banks operating nearly 1,300 overseas branches. No other country could match the size and depth of

British multinational banking. American banks, for example, operated only a handful of foreign branches before 1914.[9] The three remaining articles in this volume discuss aspects of the international banking activity centred on London.

Cottrell examines the nineteenth-century origins of British multinational banking. A distinguishing feature of the British overseas banks of this period was their separation from domestic banks. In other countries domestic banks established foreign branches or affiliates, but in Britain the overseas banks were 'free-standing' corporate entities with no equity links with domestic banks, and no domestic business themselves. Cottrell shows, however, that this general picture needs some qualification. The London private bank of Glyn Mills promoted and, sometimes, provided senior management for a cluster of British overseas banks active in Europe, Latin America and elsewhere, suggesting that there were greater links between domestic and overseas banks than has been supposed. Further research is necessary to ascertain whether the family of overseas banks promoted by the Glyns functioned as any kind of real group, or simply went its diverse ways. The last history of Glyns was published in 1953,[10] and a new study of that enterpreneurial bank is badly needed.

Some of the British overseas banks founded in the nineteenth century continued, in one form or another, in existence throughout the twentieth century and into the 1990s. Standard Chartered, the Hongkong & Shanghai Banking Corporation and ANZ (domiciled in Australia since 1976) all trace their origins back to nineteenth-century British overseas banks. Other parts of the British overseas banking empire found homes within the Barclays and Lloyds banking groups. During the twentieth century, the British multinational banks faced enormous changes to their environment, as the international use of sterling declined, the British Empire was replaced by independent nation states, and as many countries developed and supported their own banking institutions. Recent research by business historians has focussed on the organisational and strategic flexibility of these British banks in the face of their rapidly changing environment. Bostock's article is a contribution to this literature.

Bostock is concerned with the role of the British overseas banks in the provision of medium-and long-term finance in British colonial Africa after the Second World War. Traditionally the British banks active in these regions had concentrated on short-term commercial lending, investing part of local deposits in the London money market. They also largely restricted their customer base to expatriate Europeans and Asians, on the grounds that lending to indigenous Africans was too risky. During and after the war the banks came under pressure to assist the economic development of these territories, while the inevitability, sooner or later, of their independence stimulated a new interest in lending to Africans. Bostock shows that there was a significant response by the British banks, three of which created new specialist subsidiaries to offer medium-term finance, while a fourth undertook such lending directly. In retrospect the new strategies of the banks appear less than radical but, she argues, at least their lending was more competent than that of the public sector agency established by the British government to promote colonial development, and at a crucial period they filled a perceived gap in the financial structures of the territories in which they operated.

The final article, by Burk, examines an abortive attempt in the early 1970s to reassemble a single Morgan international bank out of the three independent British and American institutions into which the old House of Morgan had divided. At a time of fast change and expanding opportunities in international finance, there appeared much to gain from an alliance between Morgan Grenfell, Morgan Guaranty and Morgan Stanley. Unfortunately, the Bank of England liked neither change in the City nor the sight of a British bank falling under the control of Americans. Differences in corporate and national culture provided further obstacles to the merger proposals, which finally ran aground at a honeymooners' hotel in Bermuda. As Burk concludes, Morgan Grenfell, fuelled by optimism about London's resurgence as an international financial centre, 'did not want to be run by Americans'. Ironically Morgan Grenfell fell into the hands of the Deutsche Bank just 15 years later, having been weakened in the era of scandal and corruption which marred parts of British corporate life in the late Thatcher era.

If national differences helped wreck the Morgan merger proposals, it is hoped that at least this collection of essays has demonstrated that they can have a positive role in stimulating new ideas and research agendas in banking and financial history. This volume is one of a number of new comparative studies in this area,[11] which will help to deepen and enrich our understanding of one of the most under-researched parts of our business past.

NOTES

1. W.P. Kennedy, *Industrial Structure, Capital Markets and the Origins of British Economic Decline* (Cambridge, 1987).
2. M. Collins, *Banks and Industrial Finance in Britain, 1800–1939* (1991), Ch. 4.
3. See the series of important contributions by R.C. Michie, including *The London and New York Stock Exchanges, 1850–1914* (1981); idem, 'Options, Concessions, Syndicates, and the Provision of Venture Capital, 1880–1913', *Business History*, Vol. XXIII No. 2 (July 1981), pp. 147–64; idem, 'Different in Name Only? The London Stock

Exchange and Foreign Bourses, 1850–1914', in R.P.T. Davenport-Hines and G. Jones (eds.), *The End of Insularity* (1988). For a positive view of the City from another perspective, see C. Harvey and J. Press, 'The City and International Mining, 1870–1914', in C. Harvey and J. Press (eds.), *International Competition and Industrial Change* (1990).

4. Y. Cassis, *Les Banquiers de la City à l'époque Edouardienne* (Geneva, 1984); idem, 'Bankers in English Society in the Late Nineteenth Century', *Economic History Review*, 2nd series, Vol. XXXVIII, No. 2 (May 1985), pp. 210–29; idem and F. Debrunner, 'Les Élites Bancaires Suisses, 1880–1960', *Revenue Suisse d'Histoire*, Vol. XXXX (1990), pp. 259–73.
5. The British 'decline' literature is too numerous to list, but recent specimens include M.W. Kirby, *The Decline of British Economic Power since 1870* (1981); S. Pollard, *The Wasting of the British Economy* (Beckenham, 1982); B. Elbaum and W. Lazonick (eds.), *The Decline of the British Economy* (Oxford, 1986); S. Newton and D. Porter, *Modernisation Frustrated* (1988); G. Jones and M.W. Kirby (eds.) *Competitiveness and the State: Government and Business in Twentieth Century Britain* (Manchester, 1991).
6. M.E. Porter, *The Competitive Advantage of Nations* (1990).
7. Ibid., pp. 348–9.
8. B.W.E. Alford, *British Economic Performance, 1945–1975* (1988), p. 86.
9. G. Jones, 'Competitive Advantages in British Multinational Banking Since 1890', in G. Jones (ed.), *Banks as Multinationals* (1990).
10. R. Fulford, *Glyn's, 1753–1953* (1953).
11. See for example Y. Cassis (ed.), *Finance and Financiers in European History, 1880–1960* (Cambridge, 1991) and H. James, H. Lingren and A. Teichova (eds.), *The Role of Banks in Interwar Europe* (Cambridge, 1991).

Conflicting Views on Fiat Currency: Britain and its North American Colonies in the Eighteenth Century

EDWIN J. PERKINS
University of Southern California

Political and business attitudes concerning the inclusion of fiat currency in the money stock differed tremendously between England and Great Britain's North American colonies in the eighteenth century. All 13 American colonies, at one time or another, embraced the emission of fiat paper as a supplement to the circulating coinage, whereas Parliament vehemently disavowed any possibility of its issuance in England and generally discouraged its usage anywhere within the British Empire. As the years passed, frequent disagreements over the management of monetary affairs within the Empire soured relations between colonies and crown. From Parliament's passage of the Current Act of 1764 until its modification in 1773, the controversy over the emission of fiat currency was, after taxation, the second most divisive issue in imperial relations, and it ranks high among the underlying causes for the American rebellion in the mid-1770s. This article examines how these transatlantic differences in theory and practice arose, and why they persisted for so long.[1]

I

England

By the eighteenth century, most political and business leaders in England held diametrically opposed opinions regarding the legitimacy of the two main forms of paper money. As a rule, they voiced few objections to emissions of paper monies by chartered banks and most private firms whenever these issuers stood ready to convert currency into coin or bullion upon demand by drawing upon their accumulated reserves. Convertible paper money was recognized both as a convenient medium of exchange and also, since it rarely depreciated, as a relatively safe means of holding wealth. At the same time, British leaders generally opposed emissions of fiat currencies by governmental bodies, including

Parliament itself, because history had shown, or at least the European history with which they were generally familiar had revealed very clearly, that fiat monies invariably depreciated and caused havoc within a national economy. Members of parliamentary committees with responsibility for colonial affairs drew upon their wisdom and experience to steer political subunits away from the potential dangers of fiat currencies. In North America, however, they met persistent opposition from local leaders who cited consistently favourable results with unconvertible governmental issues.

To round out the argument before proceeding to more controversial matters, we should discuss briefly the form of paper money to which few critics in Britain raised substantial objections, namely currencies and banknotes issued by chartered banks and private firms. The origins of circulating private monies can be traced mainly to the functions of goldsmiths. They issued warehouse receipts to depositors of specie, and these receipts evolved into negotiable instruments which circulated as money, starting in the seventeenth century. At first goldsmiths held one hundred per cent reserves, but over the years they discovered that holding only fractional reserves against their note issue was reasonably prudent. Later several mercantile houses also entered the financial services market, providing banking and other more sophisticated financial services for their regular customers. Firms engaged in banking made loans both through deposit creation and the issuance of non-legal tender promissory notes convertible into coin at their premises.

In 1694, as is well known, Parliament granted a limited-liability charter to the Bank of England. During the next six decades, three public banks in Scotland likewise received limited-liability charters.[2] These chartered institutions issued currencies supported by specie reserves. The Bank of England emitted currency only in large denominations so that few of its bills circulated among the general population, but the Scottish banks printed currency in small denominations – £1 and even lower – and paper money eventually replaced much of the circulating coinage in Scotland. In both England and Scotland, the paper monies of the chartered banks were convertible into specie upon demand, and despite the limited liability clauses in their charters, the public had faith in their solvency and viability.[3]

Non-chartered private bankers in England and Scotland operated without the protection of limited liability. If specie reserves proved inadequate or loans went sour, currency holders were free to proceed through the courts against the business and personal assets of issuers. The unlimited liability of currency issuers gave the appearance of safety which led most public figures to adopt a tolerant attitude toward the operations of private bankers, including many firms operating on a small scale. In connection with negotiations over an extension of the charter for the Bank of England in 1708, however, the new regulations stipulated that no unchartered business firm with more than six partners was permitted to issue currency anywhere within the empire, thereby excluding large joint-stock enterprises from entering this financial activity.

D.M. Joslin estimated that the number of private bankers in London, which stook at 24 in 1725, had risen to 51 by 1776.[4] Private banks typically held greater deposit than currency liabilities, and specie reserves were normally more than adequate to permit continuous conversion. Only five bankruptcies among London's private bankers occurred between 1745 and 1771, and there is no indication that the holders of private monies by these five firms ever suffered any serious losses. Until the credit crisis of 1772, which came late in the North American colonial era, few Scottish banks had failed.[5] The outstanding record of private bankers in supporting the value of their currency issues led policy-makers in Great Britain to look favourably on paper money supported by specie reserves in the first six decades of the eighteenth century.

On the other hand, English political leaders were nearly unanimous in their opposition to the emission of inconvertible fiat currencies by governmental bodies. Their views reflected prevailing monetary theories and were buttressed by historical precedent. The prime objection to fiat monies was the danger of a steady and irreversible depreciation, which could arise because of over-issue and inadequate backing. The irregular discoveries of gold and silver set reasonably finite limits on monetary stocks consisting of coins minted from precious metals as well as currency issues supported by adequate reserves of specie, whereas huge volumes of fiat paper in denominations, large and small, could be printed by irresponsible governments within days. Without effective controls, the temptation to resort to the printing press to acquire spending power, rather than through the mechanism of taxation or public borrowing, was viewed as simply too great for any government to resist once the barrier had been breached. Over-issue led invariably to depreciation, which cheated lenders, unduly rewarded borrowers, and left a nation's financial system in disarray.

Moreover, recent experiences in Europe supported what prevailing theories about fiat monies had predicted. The only sustained government experiment in the issuance of non-metallic monies by the English crown in the seventeenth century had ended disastrously. Starting in 1667, during the reign of Charles II, the Exchequer began emitting what soon became negotiable orders; large denomination orders were issued to persons making specie loans, while amounts as low as £1 to £5 went to purchase routine supplies. These so-called Exchequer Orders were tax anticipation notes, meaning that as taxes were subsequently collected, the outstanding orders were scheduled for redemption in the exact sequence as originally issued. The orders carried an interest rate component and thus increased in redemption value over time. Since the orders were easily transferable, they became a convenient medium of exchange – in other words, paper money.[6]

Exchequer Orders held their value relative to coin for several years. The initial series were redeemed according to plan, and the holders of orders still in circulation remained confident about their ultimate redemption in specie. But the crown was pressed for additional financing to support military spending. As a convenient alternative to raising taxes, more paper was issued, and the redemptions of prior orders began to run behind schedule. Once public doubts had arisen, the paper began passing at discounts *visàvis* specie. In 1672, only five years after the inauguration of the programme, the Exchequer suddenly stopped payment on most of its interestbearing orders. Estimates of the aggregate sums outstanding range from £1.3 to £2.25 million. Most of the suspended orders were held by persons of substantial wealth who presumably held them as an investment vehicle; two goldsmiths alone accounted for approximately 60 per cent of the total. How many orders actually circulated as part of the money supply is unknown, but this failed experiment with a variation of fiat currency had a powerful influence on the attitudes of later generations.

The lessons learned under Charles II confirmed the suspicions of critics about the dangers of experiments with fiat monies. Without any means of converting the Exchequer Orders into specie at face value upon demand, holders were completely dependent on the resolve of the crown to collect sufficient taxes in the future, and, second, to use those revenues to redeem debt obligations on schedule. The stoppage of payments in 1672 was proof enough of the inherent dangers for the vast majority in Parliament; thereafter members were adamantly opposed to any scheme designed to permit the emission of any financial instrument which might function as fiat paper. Despite a shortage of silver coins of intermediate values to promote the convenient exchange of goods and services in eighteenthcentury England, Parliament held to a strictly metallic standard.

The prejudices against paper money were reinforced by the financial scandal in France linked to the infamous Scotsman, John Law. After gaining the confidence of the regent for Louis XV, Law was permitted to open a chartered bank in 1716 to aid the government in financing its outstanding debt. He eventually issued an enormous volume of paper notes supposedly backed in full by specie resting in the bank's vaults; but, in truth, the vaults were virtually empty. The whole scheme finally collapsed in 1720, disrupting temporarily the French financial system and its national economy.[7]

Because of the fiascos in England in 1672 and France in 1720, objections in Parliament were so great that members never gave serious consideration to any proposal for the emission of any form of fiat currency in the home economy or any British dominion. Ample reservations existed about the propriety and practicality of the unproven system of fiat currency. Some persons held very strong views – arguing that all paper money, including convertible notes as well as fiat paper, was an evil concept which contradicted every established principle of nature, the will of God, or higher authority in general. Morality and economics were frequently intermixed in discussion of monetary affairs in general, and with reference to fiat paper in particular. When paper money in small to intermediate dominations finally entered the English economy, it was issued strictly by private banks, not Parliament. Indeed, paper money was not commonly held by the English public until very late in the eighteenth century, many decades after its widespread acceptance as a convenient medium of exchange in several North American colonies and Scotland.

II

North American Colonies

Public attitudes toward the issuance of fiat monies by governmental units were radically different in the 13 colonies than in England. In North America, pragmatism and a fair degree of selfrestraint triumphed over theoretical abstractions and moralistic pronouncements in most colonies. Based on their own experiences, the colonists in over half the North American provinces concluded that fiat currency, when properly backed either by public taxation or private mortgages, provided a useful supplement to the money stock. It augmented, but never permanently displaced, the foreign coins, mainly Spanish in origin, which circulated among the population. All 13 colonies experimented with some form of fiat currency. Despite instances of heavy depreciation in five colonies, all of which occurred during the first half of the eighteenth century, nine legislatures continued to emit paper money until the outbreak of the American rebellion in the 1770s. Moreover, seven state legislatures remained active in monetary affairs in the 1780s – until ratification of the Constitution outlawed new issues of fiat monies by state governments in the US federal system.[8]

The conflicts surrounding fiat currency in the colonial era pitted the Board of Trade in London, which claimed the authority to disallow any local acts that violated English law or its interpretation of parliamentary intent, against separate and distinct provincial legislatures.[9] After the Exchequer's stoppage in 1672, the membership of the Board of Trade reflected the strong reservations of parliamentary leaders about the propriety of fiat monies at home and abroad. In later years, board members were pressured to uphold their convictions by British mercantile creditors who were becoming increasingly fearful about the exchange risks associated with debt collections in colonies where fiat monies had legal tender status. Accordingly, Parliament passed two acts, one in 1751 and a second in 1764, which limited the powers of colonial legislatures to issue fresh emissions of currency. The latter act, and the board's efforts to enforce it, sparked off heated political opposition in North America. Beyond New England, colonial leaders viewed the legitimacy of fiat money in an entirely different light, and they increasingly resented the interference of English officials in this sphere of their domestic affairs.

The initial emission of fiat currency, typically called 'bills of credit' in this era, came in Massachusetts in 1690. The treasury was short of funds to cover the salaries of soldiers returning from a military campaign, and the legislature resorted to the printing press as an expedient. Over the next few years, these paper monies were retired on schedule through tax collections. The success of the first paper money scheme encouraged the Massachusetts legislature to repeat the experiment again and again over the next half century, and other colonies soon became imitators. When Virginia joined the ranks in 1755, every colony had become involved in the process of issuing and redeeming fiat currency. Whenever any of the provincial legislatures authorised fresh currency emission, it usually specified the future redemption date, ranging from two to 20 years depending upon a host of considerations. Currency issues were retired either in stages or all at once in the maturation year.

Colonial currency was invariably designated as legal tender in the payment of provincial taxes and sometimes in the settlement of private debts. There was little uniformity regarding the terms and conditions of consecutive issues even within a single colony; some included an interest rate component, others had none. Currency was issued in a range of denominations, from large bills like £20 colonial down to amounts as low as one shilling in four colonies.[10] Over half the bills in circulation were for amounts less than ten shillings, which made them widely accessible and convenient for routine purchases of everyday items. (In this respect, the colonies mirrored Scotland where banknotes in small denominations circulated widely as well.) The currency issued in one colony frequently spilled over the borders into neighbouring colonies, where it was accepted on a voluntary basis and valued at prevailing exchange rates. For example, a merchant active in the city of New York, in addition to possessing quantities of Spanish, Portuguese, Dutch, and English coins, might also hold in his cash box the currencies of New York, Pennsylvania, and New Jersey.

Colonial currency fell into two broad categories. What distinguished the two were differing backing techniques, meaning the mechanisms by which they supposedly were to maintain their face value relative to coin, bullion, and foreign exchange. In one category were essentially tax anticipation notes like those first issued in Massachusetts in 1690. The provincial legislatures issued currency with the explicit proviso that outstanding sums would be fully retired from proceeds of future tax collections. Some emissions stipulated the payment of interest. (The interest-bearing bills of credit were similar in character to the Exchequer Orders issued in the reign of Charles II.) A final extinction date ranging from two to 20 years was established for each authorised series. When legislatures acted responsibly by moderating the volume of paper in circulation and diligently followed the redemption schedules, the value of their currencies remained fairly stable for decades – with Connecticut the sole exception because of unusual circumstances.[11] New York, Pennsylvania, New Jersey, Maryland and Virginia all had excellent records of paper money price stability.

The first Massachusetts issue had been prompted by a financial emergency, but colonial legislatures in subsequent decades discovered new reasons for emitting fiat paper. An emergency or minor fiscal crisis was not a prerequisite for legislative action after 1710. Some issues were authorised simply to provide the population with monies in small, convenient denominations – for example, in Maryland in the 1730s – or because voters decided to delay the imposition and collection of taxes for a few additional years. In Pennsylvannia in the 1720s, the legislature, in a move foreshadowing the techniques of Keynesian deficit spending, voted to emit fiat currency in an effort to stimulate local demand and reverse an economic downturn.[12] The local economy, in fact, revived soon thereafter, and legislative supporters of the currency emission claimed at least partial credit for the favourable outcome. The need to finance military adventures, mainly against Indian tribes on the frontier or French forces in Canada, continued to be cited as the prime justification for the authorisation of new emissions of fiat currency in most colonies. Nonetheless, in regions where fiat currency was still legally permissible after mid-century, it remained a vital component of the money stock irrespective of prevailing military or political considerations.

The American experience with fiat paper was less than perfect, however, and during the first half of the century some currencies lost purchasing power and steadily depreciated. Several colonies became increasingly lax about retiring outstanding currency. Previous emissions were simply rolled over and kept in circulation because citizens instructed their representatives not to vote the required taxes. In these instances the value of paper money depreciated sharply and irreversibly in relation to coins and financial instruments denominated in sound foreign monies – such as sterling bills of exchange.

The main offenders were the New England colonies – Massachusetts, Connecticut, New Hampshire and Rhode Island – from 1730 to 1750 plus the Carolinas (North and South were then a united province) from 1710 to 1725. Their performances paralleled what sceptics in England had predicted about the likely outcome of risky experiments involving fiat currencies. Parliamentary restrictions were therefore imposed. South Carolina was allowed to maintain indefinitely the volume of paper circulating as of 1731, but it was not permitted to add any new monies – except temporary emissions during wartime emergencies. With passage of the Currency Act 1751, Parliament likewise outlawed any new emissions of fiat monies in New England; currency issues already outstanding were permitted to circulate until their scheduled maturity dates, however.[13] To facilitate a speedy transition from paper to hard money, Parliament paid a substantial subsidy – mostly in Spanish coin – to reimburse the colonies for expenses incurred in recent military campaigns against the French in Canada. To permit some flexibility in managing periodic budget deficits, the New England colonies were allowed to issue treasury notes paying up to the legal interest rate and maturing in two years or less. The vast majority of these notes were held as short-term investments and did not circulate as currency, according to Leslie Brock, the most dedicated scholar of colonial monetary systems.[14] After mid-century the four New England colonies reverted to monetary systems based primarily on coinage until the rebellion. Meanwhile, the other nine colonies in the middle and southern regions retained the privilege of maintaining fiat currency as a component of their money stock, although every new legislative act was routinely subject to review by the Board of Trade and Privy Council in London and possible disallowance.[15]

In the second monetary category was currency issued through the auspices of governmental loan offices, which functioned as agencies of the provincial legislatures. These offices were usually called land banks by contemporaries, but the name was an unfortunate misnomer according to modern standards because they neither accepted deposits nor performed a range of financial services. Instead, these governmental agencies granted mortgage loans to citizens with sufficient equity in real properties.[16] In making these loans, they issued freshly printed currency which was often indistinguishable in design from tax anticipation notes – the alternative form of fiat currency described above. In authorising a new emission of currency, legislatures frequently allocated a certain sum to meet the recurring expenditures of government and a complementary amount for issuance through the loan office. In most colonies both forms of fiat currency circulated in tandem throughout the provincial economy.

Colonial borrowers were typically eligible to borrow amounts ranging up to one-half of the market value of land and one-third of the market value of residences. The latter provision allowed some artisans to obtain loans, although the vast majority of borrowers were yeoman farmers and owners of large agricultural estates. No restrictions were placed on the use of borrowed funds; most borrowers used the proceeds to invest in other productive assets, but they were free to spend the money on high living and luxury goods as well.

To guarantee wide access to credit facilities, the legislatures placed limits on how much money an individual could borrow from the loan office. In New York, for example, the minimum loan was £25 colonial up to maximum of £100 colonial. Most colonies had similar programmes designed to prevent a few wealthy persons from depleting the pool of loanable funds. Loan terms typically ran from eight to 12 years for initial borrowers, with amortisation schedules stipulating annual installments of interest and principal. The currency collected to cover the repayment of principal was either retired from circulation or reloaned to other eligible borrowers.[17]

This mechanism of issuance was highly conducive to the prevention of monetary depreciation, since in the absence of a collapse in real estate values, which never happened in the colonies on a grand scale, the currency was amply secured by private mortgages. Meanwhile, the currency was in steady demand because borrowers were required to make annual payments consisting of accrued interest plus a fraction of the principal to the loan office. The responsibility for repayment of the loans, and thereby the retirement of outstanding currency, rested on the shoulders of private parties, not on the will of the elected legislators to approve the collection of new taxes. If a debtor failed to repay an outstanding mortgage, the loan office foreclosed, sold the property, and used the proceeds to sink the paper money. Defaults were low and losses rare – with the exception of the operations of loan offices in South Carolina and Rhode Island prior to 1750, where hundreds of borrowers conspired to evade repayment. Elsewhere, however, this form of asset-backed currency generally had an outstanding record in terms of maintaining its value relative to specie and other sterling substitutes.

In addition to injecting a reliable currency into the overall money stock, these mortgage loans generated a steady stream of interest income for provincial governments. Interest rates varied among the 13 colonies, climbing as high as 12.5 per cent in the Carolinas early in the eighteenth century. In the middle colonies, government loans carried interest rates from 5 to 6 per cent, which were extremely low rates for a region chronically short of long term capital. In Connecticut the rates fell to as low as 3 per cent in 1740.[18] The low rates on public funds reflected, in part, religious concerns about usury; in most colonies the legal maximum on private loans, irrespective of the length of maturity dates, was restricted to 5 to 8 per cent. The legislatures welcomed these interest revenues as a supplement to tax collections. In several colonies – including New Jersey, Pennsylvania, and New York – interest revenues from loan offices covered nearly all provincial expenditures in some years. As a result, the tax burden imposed on the general population by their legislatures was slight, or even zero, in certain provinces for years.[19]

III

Private Monetary Initiatives

Although the 13 colonial legislatures were far and away the overwhelming issuers of currency, in order to lay claim to a reasonable degree of comprehensive coverage, we should also mention a few abortive initiatives by private parties. None of these private monetary experiments were sustained. Indeed, one of the most lingering and perplexing mysteries relating to colonial financial history, generally speaking, is why no individual issuers – or partnerships with up to six members, as permitted by British statute law dating back to 1708 – ever developed a long-term commitment to the issuance of monies convertible into coinage upon demand?[20] Why did no American counterparts of English private issuers arise in the leading American port cities – Philadelphia, New York, Boston, Newport, and Charleston? In London, not only did firms which had evolved from goldsmiths engage in this activity but sundry mercantile firms sometimes participated in private currency issuance as a sideline – a profitable means of employing capital and diversifying business interests.

Several possible explanations have been offered to account for the American entrepreneurial failure. Some have suggested that there was too little hard money in the colonies to support a convertible currency or, alternatively, that private parties had insufficient capital resources to enter the private banking field. Neither argument holds up to scrutiny. Substantial amounts of specie routinely circulated throughout the economy with the exception of a few crisis years, and merchants and other potential bankers faced no formidable obstacles in adjusting their asset portfolios to include adequate specie reserves. Most firms failed to accumulate hoards of specie not because of its scarcity but because it was a sterile asset without earning power. Moreover, entrance into the banking field did not require a large capital – indeed no minimum was necessary either from a legal or practical standpoint. So long as a private party maintained sufficient reserves against outstanding currency liabilities, the banking sector could be entered on a small scale and then expanded gradually over time, increasing in unison with the enhanced reputation of these private monies and the issuer's asset base. Numerous Philadelphia merchants, plus merchants in other urban centres, appear to have possessed the acumen to have diversified their business activities into a broader range of financial services, including private currency issue, yet to date none have been identified as making a significant commitment to the banking field.

On three separate occasions, large groups of merchants acting in concert did create private mechanisms for issuing paper obligations which contemporaries believed had the potential of circulating as a medium of exchange. All were relatively short-lived experiments. One arose in Massachusetts in 1733, when negotiations between Governor Jonathan Belcher and the colonial legislature over a bill to authorise the emission of additional public monies had stalled. In response, numerous Boston merchants agreed among themselves to issue up to £100,000 in private note obligations redeemable in three stages over 10 years and compounding in value at the rate of 6 per cent per annum. The merchants planned to introduce the notes into the economy by offering them to creditors willing to accept the paper voluntarily in the settlement of outstanding debts and by lending them to persons offering good security. Belcher protested the actions of the merchants and questioned their legality, but the colony's attorney general ruled in December 1735 that the notes did not violate any British laws, including the statute restricting currency issuance to private unincorporated firms with six principals or less. Surviving samples indicate that, while the notes often listed three to six signatures, their redemption in specie was not the joint responsibility of all the merchants who had agreed to co-operate in establishing the terms of issuance. Since the Boston merchants had never formed a joint-stock company with transferable shares, they likewise were not governed by the terms of the Bubble Act of 1720.

Because the notes compounded at 6 per cent interest, their value soon rose to a premium *via-à-vis* the outstanding public monies, and the vast majority were soon hoarded and held as investments until their redemption dates.[21] Given these circumstances, the Boston merchants' notes do not seem to meet the criteria for classification as a circulating currency; they became instead an innovative and unusual source of intermediate and long-term financing for the merchant issuers, who were responsible for their redemption in stages – three-tenths after three years, another three-tenths after six years, and four-tenths and final retirement in the tenth year. Their characteristics suggest that these notes were forerunners of the commercial paper that became a steady source of funding for many firms in the larger commercial centres in the nineteenth century.

In short, these instruments broadened the scope of local financial markets, but they did not provide a private substitute for governmental fiat issues.

Less than a decade later, also in Massachusetts, two separate groups of investors made formal application to the legislature for charters to create private banks with the authority to issue currencies backed by two different sets of assets. Several hundred citizens from across the colony, led by mercantile organisers in the eastern towns, but including a number of persons of moderate landed wealth, sought permission to create a private land bank.[22] The currency was to be secured by loans against mortgaged property, and its mode of operations were designed to resemble very closely the public land offices which had functioned for several decades. The second group composed largely of a rival group of Boston merchants, generally more wealthy than the first, proposed to issue currency to be supported through the gradual accumulation of a specie fund over a period of 15 years to provide the means for redemption.

The legislature granted the two charters in 1740, and company officials promptly issued around £49,000 against mortgaged real estate and roughly £120,000 against the projected silver pool. Within weeks, Governor William Shirley, who had only recently taken office, suspended the charter bill, dissolved the bank, and promptly submitted the whole issue to imperial officials for resolution. Shirley was on solid ground in challenging the legitimacy of the whole project since Parliament had reserved for itself the authority to grant charter powers to business enterprises, and just to close any loopholes, it formally extended the Bubble Act to the colonies in 1741. By June 1742 two-thirds of the land bank currency and nearly three-fifths of the specie bank currency had been recalled, and commissioners were appointed to oversee the steady withdrawal of the remainder.[23]

The third instance of a collective private initiative on the monetary front occurred in Connecticut in 1732. A group of over 170 persons drawn from 53 towns were associated with the New London Society for Trade and Commerce. According to historian Bruce Stark, the members 'did not differ markedly from the rest of the population'; over 70 per cent with identifiable occupations were farmers – with merchants, ship captains, artisans, lawyers, and physicians accounting for the remainder.[24] Sponsors received formal permission from the legislature to establish a joint-stock company under a charter reasonably similar to those granted to parishes in the Congregational church, the dominant religion in the colony. Adopting an expansive view of the latitude expressed in the charter terms, the company's elected officers quickly moved to create a private land bank. They made plans for the issuance of up to £30,000 secured by first mortgages against the lands of borrowers, many of whom where simultaneously stockholders.

The New London Society issued about £15,000 between October 1732 and January 1733. These bills had no built-in interest rate component, and therefore circulated as money just as the issuers had intended. But this monetary experiment stalled in mid-January 1733. Critics alleged that the society was exceeding its charter powers. In response to rising complaints, the legislature prohibited the issuance of any additional monies on the grounds that the enabling legislation had not granted the society the explicit right to print its own currency. In a counter effort designed to resolve the controversial affair, the legislature authorised the issuance of £50,000 in currency through the public loan office, with the stipulation that up to £15,000 be made available to members of the New Haven Society for the purpose of calling in the outstanding circulation. The society's leadership accepted these terms, and the private bank began calling in its monies and wound up its affairs over the next few years. Thus ended perhaps the boldest venture by a private firm to establish a competitive currency in the colonial era. The plan was killed by internal economic and political rivalries, although it seems doubtful that the original legislation, even if allowed to stand in Connecticut, would have survived a thorough review by the Board of Trade in London since the whole scheme appears to have been in direct conflict with provisions of the Bubble Act and possibly the 1708 statute regarding the issuance of currency by unchartered firms with multiple partners.

IV

Conflict with Board of Trade

One of the major disputes between the North American legislatures and the Board of Trade in London during the two decades before the general rebellion centred on provisions in currency legislation related to the settlement of private debts. Colonial proponents of legal tender status for private debts claimed the requirement was necessary to maintain currency values, and they often prevailed in legislative debates. Although members of the board were always sceptical about legislative acts calling for the fresh issuance of fiat currency, they were generally willing to approve, albeit reluctantly, colonial legislation which stipulated legal tender status for public payments to tax collectors and governmental loan offices. But the board raised strong objections to provisions calling for legal tender status in private transactions, especially among debtors and creditors.

The board was responsive to the concerns of English merchants who conducted substantial trade with the colonies based on the extension of credit for as long as 18 to 24 months.[25] As the volume of Anglo-American trade grew after mid-century, English merchants became ever more fearful about being forced to accept payment for past-due debts in colonial currencies which fluctuated in value. Or stated in slightly more technical terms, English creditors were increasingly reluctant to assume the perceived risks associated with transactions denominated in colonial currencies. They preferred payment in specie or its equivalents – coinage or reliable bills of exchange drawn in sterling on accounts maintained in England.

This problem was difficult to assess and resolve because different colonies had different experiences in regard to the amplitude of fluctuations in currency values. Moreover, the attitudes of English creditors shifted from year to year as well. When the values of colonial currencies were trending downward, English anxieties heightened; but when news arrived in London confirming the rebound in currency values, the merchants' concerns abated. As a consequence, uncertainties and inconsistencies governed decision-making. The Board of Trade had hoped to formulate policies with universal applicability but different financial realities in individual colonies at different times made the achievement of that goal impossible.[26]

When the board finally decided to take action, it moved in a heavy-handed manner. Under pressure from English creditors active in the American trade who wanted iron-clad protection from potential losses arising from fluctuating currency values in North America, the board induced Parliament to pass the Currency Act of 1764. The Act forbade new paper emissions which included any legal tender provisions whatsoever, private or public. The members' biases against any form of fiat currency was fully evident in drafting this Act. The new law applied to the nine colonies outside of New England where new paper money issues were still permissible after 1751.[27]

The colonial legislatures effected by this legislation were indignant. They objected because, in most cases, their currency issues had been managed responsibly for decades and none had experienced irreversible depreciation. Currency values had sometimes fallen but invariably rebounded. Second, they saw no logical reason for denying legal tender status for public transactions since private creditors, including London merchants, were not be threatened by such provisions. The Currency Act of 1764 was viewed as nothing less than an attempt to curtail the use of fiat currency, which ran contrary to the wishes of colonial voters, and their leaders reacted defiantly. Some colonial leaders later charged that it was all part of a conspiratorial British 'plot' to exert increasingly greater control over events in North America.

Over the next decade, the legislatures continued to pass legislation authorising issuance of new currency with legal tender provisions irrespective of Parliament's prohibition. By threatening to refuse payment of annual salaries, the legislatures coerced their respective royal governors into submitting new currency laws to the Board of Trade for approval. The board predictably disallowed some Acts, but after listening to special pleadings of colonial agents stationed in London, it reluctantly let others stand. In the early 1770s, for example, the board permitted both Pennsylvania and New York to emit currencies which were designated as legal tender in public payments.

The prolonged controversy was finally resolved in 1773. Upon the board's recommendation, Parliament amended the law to allow the continued issuance of fiat currency with legal tender status in all transactions involving local and provincial governments, but not in private transactions. British creditors voiced no objections to this alteration in the statute since they remained fully protected from the risks of fluctuating currency rates in the colonies. In retrospect, the extension of the law to public sector payments in 1764 had served no useful purpose, and wiser heads sponsored its deletion. The English effort to root out the heresy of fiat paper and thereby purify the North American financial system was perhaps a well intentioned paternalistic policy, but it proved extremely unpopular in the colonies.

Some colonists wanted wholesale repeal of the 1764 Act, but most were willing to settle for an easing of its harsh terms.[28] Yet it took nearly a decade of unproductive wrangling to accomplish that end. The issue was difficult to resolve because imperial officials and colonial leaders possessed radically divergent opinions about the propriety of fiat currency. The contest of wills, which raged concurrently with even more heated debates over the new taxes prescribed in the Stamp and Townshend Acts, left many leaders on both sides suspicious about the motivations of their transatlantic adversaries.

With the benefit of two centuries of hindsight and a clearer understanding of how monetary affairs unfolded in the colonies, it seems fair to conclude that the Board of Trade's reservations about the currency emissions of the middle and southern colonies in third quarter of the eighteenth century were overdrawn and exaggerated. Contrary to English expectations, all nine colonies had managed their currency issues exceedingly well after 1750; none had suffered irreversible depreciation. Their legislatures had exercised restraint in authorising new issues, and in no case had Gresham's Law taken effect – that is, fiat currency had not driven coinage out of circulation since paper and coin remained complementary components of the overall money stock. Tax revenues were collected on a regular basis to sink the colonies' tax-anticipating notes, while individual borrowers paid off their mortgage notes in timely fashion and provided the funds to redeem the currency issued through government loan offices. Occasionally, English mercantile creditors suffered minor losses before the mid-1760s because of the volatility of currency rates over a period of several years, but colonial courts usually took into account changes in the market value of monies when adjudicating cases related to private debts long past due. Nevertheless, English fears of potential losses in distant markets were genuine, and the compromise solution reached in 1773 was prudent and sensible under the circumstances.

Although most English critics condemned the American attachment to fiat paper, almost coincidental with independence, Adam Smith offered a more sympathetic view in the text of his famous inquiry into the true wealth of nations. First, Smith argued that the use of fiat currency was a choice deliberately made by the colonists rather than an unwanted outcome necessitated by the scarcity of metals – an argument that many contemporaries had erroneously advanced. The substitution of paper for coinage was a perfectly rational decision, Smith asserted, because it allowed the colonies to optimise the economic returns on the resources at their disposal; in other words, they could make a partial substitution of specie with paper and thereby export a portion of their hard monies overseas to acquire other more productive assets. Smith was reluctant to endorse fiat currency as a superior mechanism to private paper backed by specie reserves, yet he readily admitted that several North American colonies had behaved responsibly in managing their unorthodox monetary systems, and he expressed admiration for those legislatures which had derived an interest revenue from granting well-secured mortgage loans to citizens.[29]

Ironically, the political and military events in the 1770s and 1780s that resulted in independence from Great Britain also forced Americans to reassess their attitudes toward the inclusion of fiat currency in the money stock. Over half of the war costs were financed by the issuance of fiat currencies by the Continental Congress and the individual states. The various fiat monies generally held their value during the early years of the war, but after 1776 they depreciated at accelerating rates. The nominal value of new currency issued between 1774 and 1779 exceeded the value of the coinage in circulation at the start of the war, and Gresham's Law went into operation. Coins were hoarded or exported. By 1780 the market exchange rate between currency and specie was 100:1 and a year later the wartime issues had become virtually worthless.

This negative experience with fiat currency during wartime conditions altered American opinions about its merits. Although seven states reissued paper money in modest amounts after the signing of the Treaty of Paris in 1783 and most of these post-war issues resisted steady depreciation, the drafters of the Constitution in 1787 voted to deny state governments the privilege of emitting fiat currency either through the device of tax anticipation notes or the operations of mortgage loan offices. Currencies already emitted were permitted to remain in circulation until their respective expiration dates in the 1790s or early in the next century, but the American experiment with fiat paper temporarily ended – not to be revived again until the Civil War emergency led both the Union and Confederate governments once again into the realm of inconvertible paper money.

As a consequence, British and American attitudes regarding the proper composition of the money stock had more in common during the last decade of the eighteenth century than at any date since 1690. In both nations the money supply consisted of coinage as well paper monies issued by private and chartered banks. During the 1780s three state-chartered commercial banks were founded in the United States in Philadelphia, New York and Boston; in the 1790s the First Bank of the United States received a charter from Congress with the privilege of opening branch offices throughout the nation. By 1800 nearly 30 state-chartered banks were in operation, and during the next decade and one half over 200 additional state-chartered banks opened their doors. Across the Atlantic Ocean, the Bank of England maintained its position as the leading supplier of paper money in Great Britain, and with the addition of the £5 banknote to its denominational structure in the early 1790s, its currency circulated much more widely among the middle classes. In Scotland, meanwhile, 18 banks of issue continued to print banknotes in amounts as small as £1 as they had done for decades. J. Clapham estimated the number of private bankers in London at the turn of the century at 'nearly seventy', while the number of country bankers in England and Wales had climbed to 370, according to L.S. Pressnell.[30]

V

Conclusion

Public attitudes about the legitimacy of fiat currency in Great Britain and its North American colonies were sharply at variance in the eighteenth century. Political and business leaders in Britain were generally receptive to paper monies continuously convertible into specie whether issued by chartered banks or private firms with unlimited liability. But they drew the line at the prospect of the government emitting a circulating paper supported either by future taxation or private mortgages. Given the failed financial experiments with fiat currencies under two kings,

Charles II and Louis XV of France, the tenuous backing for these monies appeared too risky for British sensibilities. That negative outlook was reflected in the rulings and legislative initiatives of members of the Board of Trade which had primary responsibility for economic affairs in the colonies.

In British dominions in North America, however, colonial leaders experienced surprising success with a system of fiat currency, especially in the region from New York to North Carolina. No banks emerged in the colonies to issue paper money convertible into specie on a sustained basis; thus that form of paper money never became a viable option in the American context. Instead the colonists supplemented the supply of coinage, which was mostly Spanish in origin, with emissions of fiat currency by governmental units. During the first half of the century, the record was uneven. The four New England colonies plus South Carolina had successful financial regimes for several decades, but the temptation to forestall collection of the taxes required to support monetary values finally proved too great. These colonies were unable to hold the financial reins in check, eventually succumbing to ruinous currency depreciation. Events in those five colonies corresponded with the expectations of European critics of fiat monies. Parliament's passage of the Currency Act 1751 moved the New England colonies back toward a hardmoney standard, where they remained until the 1770s.

Eight other colonies managed their fiat emissions much more effectively, however, and none fell victim to irrepressible depreciation. These governments were genuine innovators in the persistent use of inconvertible public monies. Their fiat currency was not only a useful medium of exchange but also a reasonably reliable store of value over the long run. Fiat monies entered the money stock in two different ways and were supported in the financial markets by two distinct backing systems. Tax anticipation issues, some with maturity dates as distant as 10 to 20 years, were emitted directly by colonial treasuries and later redeemed from public revenues. Government loan offices – usually called land banks in the eighteenth century – issued currency to citizens mortgaging their properties for periods up to 15 years, and principal repayments, typically amortised over the life of the loan, provided the mechanism for retiring the paper. If borrowers defaulted, the property was sold and the proceeds were used to accomplish the same purpose. Meanwhile, the annual interest payments on these mortgage loans was often sufficient to make a substantial dent in provincial budgets, which were low since Parliament provided most of the funds required to defend the Empire on land and at sea, including the North American continent and North Atlantic Ocean.

Despite the solid record of these eight colonies, the Board of Trade, its members philosophically opposed to fiat currency and under pressure from London merchants worried about credit risks associated with paper money, manoeuvred through Parliament the Currency Act of 1764, which outlawed future emissions of fiat monies. Already in a rebellious mood, the colonists protested vehemently; their legislatures ignored the new regulations, authorised new emissions, and then bullied their governors into recommending approval to the Board of Trade. The controversy lasted until 1773, when a compromise was negotiated which allowed the colonies to continue issuing fiat paper so long as it had no legal tender status in private debts.

On the eve of the War for Independence, fiat currency remained extremely popular in more than half the North American colonies. In several regions it had been a component of the money stock for nearly half a century. It is not surprising, therefore, that the Continental Congress and the new states relied heavily on fiat currency to finance the war effort. But on this occasion the sums issued were too great and the taxes imposed too low. Without adequate backing, the massive wartime issues succumbed to a persistent depreciation, carrying their relative values down to virtually zero by 1781. Despite these problems, currency finance pro-vided most of the purchasing power necessary for the American military to wage an ultimately successful war over six long years. Nonetheless, this episode discredited fiat paper in the minds of many of its former supporters. Although seven state governments revived their currency systems in the 1780s and experienced little or only modest depreciation, the new US Constitution eliminated fiat currency as a future option for state and local governmental units. Meanwhile, banking institutions were established for the first time on the North American continent in the 1780s, and they issued notes convertible into specie upon demand. Before the end of the century, the new nation had chartered the First Bank of the United States, modelled on the Bank of England, and the several states had chartered nearly 30 additional private banks.

Oddly, stark Anglo-American differences over the composition of the money stock, which had divided Crown and colonies for over half a century before the American rebellion, dissipated in the post-war era. The colonies had refused to conform to British expectations regarding the role of fiat currency in their respective economies, but once free and independent, and given the experiences of wartime finance, the new American Constitution drafted in 1787 reflected the more conservative attitudes that had prevailed in Parliament throughout the eighteenth century. Fiat currency disappeared from the American financial system, and it was not reintroduced until the Civil War emergency nearly three-quarters of a century later. By the 1790s American and British theory and practice were finally in accord regarding the legitimacy of only two forms of circulating money: coinage and banknotes supported by specie reserves. Yet, the American colonies had demonstrated the viability of a monetary system based on fiat currency; their activities foreshadowed the abandonment of the gold standard in the twentieth century and the adoption of fiat currency as a universal standard in the modern world.

NOTES

1. Comparative studies of monetary systems in Europe and North America in the eighteenth century are rare. The only published essay to my knowledge is in Spanish by the American economic historian Eugene White, '?Fueron inflacionaries las finanzas estatles en el siglo XVIII? Una nueva interpretacion de los vales reales', *Revista de Historia Economica* Año V. No. 3 (1987), pp. 509–26. That article was preceded by the author's unpublished manuscript, 'Inflationary Finance in the 18th Century: A Comparative Study of Colonial America, Spain and France' (1986), which is available upon request by writing to Economics Department, Rutgers University, New Brunswick, NJ, USA 08903-5055.
2. J. Clapham, *The Bank of England*: Vol. I, *1694–1797* (Cambridge, 1966 ed.), pp. 1–52; S.G. Checkland, *Scottish Banking: A History, 1695–1973* (Glasgow, 1975), pp. 1–135; C.W. Munn, 'The Emergence of Joint-Stock Banking in the British Isles: A Comparative Approach', in R.P.T. Davenport-Hines and Geoffrey Jones (eds.), *The End of Insularity: Essays in Comparative Business History* (1988), pp. 69–83.
3. Some scholars argue that limited liability chartered banks were *de facto* sounder than private banks with unlimited liability; see J. Carr, S. Glied and F. Mathewson, 'Unlimited Liabitity and Free Banking in Scotland: A Note', *Journal of Economic History*, Vol. XLIX (1989), pp. 974–8.
4. D.M. Joslin, 'London Private Bankers, 1720–1785', *Economic History Review*, 2nd series, Vol. VII (1954), pp. 167–86.
5. Checkland, *Scottish Banking*, Table 2, pp. 134–5.
6. Sir Albert Feavearyear, *The Pound Sterling: The History of English Money*, 2nd revised edition by E. V. Morgan (Oxford, 1963), pp. 111–16; R.D. Richards, *The Early History of Banking in England* (1929); K. Horsefield, 'The "Stop of the Exchequer" Revisited', *Economic History Review*, 2nd series, Vol. XXXV (1982), pp. 511–28.
7. The best analysis of the Law scandal is L. Neal and E. Schubert, 'The First Rational Bubbles: A New Look at the Mississippi and South Sea Schemes', University of Illinois working paper no. 1188, Sept. 1985; see also Neal, *The Rise of Financial Capitalism: International Capital Markets in the Age of Reason* (New York, 1990), Chs. 4–5. A lively account is found in J. K. Galbraith's *Money: Whence It Came, Where It Went* (Boston, 1975), pp. 27–34; also see C. Kindleberger, *A Financial History of Western Europe* (1984), pp. 96–8.
8. For general information on colonial finance in the eighteenth century, the following studies are helpful: L. Brock, *The Currency of the American Colonies, 1700–1764: A Study in Colonial Finance and Imperial Relations* (New York, 1975), a reprint of his 1941 dissertation; E.J. Ferguson, 'Currency Finance: An Interpretation of Colonial Monetary Practices', *William and Mary Quarterly*, 3rd series, Vol. X (1953), pp. 153–80; J.R. Hanson, 'Money in the American Economy', *Economic Inquiry*, Vol. XVII (1979), pp. 281–6; idem, 'Small Notes in the American Colonies', *Explorations in Economic History*, Vol. XVII (1980), pp. 411–20; E.J. Perkins, *The Economy of Colonial America*, (New York, 2nd ed. 1988), pp. 163–88; T. Thayer, 'The Land Bank System in the American Colonies', *Journal of Economic History*, Vol. XIII (1953), pp. 145–59; R. Weiss, 'The Issue of Paper Money in the American Colonies, 1720–1774', *Journal of Economic History*, Vol. XXX (1970), pp. 770–84; R.C. West, 'Money in the Colonial American Economy', *Economic Inquiry*, Vol. XVI (1978), pp. 1–15; and E. Wicker, 'Colonial Monetary Standards Contrasted: Evidence from the Seven Years' War', *Journal of Economic History*, Vol. XLV (1985), pp. 860–84.
9. Older accounts of American monetary and political history stressed internal class

conflicts – debtors versus creditors – but more recent studies have exploded the myth of a citizenry divided by class status. Members of all occupational groups in the colonies, including most merchants, supported the concept of including some type of fiat currency in the money stock although they may have differed at times over the exact terms of issuance and redemption.

10. Colonial pounds were not the equivalent of sterling pounds in England. The colonists rated Spanish coins, and other foreign coins, at values higher than their respective mint ratios in England in order to discourage coinage exports. The same principle of overvaluation applied to fiat monies; their values corresponded with the ratings assigned to foreign coins, and, to make the story even more complicated, those ratings varied from colony to colony. For example, at the official par, £100 in England translated into £133.33 colonial in Massachusetts, £166.67 colonial in Maryland, and £700 colonial in South Carolina in the mid-eighteenth century. No public or private institutions tried to maintain fixed exchange rates among currency, coin, and foreign exchange. The only fixed standard was the rate at which colonial governments would accept monies in tax and mortgage payments as well as other miscellaneous transactions with the general public.
11. Average yearly exchange rates for colonial monies during the eighteenth century are listed in J. McCusker, *Money and Exchange in Europe and America*, 1600–1775 (Chapel Hill, 1978). In the first half of the eighteenth century, the Connecticut legislature exercised reasonable restraint in its issuance policy but the currency depreciated heavily nonetheless because so much intermingling had occurred with the monies of Massachusetts and Rhode Island, where self-restraint was not practised. Connecticut was tainted by the excesses of its immediate neighbours, and the colony was prevented from issuing new paper by the Currency Act of 1751.
12. R. Lester, 'Currency Issues to Overcome Depressions in Pennsylvania, 1723 and 1729', *Journal of Political Economy* (1938), pp. 324–75.
13. This information comes from a microfilm copy of an incomplete, but nonetheless very lengthy, unpublished manuscript recently deposited in the archives of the Alderman Library, University of Virginia: L. Brock, 'Manuscript Draft for an Unfinished Book on Currency in Colonial America'. The author's plan was to carry forward his monetary history from 1764, where his earlier work left off, through the 1770s. In addition, the manuscript contains a long chapter on Massachusetts finance in the 1730s.
14. Brock, *Currency of the American Colonies,* p. 274.
15. The size of the permanent paper money issue in South Carolina was frozen after 1731; the proclamation rate was set at 7:1 *vis-à-vis* sterling and it remained fixed at that rate until the rebellion.
16. In London many private bankers held mortgage assets, according to Joslin, 'Private Bankers', p. 176.
17. Sums reloaned to new borrowers were always for progressively shorter periods of time, an arrangement necessary to make the maturity dates of new loans coincide with the assigned expiration date of a specific currency emission. Assume, for example, the legislature had authorised a currency emission with a life of 10 years. Loans made in the third year after passage were limited to seven years, loans in the sixth year after passage were limited to a four-year term, and loans in the eighth year matured in only two years. The principal of every outstanding loan associated with a specific issue of currency came due in the final year irrespective of when the loan was contracted. When the currency authorisation for an existing loan office expired, a new authorisation often followed within a year or two.
18. B. Stark, 'The New London Society and Connecticut Politics, 1732–1740', *Connecticut History*, Vol. XXV (1984), pp. 1–21.
19. M. Schweitzer, *Custom and Contract: Household, Government, and the Economy in Colonial Pennsylvania* (New York, 1987); T.L. Purvis, *Proprietors, Patronage, and Paper Money: Legislative Politics in New Jersey, 1703–1776* (New Brunswick, NJ, 1986).
20. Instances of merchants issuing 'IOUs' or various forms of credit vouchers that later circulated among the populous as a medium of exchange, especially in remote rural

areas, have sometimes been cited as evidence of the existence of competitive monies issued by private individuals in the seventeenth and eighteenth centuries; but, in my view, the overall effect of these activities have been exaggerated and, irrespective of the circumstances, the conclusions drawn can be highly misleading. So far as I know, the volume of private paper was always small relative to the size of the aggregate money stock; few, if any, issuers maintained specie reserves and promised convertibility; and, most damning in this context, no issuer expanded these alleged private monetary operations over the decades and emerged as the equivalent of English private bankers, who were typically called merchant-bankers by residents of North America. Some colonial merchants and shopkeepers probably did experiment with the issuance of limited volumes of financial instruments which approached the status of money or at least near-monies – and given the shortage of capital and the absence of legal prohibitions against private issues – some experimentation seems almost inevitable; but the question remains: why did a valuable and frequently very profitable financial service based on lending currency against specie reserves never develop more fully before independence? In theory, both private and public monies could have circulated simultaneously with no negative consequences; the only necessary condition was that no fixed exchange rate be established by law, thereby permitting routine swaps at fluctuating market prices.

21. A. McFarland Davis, 'Currency and Banking in the Providence of Massachusetts-Bay', *Publications of the American Economic Association*, 3rd series, Vol. I No. 4 (Dec. 1900), pp. 1–445, and continued in Vol. II No. 2 (May 1901), pp. 1–332. Although technically an article, the overall length is longer than most books. This turn-of-the-century economic historian produced some the earliest and most detailed accounts of the financial history of colonial New England. For the author's discussion of specie and land banks, see Vol. II, pp. 102–29.
22. G.A. Billias, 'The Massachusetts Land Bankers of 1740', *University of Maine Studies*, 2nd series (1959), pp. 1–53. Billias studied the social origins of the sponsors and discovered, contrary to the assertions of previous scholars, that they were not poor and middling farmers but mostly persons of substantial wealth, including several Boston merchants.
23. Davis, 'Currency and Banking', Vol. II, pp. 130–67. The specie bank scheme seems at first glance to duplicate reasonably closely the type of private banks which British opinion makers found unobjectionable. Yet the terminology employed by the colonists was deceptive, and it disguised some critical differences. The issuers did not promise convertibility from the outset nor at any time for the next decade and one half; instead, the plan called for accumulating the specie required to back the currency over the life of the issue and then drawing on the fund for redemption at the maturity date. A comparable system was adopted in Maryland to support that colony's public monies, although the fund accumulated was not specie but stock of the Bank of England, which could, of course, have always been sold for specie since active markets existed.
24. Stark, 'New London Society', pp. 1–21.
25. For information on the growth of trade and credit, see J. Price, *Capital and Credit in British Overseas Trade: The View from the Chesapeake, 1700–1776* (Cambridge, MA, 1980).
26. For a discussion of these shifts in British mercantile attitudes, see J. Ernst, *Money and Politics in America, 1755–1775* (Chapel Hill, 1973). In recent years a sharp debate has emerged among several monetary historians regarding whether specie flows, reflecting theories related to the quantity theory of money, or effective backing systems were responsible for maintaining currency values. Ron Michener argues the former position in 'Fixed Exchange Rates and the Quantity Theory in Colonial America', in K. Brunner and A.H. Meltzer (eds.), *Empirical Studies of Velocity, Real Exchange Rates, Unemployment and Productivity* (Amsterdam, 1987), pp. 233–307, and 'Backing Theories and the Currencies of Eighteenth-Century America: A Comment', *Journal of Economic History*, Vol. 48 (1988), pp. 682–92; Bruce Smith supports the backing hypothesis in 'American Colonial Monetary Regimes: The Failure of the Quantity Theory and Some Evidence in Favor of an Alternative View', *Canadian Journal of Economics*,

Vol. XVIII (1985), pp. 531–65; 'Some Colonial Evidence on Two Theories of Money: Maryland and the Carolinas', *Journal of Political Economy*, Vol. XCIII (1985), pp. 1178–1211; and 'The Relationship between Money and Prices: Some Historical Evidence Reconsidered', *Quarterly Review: Federal Reserve Bank of Minneapolis*, Vol. 12 (Summer 1988), pp. 18–32. On balance, I am in agreement with Smith; this essay therefore reflects the outlook of scholars supporting the so-called 'backing' theory in determining currency values.

27. J.P. Greene and R. Jellison, 'The Currency Act of 1764 in Imperial–Colonial Relations, 1764–1776', *William and Mary Quarterly*, Vol. 18 (1961), pp. 485–518; J. Ernst, 'Genesis of the Currency Act of 1764: Virginia Paper Money and the Protection of British Investments', *William and Mary Quarterly*, Vol. 22 (1965), pp. 33–74.
28. Two chapters in Brock's 'Manuscript Draft for Unfinished Book' are devoted to the unsuccessful colonial effort to obtain the repeal of the 1764 act.
29. Adam Smith, *An Inquiry into the Nature of Causes of the Wealth of Nations*, (1776); see his discussion of colonial finance in chapter III, entitled 'Of Public Debts', in book V. At one point in the contest between crown and colonies in the prewar decade, Benjamin Franklin offered a novel suggestion regarding the possible establishment of a currency-issuing continental loan office under direct parliamentary control. Franklin suggested that the interest earned on colonial mortgages could then be used to offset a portion of British defence expenditures in North America, thereby reducing the need for generating tax revenues in the colonies. The idea was never given serious consideration, however, because of the board's bias against fiat currency and the political fear that the continental financial institution with branches in all 13 colonies might serve to unite them to an even greater extent than already existed.
30. J. Clapham, *Bank of England* (Cambridge, 1948), Vol. I, p. 48; L.S. Pressnell, *Country Banking in the Industrial Revolution* (Oxford, 1956), p. 11; and C.P. Kindleberger, *A Financial History of Western Europe* (1984), p. 83.

The Coalescence of a Cluster of Corporate International Banks, 1855–75

P.L. COTTRELL
University of Leicester

Many qualities contributed to London being the global financial epicentre during the 80 years, or so, before 1914. One was the presence within the 'City' of offices of British corporate overseas banks – institutions whose spheres of operations lay outside the formal Empire and which Baster has aptly dubbed the 'Anglo-International Banks'.[1] In 1914 the shares of 24 such banks were quoted on the London Stock Exchange and, although most – some 14 – were relatively recent creations, six had either been established in the 1860s, or their direct forbears had been formed during that decade. Moreover four of that six had strong mutual associations arising from interlocking directorships, which in turn radiated out from that very particular London 'private' bank – Glyn, Mills.[2] In 1914 H.A. Lawrence of Glyns was a director of the Anglo-Austrian Bank, the Bank of Roumania and the Imperial Ottoman Bank, while M.G.C. Glyn was a director of the London & Brazilian Bank.[3] The purpose of this present article is to examine this involvement of Glyns in the early, mid-century, development of British overseas corporate banking.

I

It is has been cogently argued that the 'new' European bank of the mid-nineteenth century evolved out of the 'old' bank, while in England's case the major element of this financial revolution was the greater development of joint stock deposit banking.[4] The activities of Glyns, and their associates, provide further evidence of this financial metamorphosis, which also points to the creation of corporate overseas banking as being an additional, English element in the European financial revolution. Moreover, these 'Anglo-International' banks were an aspect of British nineteenth century foreign direct investment, often being constituted as 'free-standing' companies.[5] The focus here will be on the creation of some of these institutions and, although they arose out of the 'old' bank, nonetheless their birth was frequently painful. Despite the merchanting and banking backgrounds of their founders, the very establishment of these banks was marked by a whole series of problems, which often proved difficult to resolve: competition for the necessary foreign concessions, constituting suitable boards of directors, obtaining management of sufficient quality, and rivalry from others – local bankers overseas and other promotional groups in London and other European financial centres. In addition, difficulties frequently arose from fluctuating exchanges – the product of natural and political forces – as well as the incidence of the trade cycle creating instability, all generating further challenges to the early success of these new banks. These are recurrent elements arising from an examination of the birth and first years of the international corporate banks formed by Glyns and their associates. As a result of the varying nature of the sources used, the approach taken in this review is a series of case studies, somewhat uneven in treatment but laid out in chronological order, rather than an attempt to synthesise the overall experience.

The analysis of the anatomy of capitalism has recently developed apace and almost a litany of 'organisation, structure and network' has been established. A common terminology is important, but it is being put aside here, because its use may imply a logic and rationality which would be misleading. 'Network' may indicate a greater bonding than was the case, hence the use of 'clusters', reflecting the more tenuous nature of some of the links involved. Caution over terminology is also being urged, since much of British corporate investment was manic. The formation of banks was no exception, with at least two such waves taking place – in the 1830s (largely domestic) and during the mid-century. Mania and logic do not lie easily side by side and it is evident that the coalescence of the 'Glyn cluster' of overseas banks was not a matter of purposeful design, but a reaction to chance and opportunity.

The opportunity to establish overseas banks during the mid-century arose generally from the emergence of the world economy, with the fall in transport costs, and Britain's dominant role within it as the major industrial, trading and financial nation. This ripe juncture was augmented by the liberalisation of British company law with regard to banks from 1857. Many took advantage, with 25 foreign banks, as well as 13 colonial banks, being effectively registered in England between 1862 and 1866.[6] The speculative froth of this mania readily lent itself to being tellingly lampooned, as with the 'Bank of Patagonia' and the 'Arungabad Bank'.[7] That bubble surfaced in early 1863, when the financial press noted the increasing promotion of 'Anglo-continental banks', but the inception of the mid-century boom and the beginning of Glyns' connection with it, had begun eight years earlier with the establishment of the Bank of Egypt.

II

Until the mid-1850s, with the exception of the Ionian Bank, British corporate overseas banking was exclusively imperial – concerned with Australia, Canada, India and the West Indies. In some cases these institutions began as local concerns, but, through the need to obtain a *British* royal charter, acquired British capital and management. This was particularly so with some Indian banks and the Oriental Banking Corporation was a prototype for such developmental reconstitution. It had started as the Bank of Western India, formed in Bombay in 1842, but was renamed in 1845 and acquired a British charter in 1851.[8] Until the liberalisation of British company law, a charter appeared to be almost a *sine qua non* of British overseas banking, the only exceptions being the Bank of Australasia (1835), the Union Bank of Australia (1837) and the Australian Joint Stock Bank (1853). Glyns were involved with one of these antipodean institutions – the Union – the first indication of its future role as midwife to British corporate overseas banking.[9] Obtaining a charter was difficult and expensive, impediments which seriously constricted bank promotions. Nonetheless the mid-century overseas banking boom was heralded by the formation of two further chartered institutions – the Bank of Egypt and the Ottoman Bank.

The Crimean war acted as a lens focussing promoters' attention upon the eastern Mediterranean, but other, longer run, forces were also acting in the same manner. From the 1830s the Asian market was the most dynamic for British cotton exports so that by the mid-1840s it took a quarter, by value, of cottons exported. Indian demand for British cottons retained this dynamism over the 1850s.[10] The eastern Mediterranean played a number of roles in this commerce – it was a source of dyestuffs, but more particularly the Suez isthmus was a critical junction in Anglo-Oriental trade. This neck of land connected the steam routes established during the 1850s in the Mediterranean, the Red Sea and the Gulf.[11] One of the specific initial aims of the Bank of Egypt was to finance this overland trade.[12]

The promoters of the Bank of Egypt obtained a charter in July 1855, but nonetheless it took some time for the bank to be established. Its prospectus was not issued until January 1856, while the bank opened for 'general' business only in July 1856. Initially it had one Egyptian office – in Alexandria, but in August 1857 a decision was taken to open in Cairo, by September for the 'winter trade'. However, again, delay occurred, the branch not commencing business until mid-1858. Some of the senior management in Egypt was European: A. St. John Forssmann, with 'extensive experience in almost all parts of the continent', was appointed on the recommendation of Weguelin, the Governor of the Bank of England, and when transferred to Cairo, his place in Alexandria was taken by Ranking, formerly a London merchant. The London manager was Robert Diggles, previously a Calcutta merchant.[13]

Although outwardly a very British concern, the Bank of Egypt had been conceived by Peter Pasquali, an Egyptian merchant of Symrna and London. This was acknowledged publicly through Pasquali receiving £7,500 out of the bank's preliminary expenses of £10,194 and, from March, 1857 he was senior manager at Alexandria.[14] According to a possibly scurrilous source,[15] in February 1855, while the Bank of Egypt was being formed, Pasquali, with an associate Stephen Sleigh, conceived the idea of establishing a 'British Bank of Turkey'. The groundwork in London was left to Sleigh. Negotiations in Constantinople were entrusted initially to a Frenchman, Mille, who was a member of the Turkish civil service. When the Turkish government indicated that their interest lay in the creation of an institution to regulate the exchanges, reform the currency and act as an investment bank, Mille was replaced by Zohrab, the former Consul-General of Turkey in London. This desire for a 'national bank', first aired by Turkish reformers in 1853,[16] continued until the early 1860s and led to Constantinople becoming a bear pit, created by the machinations of competing putative concessionaires, local and European.

In their endeavours Sleigh and Pasquali faced three interrelated problems, which generally confronted other bank promoters – obtaining Turkish permission, negotiating a British charter, and constituting a board of directors, since the ratification of both the Turkish authority and the charter required the submission of the bank's proposed board. Moreover, with respect to the charter, an additional difficulty arose from the bank's operations lying outside the jurisdiction of the British crown, but Sleigh demonstrated that Indian banks had been incorporated with powers to operate in China, and elsewhere, thereby establishing the necessary precedents. The Pasquali group regarded gaining a suitably prestigious chairman as the key to the construction of their prospective bank's board. They approached Layard, who agreed, providing the 'City' would back the insitution. This led Sleigh to turn, *via* an intermediary, to Glyn, Mills. Apparently the London private bank gave its conditional support to the venture; Sleigh first had to obtain the charter and the firman. By 13 August 1855 the Privy Council had approved the draft charter, so that the remaining, but now overriding, problem in London for the Pasquali-Sleigh group was the composition of their bank's directorate. This became acute from October 1855, when it was evident that rival schemes were afoot, and consequently Sleigh spoke to W.R. Drake, a solicitor, an associate of Glyns, and also involved in promoting the Bank of Egypt. Glyns restated their support, but it remained premised upon securing the charter and the firman.

In early 1856, with Rothschilds also interested in establishing an 'Ottoman Bank', according to Sleigh, Glyns acquired the interests of the Pasquali group and tentatively named as directors J.J. Cummins and R. Campbell, both on the board of the Union Bank of Australia. A fresh petition for the charter was now required, as Drake had determined that the British authorities opposed Pasquali's involvement, as 'it was thought [he] had quite enough on his hands in the Bank of Egypt'. Further, the competition was becoming fiercer; in early February 1856 an Anglo-French group, headed by Trouvit-Chauval and backed by Hankeys of London and Weikersheim, a Viennese banker, obtained a firman for a National Bank of Turkey. George Glyn and Drake decided to acquire the Trouvit-Chauval firman for £7,000 and make Hankey and Weikersheim directors of their proposed bank, named on 8 February the Ottoman Bank. H.A. Bruce, M.P., and G.T. Clark also agreed to be directors, the full board being formally constituted on 11 February, with a prospectus issued on 13 February. *The Times* noted that the terms of the charter for the Ottoman Bank 'were precisely similar to the Bank of Egypt'.[17]

There still, however, remained the question of the firman, as Zohrab doubted the validity of the Trouvit-Chauval concession. To resolve this dilemma, Layard and Glyn saw Aali Pacha and Clarendon in Paris at the end of February. The need was pointed up by further competitors, including Foulds of Paris, working with Sina of Vienna. By early March more were in the field at Constantinople: Atkinson Wilkin, acting on behalf of another London group, and even Trouvit-Chauval once again. Zohrab obtained a fresh firman on 27 March,[18] ratified on 7 April, but then opposed by Stratford de Redcliffe, the British Ambassador at Constantinople, following an intervention with Clarendon by Layard. According to Sleigh, Layard then took delivery of the firman that Zohrab had obtained, ultimately leading to recriminations between the Pasquali group and its Glyn successors.

III

After a somewhat murky beginning, the position of the Ottoman Bank was made more complex by the Turkish charter of reforms of 1856 – Hatti-Humayoun – of which article 37 stated:

> On s'occupera de la création de banques et d'autres institutions

> semblables pour arriver à la réforme du système financier et monetaire, ainsi que de la création de fonds destinés à augmenter la source de la richesse publique et matérielle de l'Empire. [*Measures will be taken to establish banks and other similar institutions to achieve the reform of the financial and monetary system, and to create funds earmarked to augment the Empire's source of public and material wealth.*]

The reforms were applied from April 1856, under pressure from a growing European mania for investment in the Turkish empire. *The Times* correspondent in Constantinople, with some dry amusement and scepticism, enumerated 14 rival banking schemes, as well as others seeking concessions for railways, gas companies and alike. The Turkish government tried to capitalise on this situation by raising once again its concerns for domestic and international monetary reform to be undertaken by an 'Imperial Ottoman Bank'. The Turkish *desiderata* for this institution were handed to the various competing foreign groups for the concession.[19]

The directors of the Ottoman negotiated over the matter but made little progress. Instead, from August 1856, discussions took place intermittently with a group aiming to establish a 'National Bank of Turkey'. Initially this was composed of traditional native bankers – Greeks and Armenians resident at Constantinople – but who also now sought the backing of European finance.[20] At the close of 1856 the Turkish government constituted a banking commission to review the projected 'national bank' which recast the matter in slightly different terms. These were also unattractive to at least four of the competitors for the concession – the Ottoman Bank, the Crédit Mobilier, Rothschilds and the consortium of local houses, but the revised concession was sought by Wilkin. He represented a London syndicate, headed by W. Gladstone, which had been seeking an opening at Constantinople since the spring of 1855.[21] It has been inferred, from the presence of S. Laing M.P., Brassey and Darby within this group, that it was a railway hunting syndicate, but the terms of the concession clearly demonstrate that the institution was designed as the Turkish equivalent of the Bank of England and the Bank of France. The Gladstone group's concession was apparently formally ratified in March 1857. It was for an issuing bank, with a cover of 50 per cent for a circulation up to £15m. The promoters' original intention was to raise the necessary capital in France and Germany, as well as England.[22]

In mid-1857 Turkish financial affairs became even more chaotic, marked outwardly by the fall of the exchange, the result of the general European economic crisis and difficulties in the Danubian provinces. This situation appears to have rendered the initial Gladstone bank concession moribund. However in 1858 the Ottoman Bank was able to issue £3m, nominal, of a Turkish loan totalling £5m, nominal, and these resources were supposedly earmarked for reforming the Turkish currency. The Ottoman Bank used the relative success of this flotation to put forward proposals for monetary reform.[23]

The mere news of the loan led to both the Turkish exchange improving and a reawakening of the interest of the Gladstone group, now operating with the Banque Générale Suisse. However the pattern of events from the end of 1858 and through the opening months of 1859 was complex. In December 1858 discussions with the Gladstone group appear to have been terminated, the Turkish government also declining the Ottoman Bank's currency reform proposals. Yet in February 1859 the Gladstone group secured a fresh firman.[24] But this too proved to be a false start, as the economy of the eastern Mediterranean in 1859 was disrupted by the Italian war. In these circumstances the Turkish government established a further commission to review financial questions, with Falconnet, the Ottoman Bank's Constantinople manager, a member. The National Bank of Turkey group made another move in October 1859 to activate its concession, through Gladstone, now working with M.E. Rodocanachi, depositing £20,000 with the Bank of England. The Turkish government responded positively, by nominating its directors, leaving the foreign concessionaires to appoint a further eight. The prospectus for the National Bank of Turkey was, at last, issued in London during the final week of 1859.[25] The subscription list closed on 7 January 1860 with 80–90,000 applications for 50,000 shares and by the end of the month it was expected that the bank would open in June.[26]

Certainly by spring 1860 Turkish finances seemed to be set fair. The Ottoman Bank was able to issue the balance of its 1858 loan, while the exchange further improved. Moreover, the Turkish authorities appeared to be establishing the necessary domestic environment for the 'Gladstone' bank to commerce business, since the proceeds of the 1858 loan were applied to withdrawing some 547.9m piastres of the paper money, leaving only 71.0m remaining. This was to meet the stipulations of the Gladstone group which called for a complete cessation of the paper circulation before the National Bank began business on the basis of the gold standard.[27] However, although the Gladstone–Rodocanachi group determined with the Turkish authorities various deadlines for the final withdrawal of paper money, other events prevented them from being met.[28] This impasse in the affairs of the still embryonic National Bank of Turkey led, in August 1860, to some of its London shareholders attempting to wind up the institution. Yet its promoters persisted, apparently hoping in the late autumn of 1860 that the new Turkish external loan, contracted with Mirès, would resolve the situation.[29] These expectations proved to be misplaced, as the frail fabric of Turkey finance was totally rent by a further series of calamities – economic, natural and political.

Continuing disturbances in Syria since 1859 seriously affected Beirout, the important mercantile centre of the Levant, to the extent that in mid-1860 the Ottoman Bank placed the books of its branch there on a man-of-war. This situation forced the Turkish authorities to resort to the printing press, ultimately to the equivalent of £8m. The uneasy situation and monetary expansion tightened local money markets[30] and from early 1861 the eastern Mediterranean was affected by a growing commercial crisis, leading to the suspension of 19 houses at Constantinople.[31] Galatz in February 1861 was flooded, which destroyed corn in store and ruined 15,000 of the town's inhabitants.[32] Bad went to worse with the arrest in Paris of Mirès for fraud, which put the external loan into doubt.[33] This Turkish financial collapse caused the effective demise of the National Bank of Turkey, although its death throes continued until 1863.[34]

The concatenation of events in the eastern Mediterranean – natural, political and financial – between 1859 and 1861 resulted in some of the Ottoman Bank's shareholders pressing for liquidation.[35] This was despite the board in March 1861 both declaring a dividend of eight per cent and putting a further £5,000 into the Reserve Fund, which then stood at £63,196, mostly in Consols. The Bank of Egypt was also in difficulties, although largely as a result of lax management. The board required Pasquali to resign in October 1860, after it had been discovered he had lent £162,000 to a member of the Egyptian ruling family and had been less than diplomatic in his efforts to recover the loan. This led to the Viceroy's family closing their accounts with the bank, and also strain in the bank's relations with Oppenheims, the Viceroy's financial agents. The imbroglio was investigated by Anstruther, the bank's deputy chairman, who managed to reduce the princely debt to £70,000. But he also discovered other 'lock-ups', totalling £120,000, largely illiquid advances on land, which it seemed in early 1861 would only be recovered at a loss. The bank's London board now publicly declared that they had always recognised that Pasquali had been a risk, phrased as 'a partiality for difficult engagements'. Further complications were caused during 1861 by exchange difficulties, but the Bank of Egypt recovered. By August 1861 the princely debt had been reduced to £30,000, the loss on the land loans appeared to be now £8,000, while, under these pressures, overheads were cut by £3,000 and the board felt confident enough to declare a dividend of seven per cent.[36]

The Ottoman Bank survived the difficulties of 1861 and, through announcing a debt of £152,000 owed by the Turkish authorities, implicitly acknowledged to shareholders that it had become primarily a banker to the state. Actually the bank was now almost in a monopoly position over Turkish government finance and it capitalised on this by floating an external loan in 1862. Once again this had the purpose of reforming the currency and stabilising the exchange. However this was now to take place under the supervision of French and English financial commissioners, appointed following the crisis in Turkish finance in 1860/61. The Ottoman issued the 1862 Turkish loan in conjunction with Charles Devaux & Co. and Glyn, Mills. The flotation was an overwhelming success, being oversubscribed seven times; it astounded the British financial press.[37] The commission on the loan enabled the Ottoman to declare a dividend of ten per cent in mid-1862 and place £15,000 to reserves, raising the latter to £93,000. As well as moving towards being the banker to the Turkish authorities, the Ottoman also developed its commercial business, opening a branch at Bucharest. Nonetheless it was the renewal of 'closer relations with the government' which was important and led the board of the Ottoman Bank to decide to double the institution's capital and seek to ease the restrictions in the clauses of its British charter.[38]

The resources of the 1862 loan allowed the withdrawal of the Turkish paper currency, which put into play yet again the question of establishing a Turkish national bank. During November 1862 Fruhling & Goschen, with Devaux, competed for the concession, but it was gained by the Ottoman with the Crédit Mobilier and its Parisian associated *banques des affaires*.[39] The new bank – the Imperial Ottoman Bank – a true multinational concern based in Constantinople, London and Paris, received its firman on 29 January 1863. However, as in the late 1850s, the prior negotiations had proved difficult, provoking a ministerial crisis. The new bank had a concession for 30 years and was to be the banker to the Turkish authorities as well as a bank of issue. It was to receive the public revenue and pay interest on the public debt for a commission of one per cent plus £20,000 *per annum*. As a bank of issue, its notes were to have initially a cover of 50 per cent, falling to 33.3 per cent after two years, but this stipulation was not effected, the European founders preferring 100 per cent cover. As a national bank, the head office was to be in Constantinople, with the Turkish government appointing a high commissioner and an inspector. The direction of the bank was to be through a committee of 20 to 25, with sub-committees, consisting of four each, in London and Paris.[40]

The creation of the Imperial Ottoman did not go totally smoothly in London. The concessionaires of the defunct National Bank of Turkey protested, but the Court of Chancery maintained that, on technical grounds, it was powerless to interfere in Turkish matters. Further, some of the shareholders in the Ottoman objected to the change in the bank's character and nature. However these objections came to nothing. With the reconstitution, each shareholder of the Ottoman received 2 shares of the Imperial Ottoman for every Ottoman share, new (1862) or old (1856), held.[41]

IV

Layard and George Grenfell Glyn did not participate in the transformation of the Ottoman as they had resigned from the direction in the spring of 1862. Layard left the board of the Ottoman on entering government office, while Glyn retired because of 'pressure of business at his own bank'. Their places were taken by the Hon. T.C. Bruce, the brother of Lord Elgin, and Pascoe du Pré Grenfell.[42] Grenfell was one of the sons of the Swansea copper smelter, Pascoe St. Leger Grenfell, and a business associate of Glyns as well as being related by marriage. Within two months the Glyn bank was involved in the promotion of the London & Brazilian Bank, its prospectus issued on 6 May 1862.[43] It was one of a number of British registered corporate international banks established before the Companies Act of that year became operative on 2 November.[44]

Part of the attraction for founding banks in the eastern Mediterranean had been the potential to take advantage of the 'turn' in interest rates as between western European financial centres and the Levant. Brazil had the same lure, and the first point of the prospectus of the London & Brazilian stressed that in Rio 'the minimum rate for the best mercantile paper at banks rules from 8 to 9 per cent'. However the growth of British trade was also a stimulus, with exports to Latin America, by value, growing markedly from 1863 and being by 1866 54.5 per cent, at current prices, above their previous cyclical peak – 1860. Imports also expanded – by 60.8 per cent as between 1860 and 1866.[45] Brazil had particular attractions with the 'Cotton Famine', ranking third, after India and Egypt, as a potential alternative supplier to the American South.[46] J.W. Cater, of R. Benson & Co., was the mainspring of the London & Brazilian, but it was established with the assistance of two of the Glyns – George Grenfell and Pascoe Carr.[47] The bank was formed in Brazil by a Brazilian decree, not a charter, but the provisions of the local law were considered in London to be conservative and therefore restrictive. The directors soon found that the Portuguese link remained critical for the Brazilian economy and, consequently, at the end of 1862 applied to the Portuguese government to open at Lisbon and elsewhere within the kingdom. In practice this objective proved to be more easily accomplished by acquiring the interests of the recently formed Anglo-Portuguese Bank.[48]

The London & Brazilian was registered on 17 May 1862 by James Alexander, Henri Louis Bischoffsheim, J.W. Cater, Philip Charles Cavan, J. Bloxham Elin, Pascoe C. Glyn, Edward Johnston, Edward

Moon, and William Freer Scholefield, who constituted the bank's first board. The legal work had been undertaken by Birchams, Drake's firm. The bank began with a nominal capital of £1m, consisting of £100 shares on which £35 was paid up during the first year of the bank's existence. There were just 43 major shareholders, each with holdings greater than 50 shares, who contributed, collectively, just over half of the bank's initial subscribed capital. Amongst them were members of the Glyn family and bank and this interest was larger since George Grenfell subscribed for 20 shares. Beyond this inner core were directors of the Imperial Ottoman Bank, such as J. Alexander with 70 shares and W.R. Drake holding 20 shares. A new element was not only co-operation with R. Benson & Co., but also Bischoffsheim & Goldschmidt, with German members of the Goldschmidt family also taking stakes – Heyman B., of Stuttgart, holding 50 and Benedict H., of Frankfurt a.M., initially 100, but of which 50 were soon sold.[49]

Like the Ottoman in the late 1850s, the London & Brazilian was rapidly subject to competition. In July 1863 the prospectus of the Brazilian & Portuguese Bank was published. It had a nominal capital of £1m dividend into £20 shares and a board of London merchants, coupled with a local board in Rio of wealthy Brazilians. This bank obtained Portuguese royal decrees and was not legally constituted to operate in both Brazil and Portugal until March 1864.[50] The Brazilian & Portuguese was badly affected by a commercial crisis at Rio at the turn of 1864, with losses of £40,000. One reaction was to rebuild its Rio committee and, although by mid-1865 the bank was once more generating a profit, no divided was declared because of exchange problems.[51] It would appear that the London & Brazilian was unaffected by the commercial convulsion at Rio. In mid-1865 its London board announced plans for a fusion with the banking interests in Argentina, Brazil and Uraguay of Barão de Mauá, the leading Brazilian capitalist of the mid-nineteenth century,[52] with the aim of establishing on 1 January 1866 the London, Brazilian, Mauá & River Plate Bank. Legal difficulties prevented this, the fusion being publicly announced as delayed until January 1867, although by then it had been rendered still-born by the 1866 crisis. However before the crash of Overend, Gurney, more competitors entered the field, with the local establishment of the Commercial Bank of Rio de Janeiro, which had one English representative on its board.[53]

V

The third bank with which the Glyns were involved during the mid-century was the Anglo-Austrian, for which George Grenfell took the first steps in January 1863. The necessary Austrian concession was gained on 5 October 1863 and during intervening months George Grenfell had had to tussle with competition from both the Rothschilds and a London speculative concern – the Union Bank of Austria. The discussions in Vienna were left to an agent, G.E. Seymour, while George Grenfell's greatest personal difficulty was the construction of a London board for his institution, on which there were vacant places even after the bank had been publicly announced.[54]

VI

Although the Glyns refrained from directly promoting further overseas banks during the 1860s and 1870s, their financial associates continued. The next institution was the Anglo-Italian Bank. Its flotation was undertaken by the International Financial Society, a finance company formed in May 1863 by London merchant bankers and to which Glyns acted as bankers. A proposal to establish this bank had been placed before the board of the International in November 1863[55] and a 'dummy' company with a capital of £2,000 was registered on 2 January 1864.[56] The International had adopted this procedure of registering dummy companies in June 1863 after nearly losing the company name of a prospective promotion, because of prior registration by other parties. During the mid-1860s financial boom there was an active trade in company names, a factor responsible for both the cluttering of the company register and the incidence of 'small' and abortive companies.[57]

The Anglo-Italian was a constituent of the wave of 'Anglo' banks formed in the mid-1860s, many of which were highly speculative concerns. The Anglo-Italian had a rationale in that Italy attracted foreign capital after the creation of the kingdom in 1859, while Anglo-Italian trade grew rapidly from the early 1850s, especially Italian exports to Britain.[58] The bank was finally registered in London on 13 January 1864 with a capital of £1m. divided into 20,000 £50 shares[59] and these were issued by the International for a commission of £10,000.[60] R. Benson and G.H. Goschen of the International signed the bank's memorandum of association, with Benson becoming a director.[61] The London merchant bank, Thompson, Bonar & Co., through C. Bell, took up a portion of the bank's capital and John Lubbock, the London private banker, was its first chairman. Two Italian merchants resident in London – Julius Bordier and Ippolite Leonino – were also involved in the formation of the bank. It took a further month for the bank's prospectus to be issued and again, as with the Anglo-Austrian, the completion of the institution's directorate seems to have been the problem.[62]

The impression made by the bank's first return of shareholders to the Registrar of Joint Stock Companies, dated 10 February 1865, a year after the public flotation of shares, is that of a 'staged', 'boom' promotion. Some 18,335 shares had been subscribed. Of these 17,590 – 96 per cent – were sold during the bank's first year of existence, but other factors, arising from Italian domestic politics, may equally have led to this high turnover.

The Anglo-Italian commenced business in Italy in October 1864 with the opening of its head branch at Turin, the Italian capital.[63] However the progress of the bank was then affected by instability within the Italian economy and politics. The post-war speculative financial bubble collapsed in 1864,[64] while domestic politics were unsettled, with a major issue being the site of the capital. Turin was not Italian enough, regarded by many as Piedmontese. Marco Minghetti, Cavour's successor, agreed with Tuscan deputies that the capital should be more centrally situated and be more 'Italian' in complexion. The question was settled in September, 1864 through a convention with France, by which Napoleon III undertook to withdraw troops from Rome within two years provided that Florence became the capital. This led to fresh uproar in Italian political life and a catastrophic fall in Turin property values. Nonetheless Lamarmona, who had replaced Minghetti, was able to transfer the seat of government to Florence within six months.[65] This affected the Anglo-Italian Bank through the costs arising from having established its Italian base at Turin.[66] On 1 December 1864 it opened a branch at Milan, managed, as at Turin, through a local committee and, in early 1865, was planning to establish, imminently, further offices at Florence and Naples. The bank was able to pay a dividend of over six per cent for 1864 and in August 1865 declared an interim divided of five per cent.[67]

The Anglo-Italian Bank was also affected by the British financial crisis of 1866 and the Italian war of that year, but its board argued that its difficulties stemmed from the Italian suspension of cash payments. In mid-1866 the directors maintained that this accounted for the difference of £8,768, as between assets and liabilities, equivalent to 13.5 per cent of the bank's capital and reserve fund. Nevertheless it was decided to persevere with the institution through a capital reconstruction. However this could only be accomplished by first winding up the old bank and then forming a new concern, registered on 15 March 1867.[68] This transformation was undertaken by the board, through initially creating a new company without any paid-up capital.

VII

Not all of the 'international' banks formed in the mid-1860s were public companies. The London & San Francisco Bank was a very private concern having initially only 10 shareholders who collectively took up 11,000 shares, thereby supplying £110,000. It was created in March 1865 by London, Parisian and Frankfurt merchant bankers, some of whom, like H.L. Bischoffsheim and H. Stern had been involved in the London & Brazilian, while F. Rodewald had been a founder of the Brazilian & Portuguese Bank, as well as a director of the London Joint Stock Bank. The other London houses involved were Huths, Morgans, and Fruhling & Goschen, all constituents of the International Financial Society. Frankfurt was represented by the private bankers J. May and R. Sulzbach and, via the latter, the Bank of Saxe Meiningen. Charles Griswold stood for the Paris market. There was no question over the bank's private character:

> no new subscriber shall be admitted unless he be approved by a majority of the shareholders, determined by votes given, as provided in Article 44 ...
>
> No shareholder shall without the previous consent of the holders of the other shares or the majority of three-fourths parts thereof, determined by votes given, (as provided in Article 44) at any time within a period of three years from the constitution of the company, sell or dispose of any of his shares.[69]

These restrictive conditions continued until August 1869, when Messrs. Russell & Sturgis of Manila were admitted as shareholders and given the same rights as the original founders. The Philippino house was represented on the bank's London board by E.H. Green. The bank developed on the western coast of America, not so much through expansion in California, but as a result of sizeable agencies in Portland, Tacoma and Seattle, although overall growth was restricted by conservative management from London.[70]

Political change affected the structures of some of the banks formed in the mid-1860s. There had been attempts since the beginning of the decade to establish a 'European' bank in Romania and another opportunity arose in 1865, when the nationalistic Couza regime authorised the formation of the Banca Roumanei. The Crédit Mobilier had been an early contender in the field, but increasing internal difficulties prevented it from pursuing the matter in 1865. Instead, after a struggle with the Société Générale,[71] the concession was gained by a syndicate composed of some of the Mobilier's associates – the Pereires and Mallet Frères – together with the Imperial Ottoman Bank and the International Financial Society of London.[72]

The new bank took over the existing agencies of the Imperial Ottoman at Bucharest and Galatz,[73] assuming their assets and liabilities for an immediate cash sum of £115,000, with a further payment of £25,000 to be made within six months. Existing accounts were to be liquidated without the Imperial Ottoman being charged a commission. An offer by the new bank to rent the property of the Imperial Ottoman at Galatz at 5 per cent was declined, as the Imperial Ottoman desired an outright sale.[74] The bank was floated during the difficult year of 1866 with the International taking 2,000 shares in the bank,[75] while the Imperial Ottoman took an interest equivalent to the capital that it had invested in the former agencies.[76] Although the bank's head office was at Bucharest, its capital was denominated in sterling. The London Committee of Imperial Ottoman Bank did interlock with that of the Bank of Roumania, so that in 1872 James Alexander, Sir W.R. Drake, Pascoe du Pré Grenfell, and L.M. Rate sat on both boards.

Similarly, with the relative autonomy of Hungary, following the *Ausgleich* of 1867, the Budapest branch of the AngloAustrian Bank formed the basis for the creation of 1868 of the AngloHungarian Bank, with a capital denominated in florins. In 1872 this bank had a London Committee composed of S.A. Beaumont M.P., F. Engelhardt, both directors of the AngloAustrian, and J. Gerstenberg, S. Reuter, and J.F. Wulff.[77]

VIII

Glyns' associates constituted further corporate international banks in the boom of the early 1870s. E. Wanklyn had been a major investor in the London & Brazilian Bank and in 1872 his AngloArgentine private bank was converted into the Mercantile Bank of the River Plate, one of 12 foreign and two colonial banks effectively registered in London between 1870 and 1873.[78] This Latin American promotion was undertaken by the London Banking Association, a private finance house, constituted by the merchant banking communities of London and Paris. One of the 'City's' representatives was H.L. Bischoffsheim, who had also been involved in the establishment of the London and Brazilian Bank.[79] Backing for the Mercantile Bank came not only directly from the London Banking Association but also from its associates – the Banque de Paris et des Pays-Bas and Henry Oppenheim – and others, such as Baron Louis d'Erlanger and Louis Beer. The London–Paris group took founders' shares in the Mercantile Bank and made a public appeal for capital. The bank prospered during the early 1870s, with dividends of 15 per cent in 1873 and 10 per cent in 1874, but went into voluntary liquidation in 1881, when it was revealed that it held the controlling interest in the Montevideo waterworks.[80] Bischoffsheim Goldschimdt, with some of the 'Glyn group', also established, in May 1872, the Banque de Constantinople,[81] while in November 1872 the Imperial Ottoman Bank formed the London Bank of Tunis.[82]

The interests behind the creation of the London Banking Association, the Mercantile Bank, and some of the other international bank promotions of the early 1870s marked the ever-increasing cosmopolitan nature of the 'City'. A further formalisation of this was the foundation in April 1871 of the German Bank of London, with a nominal capital of £600,000. Its board was composed of some of the 'fringe' associates of what has been called here the 'Glyn group', namely E.H. Green, F. Rodewald, and R. Sulzbach, all directors of the London & San Francisco.[83] This bank was reconstituted in 1879 and in February 1913 changed its name to the London & Liverpool Bank of Commerce, while its share capital was acquired by the British Overseas Bank in 1923.[84]

IX

The role of the 'Glyn group' in founding international corporate banks continued on into the late nineteenth century. During the early 1880s it established the English Bank of the River Plate, directly replacing the failed Mercantile Bank of the River Plate, and designed to compete with the highly successful London and River Plate Bank formed in 1862.[85] The issue of the bank's £1m nominal capital was undertaken by the International Financial Society for a commission of £5,000.[86] The bank acquired an experienced manager, E.R. Duffield, who had previously been the Rio manager of the Brazilian and Portuguese Bank, but it fell victim to the Baring Crisis and could not be reconstituted. This trait of the Glyns can be traced further, the bank being part of the underwriting syndicate for the flotation of the capital of the Imperial Bank of Persia in the summer of 1889, while Geoffrey Glyn, the eldest son of Pascoe Glyn, went on to the bank's board.[87]

X

The continuing role, from the 1830s to the 1880s, played by the Glyns in the creation of British corporate international banks was remarkable, even more so when the activities of their associates are also included. However this 'Glyn group' was largely a promotional bloc, albeit one that also provided senior management, through directorships, to the banks that it founded. The capital for these institutions came largely from the 'City' and the south-eastern 'metropolitan area', as Table 1 shows.

Unfortunately source restrictions only enable three of the banks to be considered, so care has to be taken with putting forward any substantial general conclusion. This geographical concentration of capital supply is not too surprising, since the south-east was one of the most populous areas of the UK and certainly the wealthiest.[88] The only other region of

TABLE 1
GEOGRAPHICAL SOURCES OF CAPITAL
(% of initially subscribed capital)

Region	London and Brazilian Bank	Anglo-Italian Bank	Commercial Bank of the River Plate
'City, and Westminster	63.3	70.0	36.7
rest of the 'Metropolis'	4.85	4.49	0.78
rest of the South East	6.98	9.01	1.72
	75.13	83.5	38.2
East Anglia	0.05	1.2	0.1
East Midlands	0.2	0.36	0.04
West Midlands	0.45	0.03	0.33
South West	3.05	4.67	0.03
North West	11.2	4.85	13.83
Yorks. and Humberside	1.95	1.17	–
North	0.45	0.35	–
Wales	0.04	0.87	*trace*
Scotland	2.35	0.6	1.8
Ireland	1.95	0.54	0.07
Foreign	3.3	1.25	45.54

Source: First returns of shareholders to the Registrar of Joint Stock Companies, PRO, BT31, 641/2691; 878/905c; 1736/6406. In the case of the Commercial, founders' shares have been excluded from the calculation.

consequence was the north-west in the case of Latin American banks, and again this is explicable in terms of the trading links of Liverpool with South America. As Table 2 reveals, it was the commercial and financial communities which were the major investors in these banks. Once more, the available sources do cloud the resolution of the question, with the high level of subscriptions from what has been termed 'Unoccupied – Male' in the case of the London and Brazilian. Yet, although all subscribers have been treated for the purposes of compiling Tables 1 and 2 on the basis of the information that they themselves declared in the relevant returns, other knowledge of many that called themselves 'gentlemen', indicates that they were either merchants or bankers.

There still remains the question of whether these banks were actually 'British', although they were largely formed under British law and promoted by the 'City'. The modern 'City', since its origins in the eighteenth

TABLE 2
OCCUPATIONAL SOURCES OF CAPITAL
(% of initially subscribed capital)

Occupation	London and Brazilian Bank	Commercial Bank of the River Plate
Unoccupied		
Male	38.6	9.17
Female	0.55	0.08
Land	0.1	–
Professions	5.7	0.29
Commerce and Finance		
Merchants	34.75	37.01
Brokers	1.46	–
Bankers	3.4	33.13
Stockbrokers	10.9	5.37
Underwriters	1.4	0.11
Retail	0.15	*trace*
Other	0.4	0.11
Industry	–	1.05
Service workers	0.1	0.11
Unknown	2.42	13.12

Source: as for Table 1.

century, had been cosmopolitan in complexion and the founding of these banks was a 'cosmopolitan' enterprise, especially in the case of the Imperial Ottoman, with its affiliates, the Anglo-Austrian, and the Commercial Bank of the River Plate. In the case of the latter, as a result of the involvement of the London Banking Association and Bischoffsheim & Goldschmidt, nearly half of the bank's initial capital formally came from abroad. This is remarkable since Latin America from the 1860s has often been regarded as a very particular part of the 'informal' British empire. However an equally valid perspective would be that, with the maturity of financial centres in continental Europe and better communications with the telegraph, the cosmopolitan world of commerce and finance had moved a stage on from requiring a central physical centre, such as London had been during the first half of the nineteenth century. The 'cosmopolitan bourgeosie', as C. Jones has termed it, was acquiring a new morphology in responding to the widening opportunities of the evolving world economy.[89] By the early 1870s this could take the form of promoting a multinational corporate international bank, with its capital coming from a number of centres, formed under one system of commercial law, but to operate elsewhere in the jurisdiction of other legal codes.

NOTES

I am grateful to M. Vollor, a referee and the editor for comments and constructive criticism on an earlier draft.

1. A.S.J. Baster, *The International Banks* (1935).
2. From 1851 this bank was called Glyn, Mills & Co., but was restyled as Glyn, Mills, Currie & Co. in 1864. It was unique in many ways: it was a major London agent for country banks, but also acted as the 'railway bank', was involved in foreign lending and undertook long term loans to domestic manufacturing. Regrettably, there is only a general history: R. Fulford, *Glyn's 1753–1953* (1953).
3. See T. Skinner, *The Stock Exchange Year-Book for 1914* (1913), Section 'Banking and Discount Companies', pp. 443–90.
4. D.S. Landes, 'The Old Bank and the New: The Financial Revolution of the Nineteenth Century', *Revue d'Histoire Moderne et Contemporaine*, Vol. III (1956), translated in F. Crouzet *et al.*, *Essays in European Economic History 1789–1919* (1969); and D.S. Landes, *The Unbound Prometheus* (Cambridge, 1969), pp. 205–10.
5. M. Wilkins, 'The Free-Standing Company, 1870–1914: An Important Type of British Foreign Direct Investment', *Economic History Review*, 2nd series, Vol. XLI (1988). See also G. Jones (ed.), *Banks as Multinationals* (1990).
6. H.A. Shannon, 'The First Five Thousand Limited Companies and their Duration', *Economic History*, Vol. II (1930–3); on subsequent developments in the 1870s, see idem, 'The Limited Companies of 1866 and 1883', *Economic History Review*, Vol. IV (1932–33).
7. See A City Man [R.M.L. Meason], *The Bubbles of Finance* (1865), a reprint of articles which had previously appeared in *All the Year Round,* and idem, *The Profits of Panics showing how financial storms arise, who make money by them, and other revelations* ... (1866).
8. See A.K. Baggchi, *The Evolution of the State Bank of India*, Vol. I, *The Roots, 1806–1876*, Part I: *The Early Years, 1806–1860* (1987), pp. 352–7.
9. See S.J. Butlin, *Australia and New Zealand Bank* (1961) and, more generally, A.S.J. Baster, *The Imperial Banks* (1929).
10. See R. Davis, *The Industrial Revolution and Overseas Trade* (Leicester, 1979); J.R.T. Hughes, *Fluctuations in Trade, Industry and Finance* (Oxford, 1960).
11. D.A. Farnie, *East and West of Suez: The Suez Canal in History, 1854–1956* (Oxford, 1969), pp. 14–57.
12. *The Times*, 26 Jan. 1856, p. 6/c.
13. Ibid., 27 July 1855, p. 7/b; 11 March 1856, p. 11/c; 29 April 1856, p. 5/b; 17 July 1856, p. 12/d; 25 Aug. 1856, p. 5/c; 14 March 1857, p. 7/a; 26 Aug. 1857, p. 4/f; 6 March 1858, p. 7/a. A.S.J. Baster, 'The Origins of British Banking Expansion in the Near East', *Economic History Review*, Vol. V (1934/35).
14. *The Times*, 25 March 1857, p. 6/c; 14 Aug. 1858, p. 5/a.
15. Anon, *Extracts from a Private Diary and Correspondence 1855–1856* (1856). This pamphlet seeks to prove duplicity on the part of associates of Glyn, Mills; much of its contents agrees with statements in the financial press.
16. R.E. Cameron, *France and the Economic Development of Europe 1800–1914* (Princeton, NJ 1961), pp. 459–60.
17. *The Times*, 13 Feb. 1856, p. 10/c; 14 Feb. 1856, p. 5/a. The prospectus entirely agrees with *Extracts from a Private Diary* ... as it names A.H. Layard as chairman, with the following as directors: J.J. Cummins, R. Campbell, both directors of the Union Bank of Australia, H.A. Bruce, M.P., G.T. Clark, G.G. Glyn, A. Hankey, H. Kingscote (Sleigh's original intermediary with Glyns) and B. Weikersheim. Bruce was a lawyer by training, was M.P. for Merthyr Tydfil from 1852 and subsequently became a junior Minister in 1862. Clark too had a landed interest in South Wales and was a J.P. and D.L. for Glamorgan, Lieutenant-Colonel of the 2nd Battalion Glamorgan Rifle

Volunteers and chairman of the Merthyr Union. The bank did not formally receive its royal charter until 24 May 1856, see G. Young, *Corps de Droit ottoman*, Vol. V (Oxford, 1906), p. 25.

18. *The Times*, 1 April 1856, p. 6/b.
19. Ibid., 5 April 1856, p. 10/c & d; 22 Aug. 1856, p. 7/b; 27 Aug. 1856, p. 8/c; 28 Aug. 1856, p. 7/c.
20. Ibid., 11 Sept. 1856, p. 8/c.
21. Ibid., 6 Jan. 1857, p. 7/a; 10 Jan. 1857, p. 8/d; 12 Jan. 1857, p. 8/a; 14 Jan. 1857, p. 5/c. It consisted of Henry Coke of Holkham, Mark Hunter of the Commercial Bank of London, E.W. Fernie (a London merchant), T.A. Chance, T. Brassey, A. Darby, A.W. Rixon and a number of M.P.s, and they may have constituted the group that Pasquali had earlier approached in the House.
22. *The Times*, 19 Jan. 1857, p. 4/a; 5 March 1857, p. 7/c; 19 March 1857, p. 10/b; 8 April 1857, p. 10/d; 15 April 1857, p. 5/c.
23. Ibid., 10 July 1857, p. 6/a; 15 Aug. 1857, p. 11/c; 27 Aug. 1857, p. 9/e; 18 Sept. 1858, p. 5/a; 23 Sept. 1858, p. 7/a.
24. Ibid., 28 Sept. 1858, p. 8/c; 2 Dec. 1858, p. 4/e; 17 Feb. 1859, p. 7/a; 9 March 1859, p. 5/b.
25. Ibid., 10 Oct. 1859, p. 8/c; 31 Dec. 1859, p. 5/a; 2 Jan. 1860, p. 7/c; 3 Jan. 1860, p. 5/a; 5 Jan. 1860, p. 4/e; 6 Jan. 1860, p. 5/a; 11 Jan. 1860, p. 7/c. The bank had two English directors at Constantinople – Black and Hanson – who were to work in conjunction with French, Greek and Armenian colleagues. Its London board was composed of Russell Ellice and R. Tubini as well as Gladstone and Rodocanachi.
26. Ibid., 27 Jan. 1860, p. 9/a.
27. Ibid., 7 Feb. 1860, p. 10/e; 15 March 1860, p. 7/a; 7 Feb. 1863, p. 12/c.
28. Ibid., 25 Aug. 1860, p. 10/e. The exact extent of the paper circulation – the caim'es or kaimes – is unclear and so consequently is the amount either redeemed, or freshly issued, between 1859 and 1861. See ibid, 18 March 1862, p. 10/c.
29. Ibid., 27 Aug. 1860, p. 5/b; 10 Nov. 1860, p. 7/a; 22 Nov. 1860, p. 9/a.
30. Ibid., 20 Aug. 1860, p. 10/b; 27 Feb. 1863, p. 10/a.
31. D.S. Landes, *Bankers and Pashas* (1958), p. 62; *The Times,* 5 Feb. 1861, p. 5/a.
32. *The Times*, 4 March, 1861, p. 6/b.
33. Cameron, *France and ... Europe*, p. 461.
34. The directors issued a report to shareholders in September, 1861. *The Times*, 6 Sept. 1861, p. 5/b.
35. Ibid., 28 March 1861, p. 5/a.
36. Ibid., 9 Aug. 1860, p. 10/a; 9 Oct. 1860, p. 5/a; 8 Nov. 1860, p. 7/a; 12 Feb. 1861, p. 8/a; 26 Feb. 1861, p. 6/a; 27 July 1861, p. 10/f; 6 Aug. 1861, p. 5/a. By the end of 1861 the El Hami debt had fallen to £25,000 and the land loans to £80,000, with the interest on the latter being serviced by rents. The El Hami debt had been further reduced to £6,000 by mid-1862. *The Times*, 18 Feb. 1862, p. 10/a; 26 July 1862, p. 12/e.
37. *The Times*, 5 Sept. 1861, p. 5/a; Landes, *Bankers*, p. 63 and fn2.
38. Ibid., 5 Sept. 1861, p. 5/a; 18 March 1862, p. 10/e; 7 May 1862, p. 6/a; 21 Aug. 1862, p. 7/a.
39. Hottinguer, Mallet Frères, Fould, Pillet Will. Ibid., 21 Nov. 1862, p. 7/a; 24 Nov. 1862, p. 7/b; 1 Dec. 1862, p. 6/a; 6 Dec. 1862, p. 7/a.
40. Ibid., 30 Jan. 1863, p. 10/a; 7 Feb. 1863, p. 12/c; 16 Feb. 1863, p. 10/c. See also C. Clay, 'The Imperial Ottoman Bank in the Late Nineteenth Century: Multinational "National" Bank?', in Jones (ed.), *Banks as Multinationals*.
41. *The Times*, 22 Nov. 1862, p. 7/a; 27 Feb. 1863, p. 10/a; 28 Feb. 1863, p. 10/a.
42. Ibid., 7 March 1862, p. 10/a; 18 March 1862, p. 10/e.
43. Ibid., 6 May 1862, p. 12/e.
44. The wave of promotions of domestic banks also antedated 2 November 1862, with formations beginning in September 1861. See P.L. Cottrell, 'Credit, Morals and Sunspots ...', in P.L. Cottrell and D.E. Moggridge (eds.), *Money and Power* (1988), pp. 45–6.
45. Calculated from B.R. Mitchell with P. Deane, *Abstract of British Historical Statistics* (Cambridge, 1962), pp. 313–27.

46. Landes, *Bankers*, p. 71.
47. D. Joslin, *A Century of Banking in Latin America* (1963), pp. 64–5.
48. *The Times*, 5 Sept. 1862, p. 5/a; 27 Dec. 1862, p. 4/d; 1 May 1863, p. 10/d; 26 Jan. 1866, p. 6/a.
49. PRO, BT31, 641/2691.
50. *The Times*, 1 July 1863, p. 13/a; 3 March 1864, p. 6/b.
51. Ibid., 18 May 1865, p. 12/b; 20 Nov. 1865, p. 7/a. During 1866 the Brazilian & Portuguese Bank was still pursuing a cautious policy, with profits being devoted both to making good the losses incurred two years previously and to building up a reserve designed to act as a buffer against exchange fluctuations. The bank's agency at Lisbon proved not to be profitable and, when it was relinquished in 1866, the whole institution was renamed the English Bank of Rio de Janeiro. Ibid., 17 May 1866, p. 6/a; 22 Oct. 1866, p. 5/b; 21 Dec. 1866, p. 7/b.
52. R. Graham, *Britain and the Onset of Modernization in Brazil, 1850–1914* (Cambridge, 1968), pp. 118, 187–8.
53. *The Times*, 18 April 1865, p. 5/e; 3 May 1865, p. 10/a; 9 March 1866, p. 10/a.
54. For a fuller account and discussion, see P.L. Cottrell, 'London Financiers and Austria 1863–1875: The Anglo-Austrian Bank', *Business History*, Vol. XI (1969), reprinted in R.P.T. Davenport-Hines (ed.), *Capital, Entrepreneurs and Profits* (1990).
55. University of Hull, Library, Records of the International Financial Society; Minutes of Board Meetings (hereafter I.B.), 26 Nov. 1863.
56. PRO, BT31, 872/881c.
57. The company in question was the Egyptian Commercial and Trading Co. which forced the International to rename, for some time, its prospective concern the Trading Company of Egypt. That the first registration was purely forestalling is indicated by both its capital of £2,000 and that its only shareholders were the seven signatories to its memorandum of association. It was informally dissolved after consenting to the registration of the International's Egyptian Commercial and Trading Co. See PRO, BT31, 787/472c. Another example is the Mauritius Land Credit and Agency, where the International's own dummy informed the Registrar of Joint Stock Companies: 'We request that you will do us the favour of cancelling our registration of a company . . . we having no intention of proceeding with it, but having registered it only for the purpose of preserving the name for another company whose documents are sent herewith'. PRO, BT31, 869/869c.
58. A. Glazier and V.N. Bandera, 'Terms of Trade between South Italy and the United Kingdom, 1817–1869, 'Terms of Trade between South Italy and the United Kingdom, 1817–1869', *Journal of European Economic History*, Vol. I (1972), pp. 9,14,16; Cameron, *France and . . . Europe*, p. 452; Baster, *International Banks*, p. 47.
59. PRO, BT31, 878/905c.
60. I.B., 7 Jan, 1864.
61. *Bankers' Magazine* (1864), p. 92; see also *Economist*, 16 Jan. 1864, p. 78.
62. *The Times*, 7 Jan. 1864, p. 6/b; 12 Feb. 1864, p. 7/a. By the time of the publication of the prospectus Sir J. Hudson and Baron Ricasoli had become directors.
63. Ibid., 7 Oct. 1864, p. 5/a.
64. Cameron, *France and . . . Europe*, p. 452.
65. D. Mack Smith, *Italy, a Modern History* (Michigan, 1959), p. 65.
66. Baster, *International Banks*, p. 48.
67. *The Times*, 23 Jan. 1865, p. 6/b; 18 Aug. 1865, p. 4/a.
68. Ibid., 28 Aug. 1866, p. 5/a; 25 Nov. 1866, p. 5/a. PRO, BT31, 1296/3295.
69. PRO, BT31, 1081/2009c, Articles of Association (31 March 1865), Nos. 7–8.
70. Baster, *International Banks,* p. 158. Another Pacific venture was the British & Californian Bank formed in 1864, the conversion of a long established San Francisco institution. It collapsed in 1866 as a result of the difficulties of one of its 'London' shareholders – the Agra & Masterman's Bank. King would appear to have confused London & San Francisco with the British & Californian; *vide* F.H.H. King, *The Hongkong Bank in Late Imperial China, 1864–1902* (Cambridge, 1987), pp. 95–6. Russell, Sturgis & Co. were also the Manila agents of the Hongkong & Shanghai Bank

from March, 1865.

71. *The Times*, 5 June 1865, p. 12/b.
72. Cameron, *France and ... Europe*, pp. 189–90; Baster, *International Banks*, p. 99.
73. Imperial Ottoman Bank, Minutes of the London Agency (hereafter I.O.B., L.A.), 14 Dec. 1864; *The Times*, 27 Oct. 1865, p. 5/b.
74. I.O.B., L.A., 5 Dec. 1865.
75. I.B., 7 Dec. 1865. University of Hull, Library; records of the International Financial Society, Minutes of Committee Meetings (hereafter I.C.), 16 Dec. 1865.
76. Baster, *International Banks*, p. 99.
77. *Bankers' Almanac* (1872).
78. Shannon, 'Limited Companies of 1866–1883'; this banking boom also involved the creation of 16 domestic institutions.
79. PRO, BT31, 1677/5957; P.L. Cottrell, *Investment Banking in England* (1985), Vol. II, pp. 495–6.
80. H.S. Fearns, *Britain and Argentinia in the Nineteenth Century* (1960), pp. 361–2.
81. I.B., 23 May 1872, 30 May 1872; Baster, *International Banks*, p. 95.
82. I.B., 28 Nov. 1872; Baster, *International Banks*, pp. 112–19.
83. *Bankers' Almanac* (1872).
84. *Register of Defunct and other Companies ... 1955* (1955).
85. Joslin, *Banking in Latin America*, pp. 108, 118.
86. I.C., 10 May 1881; I.B., 12 May 1881.
87. G. Jones, *Banking and Empire in Iran* (Cambridge, 1986), pp. 26–29.
88. In 1881 Greater London had a population of 4.77m., about 16 per cent of the total population of Great Britain: Mitchell with Deane, *Abstract of Historical Statistics*, pp. 6, 19. On the distribution of wealth see W.D. Rubinstein, 'The Victorian Middle Classes: Wealth, Occupation and Geography', *Economic History Review*, 2nd Series, Vol. XXX (1977).
89. C.A. Jones, *International Business in the 19th Century* (1987), p. 94.

Financial Elites in Three European Centres: London, Paris, Berlin, 1880s–1930s

YOUSSEF CASSIS

University of Geneva and Business History Unit, London School of Economics

Bankers, and more generally financial elites, are rarely included in the discussions on entrepreneurs and the main questions they raise, whether in terms of ownership and management or in terms of social mobility. The object of this article is to consider the financial elites of the three major European economies from the 1880s to the 1930s. The differences between the English, French and German banking systems are relatively well known and the relationships between financial structure and economic development have been for several decades a central issue in economic and business history. Bankers and financiers have remained absent from these debates and analysis. An important question is whether a different type of banker and financier, defined both in terms of professional activity and social status, existed in London, Paris and Berlin; and if there were significant differences, to what extent they were the product of the banking system prevailing in each country, and in turn whether the socio-professional characteristics of a financial centre had any incidence on the interaction between finance and the 'real' economy.

These questions will be considered in a comparative perspective. It will be argued that the earlier emergence of a professional banking elite in Germany appears unlikely to have had long-term economic implications. In a first section, the main attributes of London, Paris and Berlin as financial centres will be briefly discussed. In a second section, the professional and business positions of bankers and financiers in the three centres will be examined, and in a third section their social status. Some conclusions will be drawn in a fourth seciton. The notion of financial elite will be primarily applied throughout this article to senior bankers and financiers, and to a certain extent to merchants and other professional groups which are found on the boards of the joint stock banks. Other groups, such as stockbrokers, money dealers, insurance brokers, commodity brokers and so on, although they will occasionally be referred to, cannot be included in the financial elite. In the first place, only a handful of them belonged to the highest ranks of the financial world; secondly, they were to be found in much greater number in the City of London than in the two other centres, particularly in Berlin, where these activities were usually undertaken by bank officials.

I

As financial centres, London, Paris and Berlin present both many contrasts and many similarities. Although all three were the financial – as well as the political – capitals of countries of comparable size, the scope of their financial activities varied considerably. This was due to the form of financial organisation prevailing in each country, their degree of development and sophistication, as well as to the role of each city as an international financial centre. In hierarchical order London came first followed by Paris and then Berlin. This order did not change throughout the period under review and indeed has not changed up to this day.

Before 1914 the position of London as the financial centre of the world meant that world trade was financed through the medium of bills of exchange drawn on London, whereas bills on Paris or Berlin were only used in order to finance the commerce of these countries.[1] The capital exported from Britain – between £3.5 billion and £4 million in 1913 – considerably exceeded the capital exported from France – about £1.8 billion – and from Germany – about £1.1 billion.[2] As a consequence, London was the leading centre for the issue of foreign loans and equity. The London Stock Exchange was larger than the Paris and Berlin stock exchanges put together; however, Paris emerged in the second half of the nineteenth century, alongside London, as an international market covering in particular Europe and the Mediterranean era, whereas Berlin had to compete with both Frankfurt and Hamburg and never managed to dominate, although it was considered to have the edge.[3] The insurance market was also much bigger in London, with the emergence, to a greater extent than in the two other centres, of large composite companies with offices in several cities in North and South America, Australia and other parts of the empire.[4] Only two German insurance companies, and not a single French one, had premium incomes in excess of £2 million in 1910 as against ten in Britain. With over £12 million premium income that year, the Prudential the largest insurance company in Britain, was twice as large as its German counterpart, the Victoria zu Berlin.[5] London's dominance of the world of insurance was also due to the unique role played by Lloyd's, first and foremost in the field of marine insurance, but also and increasingly from the early twentieth century through its capacity to insure new risks.[6] Many commodities were traded primarily if not exclusively in London, and markets such as the Baltic Exchange or the London Metal Exchange had no equivalent in the two continental centres.

These business opportunities attracted many foreigners to London, whether individuals or institutions. It has been observed that in the foreign governments bonds market of the London Stock Exhange, French and German could be heard as often as English[7] and that the foreign exchange business in the City of London was almost entirely in foreign hands. From the 1870s on, all the leading European and American banks opened a branch in London; the number of branches of foreign banks in the City amounted to about 30 in 1913.[8] The London bankers were fully aware of the attractions the City offered to foreign banks. Alexander Goschen, a partner in the merchant bank Frühling & Goschen and a director of the London Joint Stock Bank, considered that there was a bigger market for everything in London and that many operations undertaken by foreign banks in the City could not be done by British banks in a European centre. According to Goschen, this explained why the English clearing banks were so reluctant to open branches abroad.[9] The overseas banks, however, ensured that many more multinational banks were based in London than in Paris or Berlin. The number of foreign branches of British banks has been estimated at 2,000 in 1913 as against 500 for French and German Banks.[10] The attractions of Paris to foreign banks should not, however, be underestimated, as about 20 of them had opened a branch there in 1914.[11]

Despite these differences at the international level, London, Paris and Berlin showed greater similarities on the domestic banking scene. In the three centres there remained until 1914 a financial aristocracy based on old family partnerships. The largest joint stock banks were also of the same size: in 1913, Lloyds Bank and the Midland Bank in London, the Crédit Lyonnais in Paris, and the Deutsche Bank in Berlin all had total assets amounting to about £100 million. The continental banks, however, worked with a larger capital than their English counterparts which, in turn, had higher deposits.[12] One reason for this difference in the structure of their liabilities lies in the banking organisation of each country. As is well known, the English banking system was much more specialised than those existing on the Continent. The English joint stock banks confined themselves to deposit banking, other operations being undertaken by the discount houses, the merchant banks, the overseas banks and the investment trusts, whereas in Germany the so-called 'universal' banks undertook all sorts of financial operations including long-term investment and the issue of securities on behalf of industrial companies. In France, the commercial banks modelled themselves on the English joint stock banks and, even though the system was less specialised than in England, there was a clear difference between the *banques de dépôts* (deposit banks) and the *banques d'affaires* (investment banks). It is nevertheless interesting to note that, although the City of London was the world's leading financial centre, and despite the beginning of Britain's relative industrial decline, the largest companies in Britain, measured in terms of paid-up capital, were not banks but manufacturing industries, whereas the reverse was true in France and Germany.[13]

The First World War put an end to London's unrivalled financial supremacy, as a result of the sale of part of British overseas investments, its abandonment of the Gold Standard and the difficulties of returning to it between 1925 and 1931, and more generally Britain's weakened economic position. However, the challenge to London's world leadership came from New York, not from Paris and even less Berlin, and this challenge was only gradual, for if the capital was henceforth in New York, experience and expertise remained in London.[14] Berlin's position was considerably weakened by defeat, inflation and reparations. The situation of Paris was somewhat different: although it never developed the range of financial services which would have enabled it to challenge London seriously, the gold reserves and the sterling assets held by the Banque de France, as a result of the overvaluation of the pound and the undervaluation of the franc, put Paris in a strong position *via-à-vis* London and enhanced its international status, particularly in the immediate aftermath of Britain's departure from gold in 1931.[15] Otherwise, despite the loss of its financial supremacy in favour of New York, London actually widened the gap which separated it from the two continental centres, and from Berlin in particular. In 1938, the capital exported from Britain amounted to $22.9 billion, as against $3.9 billion for France and $700 million for Germany.[16] The London Stock Exchange remained far larger than its continental counterparts, as did the insurance market and the insurance companies. As far as the clearing banks were concerned, after the amalgamation movement of 1918 which gave birth to the 'Big Five', they now outdistanced in size their French and German competitors, both in terms of capital and deposits.[17]

II

The professional position of financial elites in London, Paris and Berlin can be compared at three levels: firstly, the respective role played by individual and corporate initiatives; secondly, the place of the '*haute banque*'; And thirdly, the management of the joint stock banks.

Because of the specialisation of the English banking system and the confinement of the clearing banks to traditional banking operations such as short-term loans, discounts or overdrafts, the City of London offered many more business opportunities for individuals or private firms, particularly in new areas of financial activity. The contrast is particularly striking between London and Berlin. Company promotion is a revealing example. In the City of London before 1914, no type of bank or financial institution such as the investment trusts were undertaking this type of operation. So the field was left open for the company promoter who mainly acted as an independent financier. Some had a reputation for honesty, like Osborne O'Hagan, others were notorious adventurers, like Ernest Terah Hooley or Whitaker Wright.[18] In Berlin, by contrast, the place of the company promoter was taken by one of the big banks' senior executives. At the Deutsche Bank, for example, Carl Klönne, one of the six members of the executive board, was responsible for industrial finance; he joined the Deutsche Bank in 1899 after having spent 20 years with a bank in Cologne, thereby acquiring a solid experience of the Ruhr industry.[19]

The differences between London and Berlin were as pronounced in the field of international finance. In England, new initiatives were taken by private firms of merchants, bankers or financiers, whereas in Germany these initiatives were usually taken by the big banks. In the oil industry, for example: in England, the Shell Transport and Trading Co. was founded and managed by Marcus Samuel, later Lord Bearsted, and his partners, whereas in Germany Deutsche Petroleum was founded in 1904 under the auspices of the Deutsche Bank; Deutsche Erdöl, however, was created by an individual entrepreneur, Rudolf Nöllenburg.[20] The financing of the Baghdad railway was taken in charge by the Deutsche Bank, whereas its counterpart in England, until the prospect of a collaboration collapsed in 1903, were Baring Brothers & Co., J.S. Morgan & Co. and Ernest Cassel.[21] In mining finance, A. Goerz & Co., a company registered in London, was backed by the Deutsche Bank, the Berliner Handelsgesellschaft and Jacob S.H. Stern, while a firm like Wernher, Beit & Co. was owned by its two partners Julius Wernher and Alfred Beit, who were originally German businessmen who had settled first in South Africa and then in London.[22] The British overseas banks were founded in the mid-nineteenth century by merchants and bankers independently from the joint stock banks, whereas their German counterparts, established a few decades later, were all subsidiaries of the big banks.[23] Whether an independent financier in the City of London fared better than a director of a large bank in Berlin will be discussed later. The question of the economic effects of each system has been for some time an open debate in English historiography, and cannot be dealt with here.[24]

The situation changed somewhat after the First World War without, however, being radically transformed. In England, individual initiatives clearly diminished with the decline of the company promoter, both in domestic affairs or in international finance. His role, however, was taken over by the merchant banks, directly or through the medium of finance houses specially set up for that purpose,[25] and not by the clearing banks despite the latter's greater involvement in industrial finance following the 1918–20 boom, or their control over overseas banks, with the creation, for example, of Barclays Bank D.C.O. in 1925 or the controlling interest of Lloyds Bank in the Bank of London and South America.[26] Where the old established private banks capable of holding their own in the same way in Paris and Berlin?

At the beginning of the period under review, the banking aristocracy, or '*haute banque*' was in the foremost position in the three centres, whether in terms of social and professional prestige or in terms of wealth and business activities. In Paris, where the word originated, the '*haute banque*' was made up of a certain number of old Protestant family banks, such as Mallet, Vernes, Hottinguer, de Neuflize or Mirabaud, with a network of European connections, in particular in Switzerland. In parallel to the *haute banque protestante*, there was a Jewish *haute banque*, whose most prominent member was of course Rothschild, as well as a Catholic *haute banque*. In Berlin, the term refers to a few private banks, mainly Jewish, such as Bleichröder, Medelssohn or Warschauer, the last one being taken over by the Darmstädter Bank in 1904. The German *haute banque*, however, was not confined to Berlin; some of its members were to be found in centres such as Frankfurt, with the Speyer and the Rothschild until the disappearance of the German branch of the family in 1901, Hamburg with the Warburgs or Cologne with the Oppenheims. The business of these banks, both in France and Germany, corresponded more or less to that of the English merchant banks, that is issuing foreign loans and financing international trade, although the German private banks were also engaged in commercial banking.[27]

In the City of London, until the last decade of the nineteenth century, two types of private banks co-existed: the private deposit banks and the merchant banks, and both can be considered as members of the *haute banque* on the basis of the wealth and social status of their partners. By the early twentieth century, nearly all the London private banks, with the exception of a few exclusive West End banks, had been taken over by the joint stock banks.[28] The London *haute banque* thus became much more similar, as far as its functions were concerned, to its continental counterpart. But the London *haute banque* was to prove the most resilient: it remained in the inter-war years, and indeed up to this day, a decisive component of the English banking sense, whereas it had lost almost all significance in Berlin and had entered a period of decline in Paris.

The financial aristocracy was stronger in London because its existence rested on a banking speciality which was not undertaken by the joint stock banks. As is well known, the two specialities of the merchant banks were the accepting and issuing businesses, and, even though competition was growing in the early twentieth century, the merchant banks were not really threatened until the First World War. After the war, they compensated for their loss of international business by turning to the domestic market, where they met with little competition from the joint stock banks.[29]

The situation was different in Berlin where the big banks were engaged in all the activities which constituted the private banks' speciality. Incidentally, it is not without interest to note that in the City of London itself the German big banks were amongst the strongest competitors of the English merchant banks in the accepting business, in particular the Dresdner Bank and the Disconto-Gesellschaft.[30] The result was that only a few very strong and very wealthy private banks could survive, at least at the top of the league. There remained about 460 private bankers in Berlin in 1902, but they were small firms, many of them being in fact brokers and commission agents on the Berlin Stock Exchange,[31] and cannot be considered as part of the financial aristocracy. In the inter-war years, after Bleichröder had become 'a shadow of itself',[32] Mendelssohn remained the only major Berlin private bank, while Warburg of Hamburg, thanks in particular to its New York connections, rose to international prominence. During the Nazi period, M.M. Warburg & Co. was 'Aryanised' in 1938 and its name changed to that of Brinckman, Wirtz & Co. in 1941, while the Mendelssohns preferred to join the Deutsche Bank in 1938.[33]

The Parisian *haute banque* remained very rich and very powerful until 1914 and beyond, and this was in no small way due to the international character of Paris as a financial centre. However, the activities of the *banques d'affaires*, the most important of which was the Banque de Paris et des Pays-Bas, were certainly encroaching on the traditional banking specialities of the *haute banque*, particularly the issue of foreign loans. It is significant, for example, that in the various Argentine loans that they issued between 1907 and 1914, Baring Brothers dealt, for the portion of the loans to be issued in Paris, with the Banque de Paris et des Pays-Bas and its two associates, the Société Générale and the Comptoir d'Escompte; in Germany, Baring's partners were the Disconto-Gesellschaft, associated with the Deutsche Bank.[34] The same is true about the financing of foreign railways, mining companies and others. In the Far East, the Banque de l'Indochine became the privileged instrument of French foreign policy, and the Banque de Paris et des Pays-Bas played the same political role in Morocco.[35] However, as David Landes showed some 35 years ago, the 'new bank' was very much a product of the old one.[36] There were members of the *haute banque* on the board of the Banque de Paris et des Pays-Bas and another important *banque d'affaires*, the Banque de l'Union Parisienne, was created and owned by the *haute banque*. Members of the *haute banque* also filled the boards of the major insurance companies, in particular the biggest one, the Compagnie d'Assurances Générales where, as late as 1926, the chairman was the Baron de Neuflize and the vice-chairman Ernest Mallet. The *haute banque* was also strongly represented on the boards of the railway companies and, most importantly, among the directors of the Banque de France. The semi-nationalisation of the Banque de France in 1936, that of the railway companies the following year and the nationalisation of the commercial banks – but not of the *banques d'affaires* – and insurance companies in 1944–46 undoubtedly diminished the control exerted by the *haute banque* over the financial sector of the French economy.[37]

Such a control was even more impressive in the City of London, where the most prominent merchant banks and merchant houses were represented, through their partners, on the boards of the major joint stock banks, overseas banks, insurance companies and investment trusts as well as on the Court of Directors of the Bank of England. This situation put the private firms in a position of collective control over the funds of huge financial institutions and gave them an economic power which went far beyond the size of their private firm.[38]

Contrary to their English and French counterparts, the German private bankers did not succeed in keeping control over the large financial institutions they had themselves created. The founders of the Deutsche Bank in 1870 were private bankers and the evolution of its relationships with one of them, Delbrück, Leo & Co., is revealing in that respect. At first, all the issue business was jointly undertaken, but as the Deutsche Bank grew stronger the relationships increasingly cooled, with the director general, Georg Siemens, having the edge over the chairman of the supervisory board, Adelbert Delbrück.[39] The identity of functions between private and joint stock banks as an explanatory factor has already been discussed. Another explanation lies in the higher status enjoyed by professional bankers in Germany, which is reflected in the differences between the management structure of the English and French banks on the one hand and of the German banks on the other hand.

In England and France, a clear demarcation separated the directors from the managers. The directors were concerned with defining the general policy of their bank and supervising its management. This supervision could be very close, through committees of the board which met regularly to control one aspect of the bank's activity. The responsibility of running the day to day business of banking was left to the managers whose ultimate status was therefore that of subordinate to the directors.

Socially, there is no doubt that the managers, including the general manager, enjoyed a lower status than the directors. The former often came from a lower middle-class social background and made their entire career in the same bank of which they were full-time salaried employees; the latter were partners in a merchant or banking firm, company directors, retired businessmen, men of independent means, sometimes former civil servants or political notabilities, and devoted only a part of their time to the bank. There were differences between the English and French banks – for example the board of directors was more involved in the management of the bank in England, whereas the social status of the managers could be higher in France. However, they were minor in comparison to the German model.[40]

Such a social and professional division did not exist in Germany. As is well known, after 1870 German companies were required to have, in addition to their executive board (*Vorstand*), a supervisory board (*Aufsichtsrat*).[41] It would be a mistake to compare the members of the executive boards to the managers of an English company and the members of the supervisory board to the directors. The members of the executive board were not only responsible for the daily routine of banking activities; they were the real heads of their bank, deciding its long-term strategy as well as its short-term tactics. They were rather in the position of the managing directors of an English bank while the members of the supervisory board could be compared to non-executive directors in England. The example of the Deutsche Bank is the most striking. In 1907, it was managed by an executive board of six members. Among them, Arthur Gwinner, usually considered as the unofficial head of the bank, was in charge of external affairs: foreign loans, foreign investments, in particular the Ottoman railway. Carl Klönne, already mentioned, was in charge of industrial finance. Rudolf Koch was responsible for the current and deposit accounts as well as the relationships with provincial banks, while Paul Mankiewitz was responsible for Stock Exchange operations. Significantly, the chairman of the supervisory board was Wilhelm Herz, at the time over 80 years old, one of the most prominent merchants in Berlin.[42]

It is important to bear in mind that the members of the executive boards were not subordinate to the supervisory board – as managers of an English or French bank with similar share of responsibility would be to the directors – and that they enjoyed the same social status. This is shown, for example, by the fact that two of them were ennobled, Arthur Gwinner and Rudolf Koch; no manager of an English bank was ever raised to the peerage during that period. Rudolf Koch was on the central committee of the Reichsbank, alongside private bankers such as Albert von Oppenheim, Julius Bleichröder or Paul Schwabach, as well as representatives of the other big banks. Apart from the fact that a clearing banker could not become a Director of the Bank of England, bank managers in England hardly ever represented their bank on the board of other companies, unlike the members of the executive boards of the German banks who could chair several supervisory boards, in particular of industrial companies. The higher social status of the members of the executive boards of the German banks in Germany is also reflected in their personal wealth. The richest of them, men such as Carl Fürstenberg, of the Berliner Handelsgesellschaft, Eugen Gutmann, of the Dresdner Bank, or Arthur Gwinner, of the Deutsche Bank, had fortunes estimated at around 16 million marks in 1911, that is £800,000. This is the sort of fortune left by a rich merchant banker in the City of London: such considerable City figures as Henry Huck Gibbs, later Lord Aldenham, or Alexander Kleinwort did not leave as much as that. Among the less wealthy, Ernest Russel, of the Disconto-Gesellschaft, had an estimated fortune of two to three million marks in 1911, that is between £100,000 and £150,000, which is well above the average fortune of the general manager of an English bank: 66 per cent of those active betwen 1890 and 1914 left an estate valued at less than £50,000.[43] This is not to suggest, however, that banking fortunes were higher in Berlin than in London. On the contrary. We will come back to that point in the next section.

The status of the professional bankers in England and France improved from the beginning of the twentieth century and in particular after 1914. An increasing number of general managers became chairman of their bank. One of the earliest and most spectacular examples is that of Edward Holden, who became chairman and managing director of the Midland Bank in 1908. Another is Frederick Goodenough who became chairman of Barclays Bank in 1917, the most private of the British clearing banks, after having been secretary and then general manager. In France, in the same year, Adrien Mazerat, general manager of the Crédit Lyonnais between 1882 and 1905, succeeded Henri Germain, the founder of the bank, as chairman. At the Société Générale, Louis Dorizon, who had started as an office boy in 1874, rose step by step to become manager in 1896, general manager in 1909 and finally chairman in 1914. Senior managers also increasingly tended to hold the position of managing-directors rather than general managers. At the Midland Bank, after Holden's death in 1919, three joint managing directors were appointed. At the Crédit Lyonnais, after Germain's death in 1905, his two sons-in-law, Edmond Fabre-Luce, originally a diplomat, and Baron Brincard, became joint managing directors, the latter becoming chairman in 1919. In France, an important factor in the rise of the professional bankers was the higher proportion of university-educated managers. In particular, the banks increasingly recruited finance inspectors to fill senior managerial positions. In the course of time, especially after World War II, this *grand corps* was to become the main supplier of French senior bankers.[44]

The integration of full-time professional bankers to the financial elite took place earlier in Germany than in England and France. All the descriptions of Berlin *Hochfinanz* before 1914 put side by side private bankers and top salaried managers of the big banks.[45] This took another generation to happen in France, and even longer in the City of London. But was this closely-knit German banking community as integrated to the upper-classes as the English and French financial aristocracies?

III

Wealth is a first indicator of social status, although not necessary a sufficient one as it usually takes a second generation to gain full social acceptance. In the three countries, bankers and financiers were the wealthiest business group in the early twentieth century. In England, according to Rubinstein's figures, 51 per cent of the non-landed millionaires and half-millionaires deceased between 1900 and 1919 were engaged in banking, commerce and other services; the proportion is 47 per cent for those deceased between 1920 and 1939. The figures are very similar for Germany: according to Dolores Augustine, the tertiary sector accounted for 47 per cent of businessmen with estates of six million marks – that is £300,000 – or more in 1911. Bankers, with 27 per cent, were the largest single group and, interestingly, formed a larger proportion than their English counterparts who accounted for 22 per cent of the businessmen worth £500,000 or more deceased between 1900 and 1919 and 19 per cent of those deceased between 1920 and 1939.[46] This reflects the wider spectrum of business opportunities existing then in the British economy rather than a greater strength of the financial sector in Germany.

Wealthy bankers and financiers – with say £300,000 or more – were in fact more numerous in Britain. The level of their fortune was also higher, although not of a different order of magnitude. The richest bankers in Berlin in 1911 were Hans von Bleichröder, with £1.5 million, Robert von Mendelssohn, with £1.3 million and Paul von Schwabach, with £1 million. Many more City of London bankers were millionaires and the largest fortunes were in the region of £2.5 million, as in the case of Lord Rothschild, the second Lord Revelstoke, or Everard Hambro. The fortune of the most successful financiers could reach greater heights, for example Sir Ernest Cassel, who left £7.3 million in 1921. Compared to London, Berlin was handicapped because of its more recent accession to the position of Germany's financial capital. The largest German banking fortunes were not in Berlin, but still in Frankfurt, with Maximilian von Goldschmidt-Rothschild, worth £8 million in 1911 – he had married the daughter of Willy von Rothschild, the last male member of the Frankfurt branch – and Eduard Beit von Speyer, worth £4.4 million. The aggregate fortune of the Rothschilds and Goldschmidt-Rothschilds in Frankfurt in 1911 reached £19.2 million:[47] the family fortune long outlived the banking house, which closed in 1911. There are unfortunately no equivalent figures for France, as the studies undertaken so far refer to businessmen as a single category without further differentiation. However, considering the concentration of millionaires in Paris and the huge fortunes of some of the directors of the Banque de France studied by Alain Plessis for an earlier period, there is some indication that banking and finance accounted for a fair share of the French millionaires.[48] Comparative analysis of the levels of fortune after 1914 remains for the moment impossible.

Education cannot be readily used as an indicator of social status. For England, education at a public school is usually considered as a criterion of absorption into the upper classes, but this can hardly be said of education at a German *Gymnasium* or a French *lycée*, even though a very small percentage of the population obtained a *baccalauréat* or an *Abitur*. Education, on the other hand, has often been linked to business performance, and in that respect the most striking feature is the comparatively low level of education of German bankers. For 1907, a sample of 20 bankers, mostly members of the executive boards of the four 'D' banks shows that the training of half of them consisted in a banking apprenticeship, while 25 per cent went to university. In England, although only four per cent of managers studied at a university during the period 1890–1914, 42 per cent of directors did so, mostly at Oxford or Cambridge. For 1927, in Germany, the proportion of apprenticeships rises to 59 per cent, 23 per cent being universityeducated; details of education are unknown for only 18 per cent. In England, for the same year, the analysis of the education of the chairmen, vice-chairmen, general managers or managing directors of the 'Big Five' produces almost identical results: 60 per cent did not go beyond secondary education, while 20 per cent studied at a university, the details of education of the remaining 20 per cent being unknown; the percentage of university-educated cases, however, rises to 40 per cent if only the chairmen and vice-chairmen are considered. In France, from a sample of bankers established on the same basis, it appears that a third pursued their studies at a university, but with no available information for more than half of the cases, the percentage is most probably underestimated.[49] Whatever the influence of German bankers on industry, it was not due to any superior level of education.

In the three capitals, bankers and financiers led an aristocractic way of life. They lived in a fashionable area such as Mayfair or Belgravia in London, the *8ème* or the *16ème arrondissement* in Paris, or the western area near the *Tiergarten* in Berlin, coupled with a seat in the country. Membership of a prestigious club was also a mark of upper-class status, primarily in London, but also in Paris; as far as Berlin was concerned, there were no such clubs and on the whole the German capital had a less active social life than the British and French ones. In the three capitals, the banking elites were geographically and socially close to the political and administrative elites, and had their entrées into higher government circles.[50]

Despite these apparent similarities, bankers and financiers in London, Paris and Berlin did not enjoy the same social and professional status in their respective country. In Britain, City bankers clearly were the most prominent business group, being on the whole richer, more integrated into the aristocracy and closer to political power than industrialists.[51] The separation between what we could call a national bourgeoisie, based on the capital, and a provincial bourgeoisie, coincided to a large extent with the separation between the City and industry, although this distinction tended to diminish from the inter-war years as the largest industrial companies increasingly moved their head office to London and the most successful industrialists were gradually integrated into the upper classes.[52]

The differentiation between a national and a provincial bourgeoisie applies even better to France. However, contrary to England, the national bourgeoisie included from an earlier date various categories of businessmen. Paris was not only the home of the *haute banque* and the large financial institutions, but of any company of some significance in France. French top industrialists were more integrated to the upper classes than their English counterparts. Members of the old industrial dynasties fully belonged to the Parisian society, the best known examples being Eugène Schneider and François de Wendel, the steel magnates.[53] The cohesion of the French business elite was certainly facilitated by the fact that the largest companies, whether financial or industrial, were often headed by former senior civil servants. However, as far as bankers were concerned, whatever their wealth and status, they could not escape the persistent hostility that the French felt towards banks, although it was more characteristic of the lower middle and rural classes than of the upper classes.[54]

Berlin, despite being the political and financial capital of the Reich, was not the home of the most important business group in Germany. Despite their involvement in industrial finance and their massive presence on the supervisory boards of industrial companies, German bankers never enjoyed the same status as their English counterparts who kept away from industry. In Imperial, as well as in Weimar, Germany the Ruhr industrialists were undoubtedly the business group enjoying the highest prestige and capable of exerting the strongest political pressure.

Their base, however, was in Düsseldorf, Cologne or Essen, although they had powerful antennae in Berlin, in particular through their professional organisations. As Gerlad Feldman put it: 'the pre-war power and prestige of German banking ... lay in its enthusiastic participation in the adventure of German industrialization'.[55]

A difference between London, Paris and Berlin, which partly explains the position of bankers in English society, is that the City aristocracy was not primarily composed of members of religious minorities. That was certainly true of the London private bankers; although they included a not insignificant contingent of Quakers, a great proportion of the latter had joined the Church of England during the period under review. But it was also true of the merchant bankers, at least as far as the most prestigious firms were concerned, apart from the Rothschilds who were in every respect an exceptional case. It is true that many of these firms had been established by foreign immigrants during or after the Napoleonic Wars, but from the second generation most of them were totally integrated into the English upper classes; they were no more part of a network of relationships characteristic of the religious minorities, but rather of a network of relationships linking together the old banking families and a number of landed families. If one adds to the merchant banks the most important merchant houses which, at least until 1914, must be considered as part of the financial aristocracy on the basis of their membership of the Court of Directors of the Bank of England, the result is that the impact of the religious minorities was much more limited in London than in Paris and even more in Berlin. As already noted, the *haute banque* in Paris was composed of several religions, but with a strong Protestant and Jewish element, while it was virtually entirely Jewish in Berlin.[56]

Not only the banking, but more generally the business elite, was less integrated into the upper classes in Germany before 1914. There was no unified dominating elite in Germany, such as the 'establishment' in Britain or the '*grand monde*' in France, based on the merger of top businessmen with another elite group. there might have been a new elite in Imperial Germany, in the sense that the aristocracy was henceforth sharing its power with the *Grossbürgertum*, that they increasingly led the same way of life, met socially and that intermarriage was becoming more frequent; the two groups might also have been functionally integrated. However, contrary to England, a complete merger, leading to the formation of a single social group, did not take place. On the other hand, the links between German big businessmen and other bourgeois elite groups were not as close as in France, where in any case the bourgeoisie did not have to share its power with any other social group. The reasons for this difference between Germany on the one hand, and England and France on the other hand, are numerous and include Germany's later industrialisation and the federal structure of its state as well as the nature of the German *Junkertum*. The specific position of the financial elites within the upper classes provides another element of explanation. As it has been suggested earlier in this article, there was no real German equivalent to the English or French financial aristocracy. In England and France, bankers were the first business group to be integrated into the upper classes, whereas in Germany the banking community was largely Jewish and so could not be absorbed fully into the dominating elite.[57]

IV

To summarise: economic power and social status do not necessarily move together and in the same direction. Despite the strong influence of the banks in the German economy, German bankers never enjoyed the same social status as their English counterparts. On the other hand, the German business community appears to have been more homogeneous, in the sense that the separation between 'owners' and 'managers' was less marked than in Britain and France.[58] German professional bankers were therefore earlier integrated to the financial elite than their English and French counterparts. The reasons for this early integration are mainly to be found in the position of the middle classes (the *Bürgertum*) in Imperial Germany. However, this integration was certainly facilitated by the existence of a supervisory board alongside the executive board, as both owners and managers basically enjoyed the same social and professional status. In addition, the existence of a supervisory board might well have helped the passage from family to managerial capitalism in Germany,[59] as it was easier than in Britain for owners to retain a certain degree of control over their enterprise without hampering the rise of salaried managers. Although this would apply more to industry than banking, there is no doubt that the subordinate status of managers in England contributed to the lasting dominance of the financial world by a City aristocracy.[60]

One should not conclude, however, that German bankers were more 'professional' than their English and French counterparts. English bank managers ran their business in a thoroughly professional manner and generated higher profits than their Continental competitors.[61] The lack of expertise of the British clearing banks in industrial financing has often been noticed[62] but must be attributed to the absence of tradition and experience in that particular field rather than to a lack of professionalism. As far as the French banks were concerned, it should be remembered that the Crédit Lyonnais was one of the very first banks to create a financial analysis department, as early as 1871,[63] and, as has been noted earlier,

French bank managers had on the whole a higher level of education than their English and German counterparts. And whatever the forms of organisation of the German 'universal' banks and their representation on the supervisory boards of innumerable industrial companies, German bank directors were very conservative during the 1920s and apparently lacked entrepreneurial spirit.[64] In any case, the management structures of the joint stock banks have so far attracted little attention from historians, especially in comparison with manufacturing industry; this should prove a fruitful field of investigation, not only at the level of the financial elites, but also of the lower strata of the banking hierarchy.

NOTES

An earlier version of this article was presented at the Metropolitan History Seminar, Institute of Historical Research, University of London. I should like to thank the participants for their helpful comments.

1. On the City of London before 1914, see Y. Cassis, *La City de Londres, 1870–1914* (Paris, 1987).
2. United Nations, *International Capital Movements during the Interwar Period* (New York, 1949).
3. R.C. Michie, 'Different in Name Only? The London Stock Exchange and Foreign Bourses, c.1850–1914', *Business History*, Vol.XXX (1988), pp.55–7.
4. See B. Supple, 'Corporate Growth and Structural Change in a Service Industry: Insurance, 1870–1914', in B. Supple (ed.), *Essays in British Business History* (Oxford, 1977), pp.70–1.
5. *Post Magazine Almanac*, 1911.
6. On Lloyd's of London, see D.E.W. Gibb, *Lloyd's of London: A Study in Individualism* (1957); C. Wright and C.E. Fayle, *A History of Lloyd's* (1928).
7. D. Kynaston, 'The London Stock Exchange, 1870–1914: An Institutional History' (unpublished Ph.D. thesis, University of London, 1983), p.200.
8. Cassis, *City de Londres*, pp.40–2.
9. Bodleian Library Oxford, Milner Papers, Vol.481, ff.10–14. On the clearing banks abroad, see G. Jones, 'Lombard Street on the Riviera: The Clearing Banks and Europe, 1900–1960', *Business History*, Vol.XXIV (1982).
10. Z. Aliber, 'International Banking', *Journal of Money, Credit and Banking*, Vol.16 (1984), pp.661–2. These figures are most probably overestimated. According to G. Jones, the number of foreign branches of British banks amounted to 1,286 in 1913. 'Competitive Advantages in British Multinational Banking since 1890', in G. Jones (ed.), *Banks as Multinationals* (1990), p.31.
11. L. Dufourcq-Lagelouse, *Les banques étrangères en France* (Paris, 1922), p.32.
12. In 1913, the total assets of the London City & Midland Bank amounted to £109 million, of Lloyds Bank to £107 million, of the Crédit Lyonnais to £99 million and of the Deutsche Bank to £92 million. However, the paid-up capital of the Deutsche Bank was £12.5 million and the Crédit Lyonnais £10 million as against £4.35 million for the Midland Bank and £4.2 million for Lloyds Bank.
13. In 1905, Imperial Tobacco, with a capital of £17.5 million, was the largest industrial company in Europe if measured in terms of nominal capital. In that year another 26 industrial companies had a larger capital than that of the largest bank, namely the Midland Bank whose capital was £3.14 million; for lists of the largest industrial companies in Britain, see P.L. Payne, 'The Emergence of the Large-Scale Company in Great Britain', *Economic History Review*, 2nd series, Vol.20 (1967), and L. Hannah,

The Rise of the Corporate Economy (2nd ed. 1982). In Germany, the largest company in 1907 was the Deutsche Bank, with a capital of 200 million marks, closely followed by Krupp with 180 million marks (unpublished list of the largest German companies in 1907 kindly communicated to me by Jürgen Kocka). The gap between the largest banking and industrial companies was wider in France: in 1907, the largest industrial companies were Saint-Gobain and Thomson-Houston, with a capital of 60 million francs, as against 250 million for the Crédit Lyonnais and 200 million for the Société Générale.

14. See K. Burk, 'Money and Power: 'The Shift from Great Britain to the United States', in Y. Cassis (ed.), *Finance and Financiers in European History, 1880–1960* (Cambridge, 1991). A good example of the lasting importance of London's expertise is given in her recent study *Morgan Grenfell, 1838–1988: The Biography of a Merchant Bank* (Oxford, 1989), pp. 86–90.
15. See P. Coste, *Les grands marchés financiers: Paris, Londres, New York* (Paris, 1932), pp. 37–71.
16. W. Woodruff, *Impact of Western Man* (New York, 1966), pp. 156–7.
17. In 1928, the capital and total assets of the largest English, French and German banks were as follows:

	Capital	*Total assets*
	in £million	
Barclays Bank	16	345
Lloyds Bank	16	395
Midland Bank	13	434
Société Générale	4	85
Crédit Lyonnais	2	78
Deutsche Bank	7.5	116
Dresdner Bank	5	98

18. On the company promoter, see J. Armstrong, 'The Rise and Fall of the Company Promoter and British Industry', in J.J. van Helten and Y. Cassis (eds.), *Capitalism in a Mature Economy: Financial Institutions, Capital Exports and British Industry, 1870–1939* (Aldershot, 1990).
19. *Neue Deutsche Biographie*; E.W. Schmidt, *Männer der Deutschen Bank und Disconto-Gesellschaft* (Düsseldorf, 1957).
20. See R. Henriques, *Marcus Samuel, First Viscount Bearsted and Founder of the Shell Transport and Trading Company, 1853–1927*, (1960); J. Riesser, *Die deutsche Gross banken und ihre Konzentration* (Iena, 1912), p. 342; F. Pinner, *Deutsche Wirtschaftsführer* (Berlin, 1924), pp. 232–5.
21. See J.G. Williamson, *Karl Helferrich, 1873–1924: Economist, Financier, Politician* (Princeton, 1971), pp. 78–110.
22. P.H. Emden, *Money Powers of Europe in the Nineteenth and Twentieth Century* (1937); entries on Alfred Beit and Julius Wernher in D.J. Jeremy (ed.), *Dictionary of Business Biography*, 5 vols. (London, 1984–86).
23. See A.S:J. Baster, *The Imperial Banks*, (1929); idem, *The International Banks* (1935); D. Joslin, *A Century of Banking in Latin America* (1963); G. Diouritch, *L'expansion des banques allemandes à l'étranger* (Paris, 1909), P. Hertner, 'German Banks abroad until 1914', in Jones (ed.), *Banks as Multinationals*.
24. I have recently discussed this question in 'British Finance: Success and Controversy', in van Helten and Cassis (eds.), *Capitalism in a Mature Economy*.
25. See an interesting case study in S. Diaper, 'The Sperling Combine and the Shipbuilding Industry: Merchant Banking and Industrial Finance in the 1920s', in van Helten and Cassis (eds.), *Capitalism in a Mature Economy*. See also Burk, *Morgan Grenfell*, pp. 91–8.
26. See D. Ross, 'The Clearing Banks and Industry – New Perspectives on the Interwar Years', in van Helten and Cassis (eds.), *Capitalism in a Mature Economy;* S. Tolliday, *Business, Banking and Politics: The Case of British Steel, 1918–1939* (Cambridge, MA,

1987); J. Crossley and J. Blandford, *The D.C.O. Story (1925–1939)* (Cambridge, MA, 1975); Joslin, *Century of Banking*.

27. See A. Plessis, *Régents et Gouverneurs de la Banque de France sous le Second Empire* (Geneva, 1985); F. Stern, *Gold and Iron* (New York, 1977); W. Treue, 'Das Bankhaus Mendelssohn als Beispiel einer Privatbank im 19. und 20. Jahrhundert', in C. LowenthalHensel (Hg.), *Mendelssohn Studien*, Bd 1 (Berlin, 1972); E. Rosenbaum and A.S. Sherman, *M.A. Warburg & Co., 1798–1938: Merchant Bankers of Hamburg*, (1979).
28. See Y. Cassis, *Les banquiers de la City à l'époque edouardienne, 1890–1914* (Geneva, 1984), pp. 23–38.
29. See S.D. Chapman, *The Rise of Merchant Banking*, (1984).
30. Ibid., pp. 121–5.
31. W. Treue, 'Der Privatbankier an der Wende vom 19. zum 20. Jahrhundert', *Tradition*, Vol. 5 (1970), p. 230.
32. Stern, *Gold and Iron*, p. 547.
33. Treue, 'Bankhaus Mendelssohn'; Rosenbaum and Sherman, *Warburg*.
34. Baring Brothers Archives, 73, Argentine Internal Gold Loan of 1907.
35. See J. Thobie, *La France Impériale, 1880–1914* (Paris, 1982).
36. D. Landes, 'Vieille banque et banque nouvelle: la révolution financière du XIXème siècle, *Revue d'histoire moderne et contemporaine*, III (1956).
37. See A. Plessis, 'Bankers in French Society, 1860s–1960s', in Cassis (ed.), *Finance and Financiers*.
38. I have discussed this point in a previous article in this journal; 'Management and Strategy in the English Joint Stock Banks', *Business History*, Vol. XXVII (1985).
39. Carl Fürstenberg, *Die Lebensgeschichte eines deutschen Bankiers* (DüsseldorfWien, 1968; 1st ed. 1938), p. 209.
40. For England, see Cassis, *Les banquiers*; for France, see Plessis, 'Bankers in French Society'.
41. See N. Horn, 'Aktienrechtliche Unternehmensorganisation in der Hochindustrialisierung (1860–1920). Deutschland, England, Frankreich und die USA im Vergleich', in N. Horn & J. Kocka (eds.), *Recht und Entwicklung des Grossunternehmen im 19. und frühen 20. Jahrhundert* (Göttingen, 1979).
42. See Schmidt, *Männer*.
43. R. Martin, *Jahrbuch der Millionäre in Berlin* (Berlin, 1913); Cassis, *Les banquiers*, pp. 28–40.
44. Cassis, *Les banquiers*; Plessis, 'Bankers in French Society'; A.R. Holmes and E. Green, *Midland: 150 Years of Banking Business*, (1986); J. Rivoire, *Le Crédit Lyonnais: Histoire d'une banque* (Paris, 1989).
45. See for example E. Achterberg, *Berliner Hochfinanz: Kaiser, Fürsten, Millionäre um 1900* (Frankfurt am Main, 1965).
46. Percentage calculated from W.D. Rubinstein, *Men of Property: The Very Wealthy in Britain since the Industrial Revolution* (1981) pp. 62–5, and D. AugustinePerez, 'Very Wealthy Businessmen in Imperial Germany', *Journal of Social History*, Vol. 22 (1988), p. 304.
47. W. Mosse, *Jews in the German Economy: The GermanJewish Economic Elite, 1820–1935* (Oxford, 1987), pp. 172–217.
48. See A. Daumard, *Les fortunes françaises au XIXe siècle* (Paris, 1973); Plessis, *Régents et Gouverneurs*.
49. Samples of English, French and German bankers for the years 1907 and 1928 established by the author.
50. Cassis, *Les banquiers*; Plessis, 'Bankers in French Society', C. Charle, *Les élites de la République, 1880–1900* (Paris, 1987); Achterberg, *Berliner Hochfinanz*: Stern, *Gold and Iron*.
51. See Cassis, *Les banquiers* and 'Bankers in English Society in the late Nineteenth Century', *Economic History Review*, 2nd series, Vol. XXXVIII (1985).
52. See P. Stanworth and A. Giddens, 'An Economic Elite: a Demographic Profile of Company Chairmen', in P. Stanworth and A. Giddens, *Elites and Power in British*

Society (Cambridge, 1974).

53. See L. Bergeron, *Les capitalistes en France, 1780–1914* (Paris, 1978); Charle, *Elites de la République*; A. Roy, *Histoire de la maison Schneider et du Creusot* (Paris, 1962); J.N. Jeanneney, *François de Wendel en République: L'argent et le pouvoir 1914–1940* (Paris, 1975).
54. Plessis, 'Bankers in French Society'.
55. G. Feldman, 'Bankers and Banking in Germany after the First World War: Strategies of Defence', in Cassis (ed.), *Finance and Financiers*. On the weight of the heavy industry see his *Iron and Steel in German Inflation, 1916–1923* (Princeton, 1977) among many other works on the subject.
56. Cassis, *Les banquiers* and 'Bankers in English Society'.
57. For further developments on this point, see Y. Cassis, 'Wirtschaftselite und Bürgertum: England, Frankreich, Deutschland um 1900', in J. Kocka (ed.), *Bürgertum im 19. Jahrhundert. Deutschland im europäischen Vergleich*, 3 vols. (Munich, 1988), Vol. 2.
58. On the salaried managers in Germany, see J. Kocka, 'Les entrepreneurs salariés dans l'industrie allemande à la fin du XIXe et au début du XXe siècle' in M. LévyLeboyer (ed.), *Le patronat de la seconde industrialisation* (Paris, 1979).
59. On the general question of ownership and management in the United States and major European economies, see the essays in A.D. Chandler, Jr. and H. Daems (eds.), *Managerial Hierarchies* (Cambridge, MA, 1980) and A. Chandler's latest book, *Scale and Scope* (Cambridge, MA, 1990).
60. Y. Cassis, 'Profits and Profitability in English Banking, 1870–1914', *Revue international d'histoire de la banque*, Vol. 34–35 (1987).
62. See for example Tolliday, *Business, Banking and Politics*, p. 179.
63. J. Bouvier, *Naissance d'une banque: le Crédit Lyonnais* (Paris, 1968), pp. 126–9.
64. Pinner, *Deutsche Wirtschaftsführer*, pp. 184–5. See also H. James, *The German Slump: Politics and Economics, 1924–1936* (Oxford, 1986), pp. 139–46.

British Investment Banking and Industrial Decline before the Great War: A Case Study of Capital Outflow to Canadian Industry

GREGORY P. MARCHILDON

Johns Hopkins University

> 'Few would deny that Great Britain's immense capital export must be counted among the most important phenomena of British and world history in the late nineteenth and early twentieth centuries. Never before or since has one nation committed so much of its national income and savings to funding overseas assets.'

So begins Michael Edelstein's detailed study of British foreign investment before the Great War. Between 1870 and 1913, Britain devoted 5.2 per cent of its gross national product to foreign lending while Germany and France, the two other major creditor nations of the world, averaged a rate of only two to three per cent of national product.[1] This flood of investment was channelled largely through British investment bankers and stockbrokers, who convinced wealthy investors, and a few of more modest means, to transfer their savings to foreign and colonial government and corporate securities. At the same time, Britain's own economic growth was slowing and her industries were losing their com-petitive edge in world markets. It is not surprising, therefore, that this unprecedented capital exodus, and the role played by the City of London banks in facilitating it, has often been perceived as one of the causes of domestic industrial decline.

One of the foremost scholars of British investment banking, Stanley Chapman, best summarises the accepted wisdom on the subject: 'Most economic historians have agreed that the London capital market was biased towards overseas investment, neglecting the opportunities of domestic industry' while 'others have seen clear evidence of lack of entrepreneurial spirit in the situation'. Chapman himself seems to agree. He explains these shortcomings by referring to the international focus of the City banks as well as their natural preference for trade and government finance over manufacturing of any origin.[2] This preference was due in part to the greater risk that attached to the recently established industrial securities market. In one of the most widely read books in economic history, David Landes explains that, by the first half of the nineteenth century, the British banking system was 'passive rather than active, responsive rather than creative' and to the limited extent that the British 'capital market did direct the flow of funds, habit and predilection combined to give the preference to overseas governments and to public utilities, foreign and domestic', over industry, foreign or domestic.[3] Alex Cairncross and William Kennedy have presented somewhat more sophisticated arguments adding weight to the 'institutional rigidity' argument or what could more specifically be called the anti-industrial bias of City banks.[4]

This perception of British banking, however, is contradicted by recent case evidence. Ranald Michie's considerable body of work demonstrates the innovative flexibility of the individuals and institutions that made up capital markets both in the City and in Scotland and their willingness to take on the risk inherent in industrial finance.[5] A case study of Foster & Braithwaite discloses that at least one City firm financed industry on a regular basis until the higher risks posed by this activity convinced the firm partners to eschew industrial financing and company promotion generally in favour of a more conservative strategy after the Great War.[6] And on the basis of his aggregate statistical study of the British capital market, Michael Edelstein argues that financial services changed rapidly in response to real economic changes suggesting institutional robustness rather than rigidity.[7]

Two recent reviews of the literature dismiss earlier simplistic arguments concerning the City's culpability in industrial decline. One concludes that, although the City was not remiss in its duty as a financial intermediary *per se*, it could (and should) have played an active and constructive role in requiring British industry to restructure.[8] The other argues that, even with the considerable research of recent years on the quantity of overseas security issues and their yields, we still have too little knowledge of individual issues and their distribution and ownership as well as the investment plans of investors and individual industrial enterprises to come to any definite conclusions about the relationship between the City and industrial decline.[9] More importantly, aside from the case evidence mentioned above as well as numerous studies of two of Britain's most venerable merchant banks, Barings and Rothschilds, we know almost nothing about the majority of financial intermediaries that were involved in these issues and their methods of operation. The latter studies in particular have led to erroneous generalisations concerning the nature of British investment banking.

The purpose of this paper is to examine some of the many other investment banks that were involved in the remarkable capital exodus during the age of high imperialism. It is a case study of a certain constellation of British investment bankers and their financing of Canadian manufacturing industry before the Great War. Evidence is presented concerning the extent to which London investment banks and their clients, the British investing public, were prepared to finance industry. Based on this evidence, an inference will be drawn as to the alleged anti-industrial bias of British investment banks.

Although a case study, this examination constitutes more than a minor chapter in the story of British foreign investment in that 'Canada was the largest borrower in the last great surge of British lending absorbing perhaps a third of British lending' between 1902 and 1914.[10] As J.A. Hobson noted in 1906, Canada was 'conscious, uproariously conscious, that her day had come ... The poor relation had come into her fortune'.[11] This 'fortune' was the wealth being generated through the rapid development of the Canadian economy, and British investment, through the London issue market, provided the largest single source of the capital used to finance this growth. Although Europeans from the continent regularly invested through the London capital market, the limited case evidence available coupled with a contemporary sample of 22 Canadian industrials indicates that the vast majority of those who purchased the Canadian industrial shares floated on the London market were in fact British citizens.[12]

One definitional problem should be disposed of immediately. There are many, often conflicting, definitions of banking. This study is confined to that branch of financial intermediation directly concerned with long-term capital advances through the sale of corporate securities commonly known as investment banking. Deposit banks, those financial intermediaries that receive 'money on deposit to be accounted for on demand by means of cheques' are of secondary interest because of their emphasis on short-term advances to industry.[13] The difficulty is in determining what is or is not an investment bank.[14] In this paper, the term will be restricted to those entities which act as principals in the market for new securities: that is, those entities that promote, issue, and underwrite new security issues as opposed to those that simply act as agents in the sale of either new or old securities to investors. The formal or legal name of the financial intermediary is unimportant; if an individual promoter, bank, trust company, or even stockbroking firm regularly acts as a principal in the new issue market it will be regarded as an investment bank. Since the vast majority of banks, trust companies, and stockbroking firms in the City acted as agents rather than as principals in providing long-term industrial capital, they should not be regarded as investment banks, but the few identified as performing a more direct role will be so treated.

Most of the great merchant banks would be considered investment banks under this definition. They merely constitute a special case because of their history. They began as general merchanting operations occasionally handling bills of exchange and acceptances. Eventually they evolved into more specialised financial intermediaries sometimes handling new issues of securities. Being established and internationally known houses, they generally handled large government debt issues. On the other hand, the smaller industrial, public utility, and mining issues became the stockintrade of a few specialised promoters and the new investment bankers, many of whom were recent Jewish immigrants from the continent. The paths of the merchant bank, the promoter, and the new investment bank sometimes crossed in competition for the railway issue business.[15]

The newer investment banks were much more connected to the activities that surrounded the London Stock Exchange than the long-established merchant banks. In fact, many of the individuals who created these banks started their careers as stockbrokers and stockjobbers. Only a handful were recognised as banks in the *Banking Almanac*, the annual directory of banks regularly used by City firms.[16] Nevertheless, these financial intermediaries were responsible for issuing and underwriting the securities of the majority of industrial and utility companies, as well as a large number of railway companies, that came from every corner of the globe to tap into the London capital market.

II

Long before a market for industrial securities existed in Canada, Canadian industrial firms obtained longterm capital from British investors through English and Scottish financial intermediaries. These investments came on the heels of large railway security flotations in London sponsored by prominent City merchant bankers. Beginning in the 1830s, the provincial authorities in what would eventually become Canada began to raise money through debentures issued by merchant banks such as Barings and Glyns.[17] Barings and Glyns then issued shares on behalf of the Grand Trunk Railway of Canada in the 1850s. Although they lost a total of £800,000 on Grand Trunk flotations by 1860, these and other investment banks continued to work raising money for other Canadian railway companies in subsequent decades. After its creation in 1881, the securities of the Canadian Pacific Railway became a favourite among British investors, and a wide assortment of the larger British investment banks, including of course the oldestablished merchant banks, were involved in the flotations which funnelled millions of pounds into the building of this transcontinental railway.[18]

The Canadian capital market was simply too shallow in terms of the number and wealth of investors to support the large blocks of securities issued by corporate leviathans such as the Canadian Pacific Railway and no industrial enterprise approached the size of this railway company until after the merger movement of 1909–12. The few large industrial enterprises willing and able to sell their securities to a national body of investors before this time were an inadequate foundation upon which to build a sophisticated Canadian securities market. Therefore, when the first large Canadian industrials did seek long-term capital in the late nineteenth century, they went to London, the most advanced and sophisticated capital market in the world until the emergence of New York as an international financial centre during the Great War. They were aided in this process by Canada's colonial relationship with Britain and by the fact that many of the families of the owners of these large enterprises originally came from the British Isles and consciously kept up their connection to the 'mother country'.[19]

One of the earliest examples of a Canadian industrial flotation in London was the Dominion Brewery issue of £240,000 worth of securities in 1889. This issue came in the midst of the British brewery flotation boom which had been initiated by the very successful Guinness share issue in 1886.[20] It is very likely that Robert Davies, the Dominion Brewery's owner, was aware of the boom and decided to take full advantage of investor sentiment in Britain by jumping on the bandwagon. Unfortunately, it is impossible to infer whether Davies or the British investment bank responsible for floating Dominion Brewery's shares, the London & Colonial Finance Corporation, was the creative force behind the decision to tap into the London capital market at this opportune moment. Nonetheless, the few documents filed with the London Stock Exchange to obtain a listing after the flotation do permit a limited investigation of this early issue.

A Canadian quite likely of British descent, Robert Davies had established the Dominion Brewery in Toronto in 1879. The business grew so rapidly during the next ten years that the firm's need for new plant and equipment outstripped the supply of earnings that could be ploughed back into the business. Davies decided to turn his operation into a limited company and publicly sell the new company's securities to British investors to raise the necessary capital in two ways. First, he was relegated to the position of one shareholder among many, although he was contractually retained as general manager of the new company for a minimum of three years. Second, not having the requisite background to carry out this form of financing himself, Davies sold his brewery to a British investment bank which in turn sold the company at an even higher price to a newly incorporated English company, the Dominion Brewery Co. Ltd. The Davies firm thus became, at least nominally, a British company although its operations and management remained entirely in Canada.[21]

A few aspects of this complicated transaction are worth noting since it anticipated some innovative aspects of North American investment banking that would eventually be adopted by British firms. In particular, the investment bank, London & Colonial Finance, took on all of the expenses as well as the risk of failure of the new issue. By purchasing the old brewery company outright it was in effect underwriting the entire issue and was compensated accordingly. Rather than receiving a cash commission, the merchant bank's traditional form of remuneration, London & Colonial Finance received 31,545 shares in the new company for its services. This constituted 13 per cent of the issue, a substantial but perhaps not excessive fee given the underwriting function performed by London & Colonial Finance and the fact that the subsequent flotation turned out to be a great success. Financial tasks involving minimal risk were farmed out to other financial specialists. The City stockbroking firm of Coates, Son & Co. was retained as brokers for the issue while a London deposit bank, the National Bank Ltd., played the more passive role of accepting applications for the purchase of Dominion Brewery's shares.[22]

The next major Canadian industrial flotation on the London market involved the Dominion Cotton Co.'s sale of £305,200 worth of debentures in London in 1895. One of the largest textile manufacturers in Canada, Dominion Cotton appointed Coates, Son & Co. rather than an established merchant bank to handle the new issue of £305,200 worth of debentures. This case illustrates the fluid nature of financial institutions in the City at this time as well as the 'stock market origins' of many of the emerging investment banks.[23] Coates, Son & Co. appears to have done everything from preparing the prospectus to conducting the flotation, receiving the share applications and registering the purchase of shares. The firm even acted as Dominion Cotton's agent in its application to have its shares listed on the London Stock Exchange.[24]

This involvement of British investment banks in directing capital towards Canadian industry, particularly that sector defined as manufacturing under national standard industrial classification schemes, accelerated in the decade preceding the Great War. The amount they raised from predominantly British investors through the London market rose steadily until 1909, when the amount jumped dramatically during the Canadian merger wave of 1909–12. During these years, large Canadian industrial consolidations were floated with great frequency in London.[25]

Table 1 illustrates the amount of capital raised for Canadian manufacturing companies on the London market between 1905 and 1913. This amount is compared in both absolute and relative terms to the annual value of all Canadian issues on the London market, which included traditionally larger items such as government and railway security issues. We see that manufacturing issues rise from an average of 4.35 per cent of

TABLE 1
CANADIAN CAPITAL RAISED THROUGH THE LONDON ISSUE MARKET, 1905–13

Year	Nominal Value of Total Canadian Issues (£000)	Nominal Value of Manufacturing Issues (£000)	Manufacturing as Per Cent of Total Issues	Actual Value of Manufacturing Issues (£000)
1905	13,530	585	4.3%	585
1906	6,428	303	4.7%	397
1907	11,204	540	4.8%	529
1908	29,355	1,059	3.6%	1,050
1909	37,412	3,981	10.6%	3,721
1910	38,454	5,619	14.6%	5,421
1911	39,856	4,965	12.5%	4,889
1912	32,457	3,435	10.6%	3,225
1913	47,636	3,428	7.2%	3,342

Source: Derived from F.W. Field, *Capital Investments in Canada* (Toronto, 3rd ed. 1914), pp. 11, 259–81.

total Canadian issues on the London market between 1905 and 1908 to an average of 12.1 per cent for the subsequent four years which are, in effect, the years of the first great Canadian merger wave. In absolute terms, we see that Canadian manufacturers received almost ten times more capital in 1910 than what they obtained in 1905 through the London new issue market. Since many of the issues were sold at a slight discount below their par value and a few were sold at a premium slightly above par value, a final column of actual value as opposed to nominal value of issues is included in Table 1. The relatively small gap between the nominal value of manufacturing issues and the actual value adds credence to the original comparison.

The investment banks involved in this remarkable transference of capital were almost all based in the City of London, although they increasingly faced competition from Canadian investment banks headquartered in Montreal and Toronto that were beginning to grab some of the risky but lucrative new issue business in Canadian industrials. Firms such as the Dominion Securities Corporation, the Royal Securities Corporation, the Dominion Bond Co., the Montreal-London Securities Corporation, C. Meredith & Co., and the Investment Trust Co. established their own houses in London at this time. Already in control of the Toronto and Montreal portion of Canadian industrial flotations, they soon began taking a slice of the much larger London issue and underwriting business. By this time as well, six of the larger Canadian deposit banks had established branches in London and were beginning to pick up some of the more routine aspects of the Canadian industrial issue business at the expense of the more established British commercial banks.[26]

Perhaps anticipating the challenge posed by these entities, some of the City investment banks recruited young Canadians into their own firms. In this way, City banks were able to assimilate the skills of North American investment banking practices while acquiring additional Canadian business. James Dunn, a broker who specialised in arbitrage operations between stock exchanges as well as in security flotations in Montreal, joined forces with Louis Fischer to form the London investment bank of Dunn, Fischer & Co. in 1905. One year later, Edward Mackay Edgar, another member of the Montreal Stock Exchange, moved to London to become a partner in the investment bank of Sperling & Co. and a member of the London Stock Exchange by 1908. A few years later, E.R. Peacock left Dominion Securities of Toronto to join Barings. All eventually became the dominating personalities in these British investment banks.[27] Some investment banks were able to specialise in Canadian business without hiring any Canadians at all, although the senior partner of the Canadian Agency, one of the largest of these firms, was the son-in-law of Earl Grey, the Governor-General of Canada, and exploited this connection to the fullest extent possible.[28]

III

In order to obtain some idea of the British investment banks involved in this significant transfer of capital to the manufacturing industry of another nation as well as their method of operation, some of the records of the London Stock Exchange were examined. Using a list of Canadian manufacturing company flotations on the London market as well as a list of new industrial merger issues floated in London, both of which were previously compiled,[29] the London Stock Exchange's index of applications for listing was searched to determine which companies had applied for listings after their floatations.[30] Although a significant number of the companies which floated an issue of securities in London before the merger wave of 1909–12 did not subsequently apply to have these shares listed on the London Stock Exchange, the later manufacturing consolidations were of the requisite size to make such a listing worthwhile. Consequently, the information derived from this survey is necessarily weighted towards the years immediately preceding the Great War.

The British investment banks involved in providing finance to Canadian industry turn out to be an eclectic mixture. It included large and established merchant banks as well as small trust companies and stockbroking firms now long forgotten. In order to determine which banks were predisposed to act as issue houses, however, it was essential to ferret out the investment bank primarily responsible for any given flotation given that many investment banks were involved in the underwriting of any single issue in order to spread the risk of failure. For example, the sample indicates that the larger merchant banks such as Lazard Brothers, Speyer Brothers, and Kleinwort, Sons & Co., were reluctant to shoulder the primary responsibility for such manufacturing issues (and therefore most of the burden of the risk of the flotation's failure), even though they were perfectly prepared to take on large slices of underwriting in a number of flotations. In one exceptional case in 1909, Speyer Brothers was prepared to take charge of the flotation of a very young but large Canadian steel company.[31]

Table 2 specifies the British investment banks that acted as the main houses of issue for Canadian manufacturing company flotations in the years preceding the Great War. It is not meant to be a comprehensive list of all the British investment banks in charge of new Canadian industrial issues. This was impossible to obtain because of the number of Canadian companies which obtained funds through the London market but never applied to have their shares listed on the London Stock Exchange and therefore left no evidentiary trail. Nor is Table 2 a representative list; those companies that ultimately obtained a quotation were without doubt the larger manufacturing companies in Canada. Nonetheless, it does provide some useful evidence concerning the types of investment bankers prepared to take on new industrial issues. For the most part, it was the smaller and more specialised investment banks that accepted the greatest risk in floating the shares of Canadian manufacturing companies. It is likely that the long-established investment banks, particularly the merchant banks, were not as willing to risk reputation and capital on the front-lines of this new industrial issue business even while some were prepared to take on a slice of underwriting.

Contrary to what occurred on the continent, where large incorporated universal banks conducted the majority of new issue investment banking, this business took on a much more personal nature in the Anglo-American world where small unincorporated investment bankers and individual promoters specialised in such work. As a consequence, individual personality played a greater role.[32] Often the institutional structure, whether a private bank, trust company, or stockbroking firm, was less important than the financier behind it. Therefore, in cases where a dominant individual personality within the investment bank could be identified, at least with respect to the Canadian flotations, the name is included in brackets below the name of the bank in Table 2.

TABLE 2

LONDON INVESTMENT BANKS ACTING AS ISSUE HOUSES IN CANADIAN MANUFACTURING COMPANY FLOTATIONS BEFORE THE GREAT WAR

Investment Bank	Manufacturing Company Issue	Size of Issue (£000)	Year
Western Canada Trust Ltd. (I.H. Benn)	Canada Iron Corporation	500	1908
	Canadian Car & Foundry	648	1909
	Canadian Car & Foundry	483	1910
	Steel Company of Canada	948	1910
	Steel Company of Canada	193	1911
	Canadian Steel Foundries	411	1911
	Cockshutt Plow Co.	772	1911
Sperling & Co. (E.M. Edgar)	Canadian General Electric	322	1906
	Canadian General Electric	411	1907
	Dominion Steel Corporation	205	1912
	British Columbia Breweries	565	1912
The Canadian Agency (A.M. Grenfell)	Canada Cement Co.	225	1909
	Canada Cotton	353	1911
The British Empire Trust Co.	Canadian Western Lumber	1,320	1910
	Canadian North Pac. Fish.	344	1910
Speyer Brothers	Dominion Iron & Steel	1,116	1909
Kitcat & Aitken (R.M. Aitken)	Amalgamated Asbestos	383	1909
Brazilian Canadian and General Trust Co.	Dominion Sawmills & Lumber	760	1910
Egerton, Jones & Simpson	Canadian Pacific Lumber	326	1911
British Foreign & Colonial Corp.	Dominion Canners	153	1913

Note: Size refers to the price at which the issue was sold rather than the par value of the security flotation.
Source: London Stock Exchange listing applications for above companies, Guildhall Library, MS 18000.

In the majority of these merger promotions, smaller issues of securities would be floated in North America concurrently with the London issues. The Canadian flotation of an industrial consolidation would often be spearheaded by a Canadian merger promoter. At the same time, a London investment bank would be retained to put together the underwriting syndicate to handle the generally much larger British flotations. These City banks were not mere employees of the Canadian promoters, however. They controlled the British issue entirely and their skill, connections, and luck determined the success or the failure of the issue. The Canadian financiers were restricted to looking on anxiously as the 'senior' transatlantic financiers released the shares of their promotions into the vast sea of the London market.[33]

The guiding hand behind Western Canada Trust, the most active issue house according to Table 2, was Ion Hamilton Benn, a 'leading figure in the City', and Unionist politician.[34] Despite the name of his firm, Benn was more concerned with the corporate flotation business than with traditional trust services. His connection with Canada began when he was a partner in Price & Pierce, London pulp and paper merchants that had interests in pulp mills and other projects in Canada. He soon became a director of Price Brothers Ltd., one of the largest pulp concerns in the country. In the course of this business, he met one of Canada's youngest and most vigorous financiers, Max Aitken (later Lord Beaverbrook), who appointed Western Canada Trust the house of issue for the Canadian Car & Foundry and the Steel Company of Canada security flotations, two of Aitken's major industrial mergers. Western Canada Trust was also a significant member of Canada Cement's London underwriting syndicate, Aitken's largest merger promotion. By successfully handling the London flotations of these industrial consolidations he helped make Aitken the most successful merger promoter of his day.[35]

Sperling & Co. was the first City investment bank to specialise in Canadian industrial flotations. It was one of the many small Anglo-German houses that branched out from stockbroking activities into the general issue business. Regarded as one of the more 'reckless' firms in the City, it was consistently prepared to take on a position of great risk in floating new issues of corporate securities.[36] In this, it was similar to the Canadian Agency, the firm created in 1906 by Arthur Grenfell, one of the partners in the established merchant bank of Chaplin, Milne, Grenfell & Co., Limited (originally Morton, Rose & Co.). Impatient with the conservative nature of Chaplin, Milne's business, but unable to convince his partners to take on the risk associated with the more speculative types of Canadian security issues, particularly the industrial and land company flotations, Grenfell set up a smaller investment bank that concentrated on this expanding Canadian business as both an underwriter and issue house.[37] The Canadian Agency was Max Aitken's first choice for an investment bank to handle the British flotations of his merger promotions but its bungling of the first Canada Cement issue infuriated Aitken and he restricted the firm's work to underwriting in subsequent flotations. Unlike Sperling & Co., which grew into one of the more significant City investment banks, Grenfell's poor choice of issue and underwriting business (and perhaps his own incompetence) bankrupted the firm by 1914.[38]

Speyer Brothers was probably attracted to the Dominion Iron & Steel flotation of 1909 because it approached the larger railway issues in size. Two years later, a much smaller issue by the Dominion Steel Corporation, the successor company to Dominion Iron & Steel, was taken by Sperling & Co. rather than Speyer Brothers perhaps because the more modest profit on the smaller transaction held appeal only for the less-established investment bank. Speyer's profit in the 1909 Dominion Iron & Steel flotation was in the form of common shares rather than a cash commission and by December 1912 it still held 11,700 common shares. Given that this was worth in excess of £100,000 and the probability that it had likely disposed of a substantial amount of its total common stock payment in the intervening three years, it is evident that Speyer Brothers made an enormous profit in this single transaction.[39]

Too little is known about the other investment banks enumerated in Table 2 to draw any definite conclusions about their role as issue houses in Canadian industrial flotations. The British Empire Trust Co. appears to have been an older and more established trust company that nevertheless decided to try out the new issue business when the flotation in question was large enough to make it worthwhile.[40] The Brazilian Canadian & General Trust Co. Ltd. may have had a similar background.[41] On the other hand, the British Foreign & Colonial Corporation Ltd. described itself as an international investment bank with a head office in London and branches in France, Holland, and Switzerland. In fact, in the only example of an issue house not setting up an underwriting syndicate, British Foreign & Colonial took on the entire risk of the relatively small Dominion Canners flotation of 1913.[42]

Kitcat & Aitken was a City stockbroking firm that appears to have taken on one industrial issue and, upon finding the whole affair less profitable than anticipated, dropped the Canadian business in favour of more traditional broking activity. Admitted as a member of the London Stock Exchange in 1905, the younger member of the firm, R.M. Aitken (no relation to Max Aitken), became interested in the Amalgamated Asbestos issue through some Canadian associates. After touring Canada to see the company's properties, he sailed back to Britain and conducted the London end of the flotation. The heavily overcapitalised company soon faced many difficulties, however, and its common shares became almost valueless, thus depriving all the issue houses and underwriters of a significant profit.[43] The case history of Egerton, Jones & Simpson and its experience with the Canadian Pacific Lumber issue of 1911 may have been parallel to Kitcat & Aitken. Certainly, this City stockbroking firm does not appear to have become an investment bank after its initial foray into the new issue business.[44]

IV

Table 2 is misleading in one very important sense. Many other investment banks, including a few exceptional stockbroking and stockjobbing firms, which are not listed as issue houses, were nevertheless involved as investment banks in these same issues as syndicate partners in their underwriting. This activity was an essential part of the new issue business of investment banking and was particularly demanding at a time when industrial securities were just becoming accepted by the average investor. While generally willing to embrace the securities of governments as well as established banks, insurance companies, railways, and utilities, investors were wary of industrial issues. This scepticism was only very gradually eroded in the decade preceding the Great War. At this time, manufacturing companies were not perceived to be as stable as railways and insurance companies, for example, and they seemed to suffer more during the periodic downswings of the trade cycle than virually any other type of business. It took very little for a fickle investing public to shun a particular industrial issue, and when this occurred underwriters had to purchase the securities knowing that they might not be able to sell them for months or possibly not at all.[45]

Underwriting was illegal under English company law until 1900, but it appears that many British investment banks engaged in this activity long before the law was changed to permit its usage.[46] In the Dominion Brewery case mentioned above, for example, the law was evaded by selling the old company to an investment bank for the purpose of the share flotation and only afterwards re-selling it to the new brewery company incorporated under English company law. After 1900, investment banks regularly engaged in underwriting activity. Indeed, in the very risky world of industrial issues, underwriting was the only means by which manufacturers could reduce the risk of raising money on capital markets sufficiently to make this a desirable form of financing. By selling its whole security issue to an investment bank, the manufacturing company was guaranteed a large amount of working capital in a very short period of time albeit at a price that exceeded smaller, short-term advances from commercial banks. Moreover, underwriting provided the most effective means by which investment banks could regularly engage in industrial share flotations without the risk of losing their entire capital base on a single issue. By having a group of other bankers and brokers agree to purchase blocks of shares not sold during the flotation, the investment bank was assured that it would not bear the entire burden of a failed flotation even though this meant giving up considerable profit to such underwriters.[47]

In the vast majority of Canadian manufacturing flotations, underwriters were paid in the common shares of the company rather than cash. This was the North American practice of high-risk financing based on the division between senior securities (preference shares, debentures, and bonds) representing the existing assets of a firm, and common shares, a speculative security intended to capture the potential value of a firm. In this way, common shares were used to lubricate the whole issue process. Promoters and issue houses accepted common shares rather than cash as payment for their services and, in turn, they paid for the services of underwriters in common shares. All were willing to take their profit in this more speculative form because the potential reward was so much greater than a simple commission payment although the risk was correspondingly greater.[48]

It is commonly believed that British investment banking was cautious and tradition-bound relative to the progressive policies of the universal banks on the continent and the innovative and aggressive, almost reckless, behaviour of North American investment banks. This is likely a consequence of generalisations based on the well documented experiences of only two investment banks: Barings and Rothschilds.[49] It is significant that while neither bank acted as an underwriter or issue house in pre-war Canadian industrial flotations, other prominent 'merchant banks' such as Speyer Brothers, Lazard Brothers, and Kleinwort, Son & Co. did play this role. It took another two decades before Barings and Rothschilds were willing to work with industrial issues.[50] More importantly, even when dealing with government debt and railway issues, both banks generally eschewed the purchase of entire issues of securities in favour of low-risk cash commission sales. It should be noted in this respect that the most important investment banker in the United States, J.P. Morgan, was reluctant to use high-risk methods of finance until the United States Steel merger flotation of 1902.[51]

The evidence that other British investment bankers did adopt new North American high-risk practice in industrial share issues can be found in the lists of common shareholders that were supplied to the London Stock Exchange each time a company made an application to have its common shares quoted. Unfortunately, only a small minority of companies made such an application. Most were satisfied with having their senior securities listed: the preference shares, bonds, and debentures actually purchased by the investing public. Common shares were used to pay off promoters, investment bankers, brokers, and even solicitors, and therefore were not used directly to raise money through a security issue. Only those companies which eventually saw an active market building up in their common shares as they passed out of the hands of the financial intermediaries and into the portfolios of institutional and individual long-term investors had a strong incentive to list their common shares. As a consequence, the evidence of the holdings of British investment bankers is limited to three of the industrial flotations listed in Table 2 but these few cases are remarkably revealing.

In the Dominion Iron & Steel flotation of 1909 most of the shares of this Canadian manufacturing company were reserved for the British market. Speyer Brothers not only acted as the house of issue but also took a large portion of the underwriting, and was compensated accordingly, as discussed above. The other major underwriter was the City stockbroking firm of George Kitchin & Co. which still had 8,785 shares worth at least £75,000 in its possession three years after the flotation. The dozen City stockbroking firms participating in the issue, mainly in the minor role of subunderwriters, also accepted common shares rather than a cash commission in payment for their services. Sperling & Co. appears to have participated in the main underwriting syndicate, while two Scottish investment trust companies from Aberdeen were involved in subunderwriting.[52]

The Canadian Car flotation of 31,500 preference shares of November 1909 turned out to be one of the most successful Canadian industrial issues floated on the London market during the Canadian merger wave, in part because the underwriting was distributed so widely. Ian Hamilton Benn of Western Canada Trust along with W. MacLeod of Fielding Son & MacLeod, a City stockbroking firm, were responsible for forming the English syndicate. The strength and depth of the syndicate is displayed in Table 3, which is drawn from the list of common shareholders on 22 August 1910. The profits of these two firms, after distribution of common stock to brokers, amounted to a par value of £544,528. Given that a $100 par value Canadian Car common stock was worth over $60 when first listed in Canada in early 1910 rising to a high of $90 in 1911, this meant that Western Canada Trust and Fielding, Son & MacLeod had a net profit of approximately £490,000, which goes far to explain the City's enthusiasm for Canadian industrial flotations. Moreover, in their personal capacities as individual underwriters, Benn and MacLeod received 1,667 common shares as remuneration which translates into a profit of over £130,000 by 1911.

Many of the underwriters listed in Table 3 are City stockbroking firms. Six of the firms, however, are specialist investment banks in the sense that they were not stockbroking firms but engaged almost exclusively in issuing, underwriting and other investment banking activities. Aside from Western Canada Trust we find Sperling & Co., the Canadian Agency, Lazard Brothers & Co. Speyer Brothers, and Kleinwort Sons & Co. on the list. The last three, of course, were large and established merchant banks although the risk they were willing to accept in this particular industrial issue was no greater than the small City stockbroking firms.[53] This implies that while such firms engaged directly in the

TABLE 3
COMMON (ORDINARY) SHARES HELD BY LONDON UNDERWRITERS IN THE CANADIAN CAR & FOUNDRY SHARE FLOTATION OF NOVEMBER, 1909

Name of City Firm	Common Shares (No.)	Minimum Market Value (£)
Western Canada Trust	10,294	126,194
Fielding Son & MacLeod	6,290	77,549
Sperling & Co.	2,477	30,539
A.V. Gehlcken (Western Trust Co.)	1.207	14,881
T.E. Jones	1,180	14,548
I.H. Benn (Western Canada Trust)	866	10,677
W. MacLeod (Fielding Son & MacLeod)	801	9,857
The Canadian Agency	580	7,151
E.F. Kelly	400	4,932
E.G. Redpath (Carr Sons & Tod)	289	3,563
F.G. Scott (Carr Sons & Tod)	270	3,329
Lazard Brothers & Co.	270	3,329
Tomkinson Brunton & Co.	262	3,230
Holland & Balfour	230	2,826
Speyer Brothers	220	2,712
Baker Mason & Co.	187	2,306
Carl Meyer	150	1,849
Kleinwort Sons & Co.	150	1,849
A.E. Bowen	135	1,664
A.G. Tontes	130	1,603
L. Gerald	112	1,381
Total Held by City underwriters	26,500	

Source: Derived from London Stock Exchange Records, Guildhall Library, MS 18000/145B/759, register of common shareholders of Canadian Car & Foundry Co. Ltd., dated 22 August 1910.

industrial issue business, they did so carefully. Although more research is needed before we can be sure, it seems likely that the large merchant banks thinly apportioned their participation over a large number of industrial issues. Unwilling to take the risk of the smaller specialist investment banks such as Western Canadian Trust and the Canadian Agency, they were also reluctant to forego the potentially large profits involved in such business and therefore ensured that they had a piece, however small, of the action.

A similar constellation of bankers and brokers was used in the Canada Cement share flotations of 1909 and 1910. Even though the underwriting is not as well distributed, we can see the same basic pattern once again being repeated. The major merchant bank involved, this time Kleinwort Sons & Co., plays a subdued role as one of smaller underwriters, while Sperling & Co., the Canadian Agency and Ion Hamilton Benn (Western Canada Trust), take up the largest chunks of underwriting. In early 1911, Sperling & Co. still had 11,970 common shares in its possession, while Benn had 4,540 shares in his possession. The other major underwriters in this issue included the London stockbroking firms of Fielding, Son & McLeod and Rowe & Pitman as well as the Birmingham stockbroking firm of Cutler & Lacy.[54]

V

This case study can only be regarded as a preliminary step in understanding the nature of British investment banking beyond the well documented but atypical cases of Barings and Rothschilds. The evidence does suggest, however, that many lesser known British investment banks, as well as some of the largest merchant banks, were willing to channel long-term capital to industry before the Great War. Moreover, there is little evidence of a systematic bias against providing capital to manufacturing companies except again in the case of Barings and Rothschilds who chose to continue raising finance for governments and large railway enterprises but eschewed industrial firms. This contrasts with American investment banks such as J.P. Morgan which added industrial companies to their traditional list of government and railway securities shortly after 1900.

The operations of the British investment banks reviewed above also indicate the absence of institutional rigidity in the City before the Great War. Individuals and firms moved with apparent ease from one category of financial intermediation into another; for example, the boundaries separating investment banking from trust companies and stockbroking firms were clearly less fixed at this time than popularly believed. Moreover, the City was a highly competitive environment. If the London investment banks did not respond to the demands of domestic, foreign, and in this case, colonial, industry, they knew that non-British investment banks would quickly establish an office in the City to take this same business.

In fact, the City banks appear to have responded very quickly to this demand by Canadian industrial firms for long-term capital. Moreover, they adopted the three basic pillars of high-risk finance: they indemnified the manufacturing company by purchasing the entire issue of securities thereby acting as an issue house; they then improved the success rate of flotations by underwriting portions of the issue before subscription was opened to the public; and finally they agreed to take their remuneration in the common shares of the company rather than a cash commission thereby staking their profit on the future viability of the enterprise. In fact, these methods might not have been 'adopted' at all. Again more research is required, but British investment banks may actually have originated many of the methods that soon became identified with North American high-risk finance judging by the methods employed in the 1889 Dominion Brewery flotation.

Even if we assume that British investment banks had a preference for foreign and colonial industry over domestic industry, we can only conclude that this was for reasons other than a 'natural preference', 'lack of entrepreneurial spirit', 'habit or prediliction'. One possible reason is that Canadian industrial firms and their financial representatives were prepared to distribute very large amounts of common stock as remuneration to issue houses and underwriters in place of the more traditional cash commission. This dramatically increased the potential profit for servicing an industrial issue but it also substantially increased the risk taken on by investment banks. Not every investment bank was prepared to accept this amount of risk, but those that did were rewarded either with an enormous profit or with a crippling liability in the form of a mound of non-transferable common stock.

Canadian industrial companies, like their American counterparts, paid a high price for this form of financing both in terms of the percentage of their share issue distributed to financiers and the long-term debt load imposed by overcapitalisation. They were prepared to pay this price because of their rapid expansion in the years immediately preceding their issues and the optimism concerning future growth. In contrast, British industrial growth had slowed to a crawl in the decades preceding the Great War and most British firms could not be as optimistic about future expansion as their North American counterparts; they therefore would have been less willing to pay the high cost involved in a North American type of security of flotation. Obtaining more incremental finance through retained earnings and the occasional short-term bank advance must have seemed a wiser strategy in the circumstances. It seems more logical, therefore, that the problem lay in the demand for capital rather than in its supply. The City's actions before the Great War appear to have been more of a response to slower domestic growth than a contributing cause of industrial decline.

NOTES

1. M. Edelstein, *Overseas Investment in the Age of High Imperialism: The United Kingdom, 1850–1914* (New York, 1982), p.3. See G. Paish, 'Great Britain's Capital Investments in Individual Colonial and Foreign Countries', *Journal of the Royal Statistical*

Society, Vol. LXXIV (1911), and C.K. Hobson, *The Export of Capital* (1914), for two contemporary accounts of this capital exodus.

2. S.D. Chapman, *The Rise of Merchant Banking* (1984), p. 98.
3. D.S. Landes, *The Unbound Prometheus: Technological Change and Industrial Development in Western Europe from 1750 to the Present* (Cambridge, 1969), p. 349.
4. A. Cairncross, *Home and Foreign Investment, 1870–1913* (Cambridge, 1953); W.P. Kennedy, 'Foreign Investment, Trade and Growth in the United Kingdom, 1870–1913', *Explorations in Economic History*, Vol. XI (1974), and *Industrial Structure, Capital Markets and the Origins of British Econmic Decline* (Cambridge, 1987).
5. These works include: 'The Social Web of Investment in the Nineteenth Century', *Revue Internationale d'Histoire de la Banque*, Vol. 18 (1979); *Money, Mania and Markets: Investment, Company Formation and the Stock Exchange in Nineteenth-Century Scotland* (Edinburgh, 1981); 'Options, Concessions, Syndicates and the Provision of Venture Capital, 1880–1913', *Business History*, Vol. 23 (1981); 'Crisis and Opportunity: The Formation and Operation of the British Assets Trust, 1897–1914', *Business History*, Vol. 25 (1983); *The London and New York Stock Exchanges, 1850–1914* (1987); 'Dunn, Fischer & Co. in the City of London, 1906–14', *Business History*, Vol. 30 (1988).
6. W.J. Reader, *A House in the City: A Study of the City and of the Stock Exchange based on the Records of Foster & Braithwaite 1825–1975* (1979), pp. 89–134.
7. Edelstein, *Overseas Investment*, chapter 3.
8. M.H. Best and J. Humphries, 'The City and Industrial Decline' in B. Elbaum and W. Lazonick (eds.), *The Decline of the British Economy*, (Oxford, 1986).
9. S. Pollard, 'Capital Exports, 1870–1914: Harmful or Beneficial?', *Economic History Review*, 2nd series, Vol. XXXVIII (1985). Also see Y. Cassis, 'British Finance: Success and Controversy', in J.J. van Helten and Y. Cassis (eds.), *Capitalism in a Mature Economy: Financial Institutions, Capital Exports and British Industry, 1870–1939* (Aldershot, 1990) for the latest review of the literature.
10. Edelstein, *Overseas Investment*, p. 287.
11. Hobson quoted in D.C.M. Platt, 'Canada and Argentina: The First Preference of the British Investor, 1904–14', *Journal of Imperial and Commonwealth History*, Vol. XIII (1985), p. 79.
12. G.P. Marchildon, 'Promotion, Finance and Mergers in Canadian Manufacturing Industry', (unpublished Ph.D. thesis, London School of Economics, 1990), pp. 45–8.
13. This is the contemporary definition of banks found in T. Skinner, *The London Banks* (1910), p. ix.
14. See for example C.J.J. Clay and B.S. Wheble, *Modern Merchant Banking* (1976), p. 8, where they unsuccessfully attempt to define merchant banks in chapter two, concluding that the 'so-called merchant banks in London are now seldom merchants and by no means always bankers'. S.L. Hayes and P.M. Hubbard fare little better in their historically valid but functionally illogical taxonomy which includes continental European banks, clearing banks, merchant banks, investment banks and securities dealers: *Investment Banking: A Tale of Three Cities* (Boston, 1990), pp. 65–8.
15. Chapman, *Merchant Banking*, pp. 39–56, 96. On British promoters, see H.O. O'Hagen, *Leaves From My Life*, 2 Vols. (1929); J. Armstrong, 'Hooley and the Bovril Company', *Business History*, Vol. XXVII (1986), and idem, 'The Rise and Fall of the Company Promoter and the Financing of British Industry', in van Helten and Cassis, *Capitalism in a Mature Economy*.
16. Although it never defines the word bank, *The Banking Almanac for 1913* only included four of the investment banks with which I was concerned: Speyer Brothers, Lazard Brothers & Co., Kleinwort, Sons and Co., and the British Foreign & Colonial Corporation Ltd. Kleinwort and Lazard were cross-listed as merchants on pp. 245–6.
17. Chapman, *Merchant Banking*, p. 94.
18. E.P. Neufeld, *The Financial System of Canada: Its Growth and Development* (Toronto, 1972), pp. 462–86; R.C. Michie, 'The Canadian Securities Market, 1850–1914', *Business History Review*, Vol. 62 (1988), pp. 40–41; Chapman, *Merchant Banking*, p. 94.
19. Marchildon, thesis, pp. 30–48; Platt, 'Canada and Argentina', p. 81.
20. P.L. Cottrell, *Industrial Finance, 1830–1914: The Finance and Organization of English*

Manufacturing Industry (1980), pp. 168–70.

21. London Stock Exchange Records at the Guildhall Library (hereafter LSE), Dominion Brewery Co. Ltd., MS 18000/21B/334, prospectus, 28 May 1889.
22. LSE, Dominion Brewery Co. Ltd., MS 18000/21B/334: Contract between Robert Davies and the London & Colonial Finance Corporation Ltd., 23 May 1889, and contract between London & Colonial Finance Corporation Ltd. and N.C. Henry, trustee for the Dominion Brewery Co. Ltd., 25 May 1989. Unfortunately, the third contract, the agreement between London & Colonial and Coates, Son & Co. fixing their remuneration as brokers, was not included in the LSE file. The prospectus simply stated that: 'Applications for Shares will be deemed to waive the specification of any such contracts ...'
23. Chapman, *Merchant Banking*, p. 60.
24. LSE, Dominion Cotton Mills Co. Ltd., MS 18000/38B/93.
25. Marchildon, thesis, p. 263–72.
26. LSE, Dominion Glass Co. Ltd., MS 18000/171B/299; Belding, Paul & Corticelli Silk Co. Ltd. MS 18000/161B/106; Ames-Holden-McCready, Ltd., MS 18000/159B/1001; G.P. Marchildon, 'The Role of Lawyers in Corporate Promotion and Management: A Canadian Case Study and Theoretical Speculations', *Business and Economic History*, 2nd series, Vol. 19 (1990); Marchildon, thesis, pp. 209–15; *Monetary Times*, 3 July 1909, p. 121; 12 Nov. 1910; p. 2021; 29 April 1911, p. 1737; 6 May 1911, p. 1812.
27. D. McDowall, *Steel at the Sault: Francis H. Clergue, Sir James Dunn, and the Algoma Steel Corporation* (Toronto, 1984), pp. 95–112; Michie, 'Dunn, Fischer & Co.'; S. Diaper, 'The Sperling Combine and the Shipbuilding Industry: Merchant Banking and Industrial Finance in the 1920s', in van Helten and Cassis, *Capitalism in a Mature Economy*; Marchildon, thesis, pp. 209–15; *Members of The Stock Exchange*, 1909–10 (1910), p. 98.
28. Earl Grey (Fourth Earl) Papers, Department of Paleography and Diplomatic, University of Durham, various correspondence between Arthur Grenfell and Earl Grey, 1907–11.
29. Marchildon, thesis, Appendix B and pp. 252–54.
30. LSE, MS 18001, card index to applications for listing. The Guildhall Library has custody of applications for 1850–1926 only; later papers are retained by the Stock Exchange.
31. LSE, Dominion Iron & Steel Co. Ltd., MS 18000/120B/202: Prospectus of £1.2 million bond issue, 5 July 1909; letter, Speyer Brothers to Secretary, Share and Loan Department, Stock Exchange, 30 July 1909; Declaration of Edgar Speyer, 30 July 1909.
32. Marchildon, thesis, pp. 6–10; K. Born, *International Banking in the 19th and 20th Centuries* (New York, 1983), pp. 161–81; R. Tilly, 'Banking Institutions in Historical and Comparative Perspective: Germany, Great Britain and the United States in the Nineteenth and Early Twentieth Centuries', *Journal of Institutional and Theoretical Economics*, Vol. 145 (1989).
33. See Marchildon, thesis, chapter 3, for a case study of Max Aitken (Lord Beaverbrook) and pp. 209–15 for a brief summary of the major Canadian promoters during the consolidation wave.
34. A.J.P. Taylor, *Beaverbrook* (1972), p. 30.
35. LSE, Canada Iron Corporation Ltd., MS 18000/123B/667; Canadian Car & Foundry Co. Ltd., MS 18000/146B/870, MS 18000/145B/759, MS 18000/149B/1136; Steel Company of Canada Ltd., MS 18000/148B/988, MS 18000/158B/825; Canadian Steel Foundries Ltd., MS 18000/155B/494; Cockshutt Plow Co. Ltd., MS 18000/153B/257; Marchildon, thesis, Appendix C; Diaper, 'The Sperling Combine', p. 77.
36. LSE, Canadian General Electric Co. Ltd., MS 18000/104B/191, MS 18000/108B/33; Dominion Steel Corporation Ltd., MS 18000/163B/331; British Columbia Breweries Ltd., MS 18000/170B/136; Diaper, 'The Sperling Combine', p. 76.
37. Earl Grey (Fourth Earl) Papers, Department of Paleography and Diplomatic, University of Durham, letter, Grenfell to Grey, 26 Aug. 1906.
38. Beaverbrook Papers, House of Lords Record Office, A/36/Killam, letter, Aitken to Killam, 3 Nov. 1909 and letter, Killam to Aitken 19 Nov. 1909; A/31/Benn, letter,

Aitken to Benn, 3 Nov. 1909; A/38/MacLeod, letter, Aitken to MacLeod, 18 Nov. 1909; LSE, Canada Cement Co. Ltd., MS 18000/146B/830; Canadian Car & Foundry Co. Ltd., MS 18000/149B/1136; Skinner, *London Banks*, p. 51; Michie, 'Dunn, Fischer & Co.', p. 198.

39. LSE, Dominion Iron and Steel Co. Ltd., MS 18000/120B/202; Dominion Steel Corporation Ltd., MS 18000/163B/331; Montreal Register of Common Shareholders, dated 19 Dec. 1912; Skinner, *London Banks*, p. 190.
40. LSE, Canadian North Pacific Fisheries Ltd., MS 18000/151B/61; Canadian Western Lumber Co., MS 18000/151B/1340.
41. LSE, Dominion Sawmills & Lumber Ltd., MS 18000/129B/320.
42. LSE, Dominion Canners Ltd., MS 18000/171B/198.
43. LSE, Amalgamated Asbestos Corporation Ltd., MS 18000/145B/744; Beaverbrook Papers, House of Lords Recorded Office, A/8/misc A, letter, W.M. Aitken to R.M. Aitken, no date; *Members of The Stock Exchange, 1909–10* (1909), pp. 3, 397; Marchildon, thesis, p. 214.
44. LSE, Dominion Canners Ltd., MS 18000/171B/298.
45. T.R. Navin and M.V. Sears, 'The Rise of a Market for Industrial Securities, 1887–1902', *Business History Review,*, Vol. XXIX (1955); Marchildon, thesis, chapter two.
46. O'Hagen, *Leaves From My Life*, Vol. I, pp. 149–56; Armstrong, 'The Rise and Fall of the Company Promoter', p. 126; D. Finnie, *Capital Underwriting* (1934), pp. 1–50.
47. C.W. Gerstenberg, 'The Underwriting of Securities by Syndicates', *Trust Companies*, Vol. X (1910); F. Greenwood, 'What Modern Underwriting Accomplishes', *The Magazines of Wall Street*, Vol. 12 (1913); L.B. Franklin, 'The Formation of Syndicates', *The Magazine of Wall Street*, Vol. 15 (1915); G. Ashmead, 'Syndicate Management and Operation', *Trust Companies*, Vol. XXXIII (1921); V.P. Carosso, *Investment Banking in America: A History* (Cam-bridge, MA, 1970), chapter 3.
48. Marchildon, thesis, pp. 23–30.
49. See P. Ziegler, *The Sixth Great Power: Barings, 1762–1929* (1988); R. Hidy, *The House of Baring in American Trade and Finance* (Cambridge, MA, 1949); J. Bouvier, *Les Rothschild* (Paris, 1967); B. Gille, *Histoire de la Maison Rothschild*, 2 Vols. (Geneva, 1965, 1967); S.D. Chapman, 'Foundation of the English Rothschilds', *Textile History*, Vol. VIII (1977).
50. Barings' 1890 Guinness brewery flotation is the one prominent exception. Chapman, *Merchant Banking*, p. 101.
51. Navin and Sears, 'Market for Industrial Securities', pp. 133–6; V.P. Carosso, *The Morgans: Private International Bankers* (Cambridge, MA, 1987).
52. LSE, Dominion Steel Corporation Ltd., MS 18000/163B/331; Montreal Register of Common Shareholders, dated 19 Dec. 1912.
53. Chapman, *Merchant Banking*, pp. 200–04.
54. LSE, Canada Cement Co. Ltd., MS 18000/153B/335; Montreal Register of Common Shareholders, dated 1 Feb. 1911.

'No Arbitrary Discretion': Specialisation in Short-Term Commercial Lending by Banks in Late Nineteenth-Century New England

NAOMI R. LAMOREAUX

Brown University

In the last two decades of the nineteenth century New England banks altered their lending practices by specialising in the provision of short-term commercial loans. Although bank loans in the region had long taken the form of short-term notes, a large proportion of the portfolios of early nineteenth-century banks had consisted of accommodation paper – that is, notes that were not connected with any specific commercial transaction and that were routinely renewed upon maturity, making them effectively long-term obligations. Accommodation loans could be – and were – used to support a wide variety of investment activities.[1] In the second half of the century, however, this type of loan fell into disfavour and, I will argue, largely disappeared from use. In its place, bankers espoused a much more restrictive type of commercial lending based exclusively on borrowers' liquid assets, a policy that made it increasingly difficult for manufacturers to obtain bank financing for their investments.

A remarkably similar transformation in lending behaviour occurred in Great Britain at around the same period of time. By contrast, banks in late nineteenth-century Germany continued to involve themselves directly in industrial finance.[2] The divergent histories of these two nations give my article a twofold purpose: first, to analyse the change in lending behaviour in New England with the aim of understanding the evolution of banking practice in that region; and second, to generate some hypotheses that might account for the different banking patterns that emerged in Germany and Great Britain. I argue that the shift toward short-term commercial loans that occurred in New England at the end of the century was the product of two historical developments: an expansion of the banking system that created large numbers of independent institutions whose behaviour was difficult to control; and the increased interdependence that resulted from the rise of deposits as a source of lendable funds, a change that made each bank vulnerable to runs triggered by the unsound practices of other institutions. By promoting strict standards for short-term commercial loans, bank reformers sought to increase the ability of directors and stockholders to monitor the lending practices of their banks and, at the same time, to limit the damage to the system that unscrupulous bank managers could inflict. As I suggest in the final section of the paper, similar problems of control developed in the British banking system in the last few decades of the nineteenth century. In Germany, on the other hand, large urban banks used exchanges of stock and other techniques to reduce the independence of outlying institutions and hence the threat to the banking system that they posed.

I

New England's post-Civil War banking system was shaped by the economic and political environment of the early nineteenth century. Scarcity of information and the modest scale of enterprise had conspired to keep credit markets localised and financial institutions small. At the same time, the general want of credit had encouraged bank directors to take advantage of their official positions to channel bank funds into their own enterprises. Records dating from the early nineteenth century show that it was common for directors and their close associates to absorb as much as 50 to 90 per cent of their institutions' lendable funds.[3]

Such an extreme degree of favouritism in the allocation of scarce resources inevitably generated resentment, and as a result, legislators were forced to make the privilege of operating a bank more widely available, both by increasing the number of charters and by lowering the minimum capital requirements for founding a bank. The result was a tremendous growth in the number of banking institutions, so that by the eve of the Civil War there were more than 500 of them in the region, or one for every 6,600 inhabitants.[4]

The elite merchants who controlled the region's oldest banks had from the first vehemently opposed this expansion of the banking system. As they saw it – quite correctly, it turns out – charters were being sought by 'those who themselves were in want of capital', and whose interest in banking had been conceived largely 'with a view to furnish funds for private speculation, or the private use of the principal stockholders'. The result, they feared, would be a flood of insufficiently capitalised banks whose fortunes depended 'on the success and solvency of the principal stockholders' and whose consequent vulnerability to failure threatened the stability of the entire financial system.[5]

But though these merchants managed in some years to block new applications for charters, in the end they succeeded only in delaying the expansion of the banking system. The problem, as they themselves realised, was a democratic political culture which made it impossible to limit opportunities that were essentially government-created. As one pseudonymous writer put it, 'under our form of government where monopolies and exclusive privileges are strictly forbidden, an important privilege cannot with any consistency be extended to one, and refused to other[s] of equal claims'. Politically, it was impossible to prevent such opportunities from being expanded in unlimited fashion. Thus a system of incorporated banks 'when once established, must necessarily be permitted to extend itself, until it shall fall under its own weight.[6]

Such a dire consequence never materialised, however, for though elite merchants were unable to prevent the expansion of the banking system, they were not so helpless when it came to regulating the behaviour of the new entrants. In order to maintain profitability, banks had to keep their currency in circulation, and this necessity gave established institutions important leverage over new banks. Under the aegis of the Suffolk Bank, an institution whose board of directors included Boston's most eminent merchants, they established a clearing house for bank notes issued within the region and required all institutions to maintain deposits of specie to back up their note issues. Banks that refused to comply would soon find their notes presented for redemption at their counters, a drain on specie reserves that no bank could afford for long.[7]

This 'Suffolk system', as it was called, worked remarkably well. The notes of New England's banks circulated consistently at or near par. Moreover, despite the fact that many new banks were organised 'by those who themselves were in want of capital', the actual danger to the financial system was slight. Because the Suffolk system placed severe limits on the size of the note issues that each bank could support, banks were generally not highly leveraged in this period. (Deposits, another potential means of leverage, had not yet become an important source of funds.) The average ratio of capital stock to total liabilities for banks in Massachusetts in 1835, for example, was a remarkable 54 per cent. The equivalent figures for other states in the region ranged from 48 to 69 per cent.[8] Because leverage ratios were so low, whenever a bank ran into financial difficulties, its stockholders were usually able to absorb any losses and keep it in operation. Even when a bank failed the consequences were for the most part confined to its own stockholders. Thus, when the collapse of the Wilkinson textile empire in 1829 brought down the Farmers & Mechanics Bank of Pawtucket, Rhode Island, the stockholders managed to pay off all the bank's creditors with the exception of themselves. In 1835 they successfully reorganised as the Phenix Bank of Providence, which rose from the ashes to enjoy a long and prosperous existence.[9]

Such outright failures were relatively rare, however. The records of the Rhode Island General Assembly between 1831 and 1845 – a period that included the contraction of 1834, the Panic of 1837, and the long depression that began in 1839 – indicate that only four of the state's 62 banks collapsed. New Hampshire's banks had an even better record; only one out of 27 failed. Banks in Maine and Massachusetts, on the other hand, performed somewhat more poorly. During this same period, seven of 56 banks failed in the former state, and 19 out of more than 120 in the latter. Most of these failures, however, occurred shortly after the Panic of 1837 and involved banks that had been recently chartered; as such they had not had sufficient time to put their operations on a solid footing before the money system collapsed. Otherwise, failures in these states were also few and far between.[10]

II

The *modus vivendi* that elite merchants had worked out in the first half of the nineteenth century was not to endure, however. By the eve of the Civil War, the Suffolk system was in disarray, a victim of the political opposition that its strict regulatory regime had aroused. Although a new institution, called the Bank of Mutual Redemption, was created to serve the same function, after the Civil War the banking system changed in ways that made the entire concept obsolete. Most significantly, under the National Banking system deposits became an increasingly important source of lendable funds. As late as 1860, for example, the ratio of deposits to capital for Massachusetts banks was still only 43 per cent. By 1870 the ratio had increased to 74 per cent, and by 1890 to 167 per cent.[11]

Once deposits exceeded – or even approached – capital as a source of funds, the likelihood increased that heavy losses would result in failures. The probability that other institutions would be affected by failures also increased, because any collapse might now undermine confidence in the banking system as a whole and, with it, the public's willingness to leave funds on deposit. The problem was that, in the eyes of depositors, individual banks had a great deal of difficulty distinguishing themselves from competitors. Although each national bank published a financial statement biannually, these documents contained no information at all about the contents of the bank's loan portfolios. Moreover, the balance sheets of many banks looked roughly similar. For example, in 1885 the average ratio of capital plus surplus to total liabilities for Boston banks was about 35 per cent, with nearly half of them falling within the range of 30 to 40 per cent. At the same time, the fact that five of the nine banks with ratios below 25 per cent were among the most successful in the city in attracting deposits suggests that savers may not have paid much attention to such information anyway.[12]

As Charles W. Calomiris and Gary Gorton have pointed out, whenever information asymmetries make it difficult for depositors to monitor the performance of individual banks, the likelihood of panics increases. Whenever depositors believe that some banks are in danger of failing but are unable to identity the particular institutions at risk, they may withdraw their savings indiscriminately, precipitating a system-wide crisis.[13] Contemporary bankers understood this danger all too well. As one writer in *Bankers' Magazine* commented, 'we are in a most important sense directly responsible for each other, and cannot avoid being disturbed by the ignorance, selfishness or immoral conduct of our most remote members'. Or, as another writer succinctly put it, 'every bank that fails through mismanagement weakens the surrounding ones'. This danger was illustrated dramatically in early 1884 when several failures, 'all attributable to the madness of speculation by bank officers', caused depositors to panic. In Vermont, for example, the failure of the First National Bank of St. Albans (allegedly caused by an 'unfortunate speculation in stocks by its president and cashier') led to a run on the National Union Bank of Swanton, even though informed opinion regarded the solvency of the latter institution as beyond question: 'to meet only $52,000 due depositors, it held $117,000 of good, short time paper'. That same year the *Bankers' Magazine* complained that 'many business men are suspicious of other banks, and, by withdrawing their deposits, are doing their utmost to bring on the very condition of things they deplore'.[14] Although national bank failures in New England during the late nineteenth century were in actuality relatively rare (there were only six failures in Massachusetts between 1880 and 1900, two in New Hampshire, and none at all in either Maine or Rhode Island), the general financial crises that periodically wracked the system kept bankers on edge. During the last two decades of the century alone, there were serious monetary disturbances in 1884, 1890 and 1893.[15]

Just as their predecessors in the early nineteenth century had developed the Suffolk system to prevent excessive note issues by large numbers of the region's capital-hungry banks, bankers responded in similar fashion to this new danger by attempting to regulate the behaviour of their colleagues. The Boston Clearing House, the region's first such institution, was originally founded in 1855 to facilitate the settling of accounts among the city's various banks. But its potential usefulness as an instrument of regulation soon became apparent. In addition to clearing cheques, the organisation could be used to instill public confidence as well as to prevent runs on its membership by serving as a lender of last resort for temporarily insolvent banks, thereby safeguarding deposits.[16] Since this service was available only to members, moreover, admission to the clearing house became a prize which could be offered as a reward for good management practices or denied as a punishment for financial transgressions. The Pacific National Bank of Boston, for example, was excluded from the clearing house because the city's leading bankers disapproved of its management 'and decidedly and successfully opposed its admission'.[17]

Unlike the Suffolk system, however, the clearing house was of only limited effectiveness as a disciplinary tool. In the first place, banks like Pacific National typically arranged to clear their cheques through allied member institutions, a practice which potentially jeopardised the latter's safety. When the Pacific National Bank failed in 1881, for example, its correspondent, Central National, faced heavy losses and had to be rescued by the associated banks.[18] Secondly, the organisation could not afford to be overly selective, because denying membership to a large number of banks would have undermined its effectiveness both in clearing cheques and maintaining public confidence in the banking system.[19] Thus membership in the clearing house was not in fact synonymous with good management, as was dramatically illustrated by the 1891 failure of one of Boston's largest banks, the Maverick National. Despite its good standing in the clearing house, the bank failed as a result of large loans to support the speculative investments of its president, Asa P. Potter, and several of its directors.[20]

Indeed, the case of the Maverick National Bank suggests that clearing-house members were so worried about financial crises that they preferred to overlook the transgressions of member banks rather than take any action that might precipitate a failure. When Potter's partner, Irving A. Evans, went bankrupt and committed suicide a month before the Maverick's collapse, rumours quickly spread that the bank itself was in trouble. The clearing house, however, took no action at all until the Winthrop Bank, of which Evans' brother was president, refused to honour one of the Maverick's certified cheques. (Potter subsequently claimed that the brother blamed him for the suicide and used this means to exact revenge.) Other clearing-house members were appalled by the Winthrop's action, but the cat was now out of the bag, and the association had no choice but to initiate an investigation, which culminated with the announcement that the Maverick National Bank was indeed insolvent.[21]

Government regulators also proved to be of little use to bankers in controlling the behaviour of their less responsible colleagues. Although the National Banking Acts prohibited loans to any one individual, firm, or corporation in excess of ten per cent of a bank's capital, this provision was relatively easy to evade and difficult to enforce. The only sanction the Comptroller of the Currency had at his disposal was to institute proceedings to revoke the offending bank's charter, a remedy far too drastic to be invoked with any frequency. As a result, the statutory limit notwithstanding, over 40 per cent of the national banks reporting to the Comptroller in

1900 had made at least one loan exceeding ten per cent of their capital.[22] The regulatory authority of the Comptroller, moreover, appears to have declined over the course of the period. Competition between the state and federal governments for the business of chartering banks led, on the one hand, to a general erosion of standards and, on the other, to an increase in the number of institutions not subject to federal regulation.[23]

III

In their drive to assert some control over the lending practices of their competitors, conservative bankers stood to benefit from the increasing numbers of men who thought of themselves as banking professionals, and who had much to gain from a shift in the way banks conducted their business. These professionals included bank employees seeking to broaden opportunities for mobility into the upper echelons of management, trade-journal publicists eager to become the nation's guides to sound banking practices, and government regulators striving to increase their authority over the banking industry. Claudius B. Patten, for example, made his way up through the clerical ranks of Boston's Suffolk and State Banks, ultimately becoming cashier of the latter institution. Subsequently, he wrote a long series of articles for *Rhodes' Journal of Banking* with the aim of promoting the sound banking practices that were exemplified by his own career, as well as providing other aspiring employees with the benefit of his knowledge and experience. His publisher, Bradford Rhodes, would later eulogise him as the very epitome of the new professional: 'he loved his profession and sought continually to formulate better and safer methods in the transaction of the banking business. ... Selfishness had no place in his nature, and he was opposed to taking out a patent on a new idea and putting it under lock and key in his own bank'.[24]

Rhodes himself had originally come to New York to work as a reporter. After a stint with the business department of the *Daily Commercial Bulletin*, he established his own bankers' trade journal, which proved highly successful and provided him with an influential forum from which to pronounce upon monetary and banking issues. By 1899 Rhodes had acquired the competing *Bankers' Magazine*, assumed the presidency of the Mamaroneck Bank and the Union Savings Bank (both in Westchester County), served several years in the New York legislature (where he chaired the Committee on Banks), and played a leading role in a variety of bankers' groups, heading the local section of the New York State Bankers Association and sitting on the executive council of the national organisation.[25]

Like Patten and Rhodes, Comptroller of the Currency John Knox began his career in private employment. After working for a succession of upstate New York banks, where he rose from teller to cashier, he journeyed westward with his brother in the late 1850s to set up a private banking firm. In 1862 he published an article in *Hunt's Merchant's Magazine* proposing the formation of a system of national banks. The article caught the attention of Secretary of the Treasury Salmon P. Chase, thus inaugurating a career in government that culminated in 1872 with Knox's appointment to a 12-year stint as the nation's chief bank regulator. Knox used the platform provided by his office to deliver numerous addresses on banking and currency matters to professional bankers' groups, and also lectured on the subject to university audiences.[26]

Men like Patten, Rhodes, and Knox joined forces with conservative bankers during the last quarter of the nineteenth century to reform management practices in the banking sector. They were particularly concerned about the prevalence of insider lending. In books on management practice, trade publications, newspaper articles, and addresses to professional societies, they aimed a barrage of criticism at bank officers and directors who enriched themselves at their own institutions' expense – at those 'who appreciate the utility of a bank – to them':

> They direct emphatically and direct in such a way as always to serve first their own interest. Their idea of a bank is that it is an institution existing mainly for their own benefit, and they do not hesitate to use it in the promotion of their own interests, however much others may suffer by their conduct.[27]

Insider lending was their primary target because it embraced the agendas of both the conservative bankers and the new professionals. As we have already seen, the bankers felt that insider lending threatened the stability of the financial system. The professionals, on the other hand, believed that it ran counter to the values of fairness and impartiality with which they had become imbued. They also recognised that so long as businessmen could secure capital for their enterprises by involving themselves in the management of a bank, the professionalisation of the banking system would be thwarted.

The most obvious solution to the problem of insider lending was to prohibit bank officers from having 'any special interest in parties or concerns that borrow money from their institutions'. Bank presidents in particular should be 'engaged in no outside interest of considerable importance'.[28] Whereas presidents had previously been chosen for their prominence in the business world, the reformers now proposed that they be selected for their expertise in banking. A likely pool of candidates consisted of men who had worked their way up through the ranks of bank officers. These men would be well-versed in all facets of bank management. More important, because they had made banking their careers, they – unlike businessmen – would be more likely to put the interests of their institutions above personal consideration, and apply strict, objective standards in evaluating applications for credit.[29]

The professionalisation of bank officers could be only a partial solution to the problem, however, because ultimate authority over a bank's lending practices rested not with its president but with the board of directors, at whose pleasure the president and other officers served. Yet it was impossible to insist that each director also forsake his outside interests, because under such circumstances no one would be willing to take on a job that involved, as one writer put it, 'a deal of gratuitous work, unwelcome and wearing responsibility, and very little of what business men deem compensation'.[30] It was in fact precisely because of his outside interests – and his consequent ability to channel business to the bank – that a director's services were valued in the first place. Moreover, because the promise of accommodation and access to credit in periods of stringency undoubtedly helped make an unremunerative job attractive to an otherwise busy man, most reformers were unwilling to support an absolute ban on loans to these officials. What they did insist was that the loans remain within legal bounds. As James G. Cannon, Vice President of the Fourth National Bank of New York and a leader of the bankers' reform movement, argued: 'if a director will give proper security, and keep within the limits prescribed by the National Bank Act, and will ask no more than his account entitles him to receive, there is no reason why he should not be accommodated as a borrower of the bank in which he is a director'.[31]

Yet because excessive loans to directors were widely recognised to be a major cause of bank failures, some means of restraining the behaviour of those who would abuse their positions had to be found. Because staff members had no authority over directors, reformers could not confine their attention solely to the issue of professionalisation, but had to focus on the lending decision itself. They had to develop a set of 'fundamental principles' to govern the granting of loans,[32] principles that could be easily applied by stockholders and conscientious directors to monitor the behaviour of less scrupulous members of the board. Most fundamental of all was the idea that banks should, to the greatest extent possible, restrict their business to the discount of 'real' commercial paper, that is, to notes issued in the course of actual commercial transactions.

IV

This preference for real bills, though frequently expressed in New England during the first two-thirds of the century, had previously not been of much influence in shaping either banking policy or practice. Now, however, the increased interdependence of the banking system and the need to check the actions of bank directors enhanced the doctrine's appeal.[33] In the first place, loans on commercial paper were considered desirable because (it was believed) they were self-liquidating: once, for example, a wholesaler had disposed of the goods he had bought from a manufacturer, he would be able to redeem the IOU he had issued to cover the initial purchase. Second, and more to the point, these loans were thought to make the lending process more objective: because a manufacturer had to scrutinise the wholesaler's standing before he risked his credit by endorsing the latter's note, bankers were relieved of the need to conduct further credit investigations. As the conservative Chicago banker James B. Forgan instructed an audience of bank employees in Providence, Rhode Island, 'the strength of the promise is not in this case of prime importance, and need not therefore be as closely considered'.[34]

Some commentators went so far as to argue that, because commercial paper bore a one-to-one correspondence to the actual wealth-generating activities of the economy, it was for all practical purposes as good as gold. As one writer explained, 'Commodities are, after all, the only things that are really wealth. . . . [I]t is only by convertibility into food, fuel, clothing, and shelter that anything becomes of value. Gold is wealth because of its convertibility; and in the same way, credit is wealth'.[35]

If credit based on real bills was tantamount to wealth, it mattered little to whom a bank granted its discounts. So long as all the notes in its portfolio were *bona fide* commercial paper, the bank was safe, and greedy directors could do it no damage. This belief was in fact built into the National Banking Acts: Section 5200 of the federal code prohibited banks from loaning in excess of ten per cent of their capital to any one person or company. But there were two exceptions to this provision. The first exempted from the limit 'the discount of bills of exchange drawn in good faith against actually existing values' – in others words, real commercial paper. The obvious presumption here was that, because such loans were based on tangible commodities, a bank would not be endangered by discounting large amounts for a single firm.[36]

The second exception, 'the discount of commercial or business paper actually owned by the person negotiating the same', is similarly instructive. Such persons were mainly expected to be professional brokers, whose growing presence in the money markets offered reform-minded bankers another means of guarding against the dangers of favouritism in loans. Not only did brokers have a responsibility to evaluate the creditworthiness of the notes they offered for sale, but by interposing themselves between banks and would-be borrowers, they made the lending process more impersonal and thus more objective. For this reason, as one eminent banker argued, 'buying paper through brokers is not without its advantages':

> Paper can be so bought with cool deliberation and free from the personal influence which the needy customer studies how best to exercise. ... The human susceptibility of the friendship, good-fellowship, neighborliness, return for favors received, sympathy for the distressed, flattery, personal interest and other extraneous considerations is eliminated. It counts for a great deal in arriving at a decision to be relieved of these influences.[37]

If bankers would only grant credit on the basis of real bills, reformers thought, the stability of the banking system would be assured. But the reformers also recognised that achieving such a goal was nearly impossible. By the late nineteenth century, real bills were declining in volume relative to other kinds of business paper, and there were simply not enough of them around to absorb the banking system's lendable funds.[38] Once banks moved away from real paper, however, opportunities for favouritism threatened to re-emerge. In calculating the amount of collateral required for a loan, for example, bankers were liable to overvalue the assets of enterprises with which they were connected, as a rash of bank failures during the early 1880s dramatically illustrated. According to trade-journal analysts, the cause of these failures was loans 'on very poor security', made by bank officers who had 'a pecuniary interest in the enterprises that received the money'. One writer surmised that the officers 'well knew in most of these cases, probably, that the securities were of a hazardous nature. And they never would have accepted such securities, except for their own interest in these outside undertakings'.[39]

In order to safeguard against such wilful misjudgement, conservative bankers began (while simultaneously espousing the real-bills doctrine) to promulgate new, objective standards for other kinds of loans. They insisted that collateral loans be backed by securities that commanded a ready market on the exchanges, so that their value could be easily assessed. They also urged banks to require financial statements from all applicants for loans, and to develop credit departments with the expertise to evaluate the information contained in them. During the 1890s, in order to encourage this practice, both the New York State Bankers' Association and the American Bankers' Association developed standard statement blanks for banks to use.[40]

Once obtained from borrowers, however, these statements had to be properly interpreted, and in the guidelines the reformers formulated for the banking community, one senses again their determination to limit directors' discretionary authority over lending. A customer's resources should be divided into fixed assets on the one hand, and quick or convertible assets on the other. Only the latter, argued the reformers, were the proper basis for loans. Even then, loans should not be made if a borrower's liabilities exceeded 50 per cent of his quick assets (the so-called '50 per cent rule').[41] By specifying that loans should be granted only on the basis of convertible assets ('those which [a borrower] not only can but, in the ordinary course of business, will, turn into money with which to pay his debts'),[42] reformers were seeking to insure that all bank loans would be as close as possible in character to discounts of real commercial paper, that is, to a type of credit instrument that they firmly believed would minimise judgement problems.

The important point here is that, although financial writers often justified their emphasis on short-term loans on grounds of liquidity alone, their primary concern was with the lending decision itself. Many bankers recognised at the time that portfolios of short-term commercial loans were not necessarily more liquid than those consisting of long-term loans, because under conditions of crisis bankers typically would renew such notes rather than risk alienating good customers or precipitating failures that would render the loans themselves uncollectible.[43] Liquidity needs, they knew, would have to be met in other ways, and it was common to recommend that a bank invest 20 per cent of its funds in high grade bonds and securities 'such as are convertible at a moment's notice', and another 20 per cent in commercial paper purchased in the open market, which would be free of any pressure for renewal at maturity. With the liquidity of the institution thus safely assured, the bank could loan the remaining 60 per cent of its funds locally for the benefit of its customers, but reformers nonetheless insisted that these loans conform to the new standards. As the writer of one article put it, they should be based only on the borrower's 'current business', which is to say, advances on 'the market value of commodities in the process of conversion into money'. If not specified for 60 or 90 days, such loans 'should mature upon the definite happening of an event which is of reasonable certainty of occurrence ... the maturity of a crop, the completion of a contract'. Loans of indeterminate length were a recipe for disaster. Especially to be avoided were 'loans which have the character of a permanent investment in the business of the borrower'.[44]

It is clear from this article that the author, who goes on to fret about the problem of insider lending, made these recommendations not primarily for the purpose of insuring liquidity, but because he believed that they were the best means of insuring that loans would be granted according to objective criteria, such that a banker could exercise 'no arbitrary discretion when he extends or refuses accommodation to the borrower'.[45] By adopting a standard for loans that resembled as closely as possible the ideal of real commercial paper, banks could avoid the entanglements between borrower and lender that distorted the latter's judgement and potentially undermined the security of the banking system.

As the writer of the article suggested, long-term loans were considered *prima-facie* evidence of such potentially disastrous entanglements between borrowers and lenders. Hence as conservative bankers redefined the boundaries of the banking business during the latter years of the century, they proscribed this type of lending entirely. James B. Forgan under-scored this point in 1898:

> One of the most fundamental principles of good banking is that the bank should not furnish the capital for its customers to do business upon. The customer should possess his own capital, and require assistance from the bank only at certain seasons and for specific purposes.[46]

Comptroller of the Currency Hugh McCulloch put the matter even more succinctly in a statement that was quoted repeatedly in the practical banking literature: 'Banks are not loan offices. It is no part of their business to furnish their customers with capital'.[47]

V

As a result of their determination to curb the practice of insider lending, then, late nineteenth-century reformers articulated a vision of sound lending policy that sharply narrowed the scope of banking operations to short-term loans based on commercial paper or easily convertible assets. The change in policy is an important one, because to the extent that it came to be embodied in actual practice, firms in the industrial sectors of the economy would have experienced greater difficulty in obtaining bank financing for their ventures. In the first place, because quick assets were considered the only proper basis for loans, the credit-evaluation process was biased against manufacturing enterprises with proportionally large investments in fixed capital.[48] Borrowers that could not meet the specified ratio of convertible assets to liabilities might be granted credit on the basis of good collateral, but this kind of loan was inevitably restricted to firms that themselves issued marketable securities (mainly railroads in the late nineteenth century) or were engaged in the buying and selling of stocks and bonds. Collateral loans could be of only limited use to most other borrowers, since businesses with the surplus funds to invest in marketable securities were not likely to be the ones most in need of funds. What manufacturers really needed were loans secured by equity in their firms, but this kind of lending was specifically frowned upon, because of the judgement problems it entailed.

Unfortunately, there is no way to test directly the effectiveness of the reformers' campaign, but evidence on changing management practices suggests that it did have a genuine effect. By 1895 two-thirds of a sample of about 30 Boston banks had presidents who were either no longer actively engaged in business or who had worked their way up through the hierarchy of bank employees.[49] Indeed, when a bank's president died or retired, there was now a growing tendency to select his successor from the ranks of banking professionals rather than prominent businessmen, as had been common earlier in the century. For example, the directors of the People's Bank of Roxbury elected their cashier president in 1886, and subsequently amended the bank's by-laws to increase his managerial authority. The cashier of the Bunker Hill National Bank in Charlestown, Massachusetts, Charles R. Lawrence, became its president in 1889. He was succeeded in 1906 by Fred K. Brown, who had replaced him as cashier. At Boston's Atlantic Bank, after President T. Quincy Browne resigned in 1898 because a business failure forced him to assign his assets – including his stock in the bank – the directors selected the bank's cashier to head the institution. Finally, the team of financiers that rescued the Massachusetts Bank at the turn of the century chose as president a Nebraskan named Daniel G. Wing, who had successfully scaled the banking hierarchy in his home state and then served as a national bank examiner and receiver for two failed Boston banks.[50]

Mergers accelerated this tendency to choose banking professionals as presidents. After the Shoe & Leather National Bank of Boston merged with the National Bank of Redemption in Boston in 1901, the directors chose as president John E. Toulmin, who had recently been brought in to serve as the Shoe & Leather Bank's director and vice president. Prior to that he had worked his way up from clerk to cashier in various local institutions and then migrated to Kansas City, where he had organized a trust company. That same year Frank W. Gale was elected president of the newly formed United National Bank in Providence, a merger of Rhode Island National Bank, Second National of Providence, Fifth National, and the National Eagle Bank. Gale had entered the employ of Providence's Third National Bank as a junior clerk at the age of 17, and had worked his way up to the position of cashier by 1889, when he was hired as secretary of the recently formed Industrial Trust Company. He moved to United National as cashier when the merger was organised in 1901, and was almost immediately promoted to president. Even venerable institutions like the Providence National Bank did not escape this trend. In 1926, the Brown family's lock on that bank's presidency, which had lasted more than 120 years, was finally broken when the institution merged with the Merchants National Bank of the same city. A year later Thomas L. Pierce was brought in from Cumberland, Maryland, to head the enlarged institution.[51]

At the same time as bank presidents were becoming more professional, new associations of bank clerks were being organised in cities like Providence and Boston. While the ostensible purpose of these organisations was to provide old age and disability benefits for their members, they also provided a forum through which upwardly mobile bank clerks could be indoctrinated with the values of their profession. Reformers were often featured speakers at association meetings, and their writings were touted as recommended reading for aspiring clerks.[52] That bank officers could absorb values that put them at odds with their own directors can be seen from the case of the Maverick National Bank. Several years before the bank's failure, cashier John Eddy had quietly resigned. As he later told reporters, 'I could not hold the position of Cashier of the Maverick Bank and sanction as I was obliged to all that I was expected to'.[53]

There is also some evidence of a renewed conscientiousness on the part of directors to their duties. During the 1870s and early 1880s attendance at directors meetings had reached an all-time low. For example, only two of the seven directors of the Boylston National Bank of Boston were present at at least 70 per cent of the board's meetings in 1880. Only three of the Massachusetts National Bank's nine directors had a similar attendance record, as did only one of the nine directors of the People's National Bank of Roxbury. By 1895, however, all six directors of the Boylston Bank were present at 80 per cent or more of the meetings, and four were there at least 90 per cent of the time. Attendance was still low at the Massachusetts National Bank, but at People's four of the directors attended at least 70 per cent of the meetings.[54] To encourage this trend, many banks began to pay their directors a nominal sum, usually $2 (sometimes more) for each meeting attended. Although these payments were largely symbolic, they reflected the power that the reformers' vision was beginning to exert over the entire banking community.[55]

Doubtless there are other explanations besides the reform campaign for each of these changes in management practice. But the point to emphasise here is not so much the cause of these changes as their effect. As bank officers became more professional, they were more likely to follow the recommendations of the reformers in their day-to-day operations. Similarly, as directors began to take their oversight responsibilities more seriously, they were more willing to use the reformers' standards in evaluating the performance of their banks' executives. Take, for example, the case of the National Shawmut Bank, which was by far the largest in Boston, the result of a merger of ten of the city's banks. Its lending business was normally handled on a day-to-day basis by its executive committee, whose decisions the board of directors assembled weekly to ratify. Each year, however, the board appointed its own agents to scrutinise the state of the bank's loan and investment portfolios. In the reports of these examiners, one finds clear evidence that the principles set down in the practical banking literature were actually being applied. In 1903, for example, the examiners chastised the bank's managers for accepting as collateral securities that were not actively traded on the market: 'we disapprove in loaning on the stock of a Corporation where we are loaning direct to the Corporation, especially to Officers, except on listed and active and saleable stocks'. The examiners also devoted a significant portion of their report to criticising 'the large and apparently permanent Loans to Corporations and Individuals which appear like furnishing a steady Capital for business enterprises'. To reduce the number of such loans the examiners recommended 'converting a certain class of Time Loans that usually have to be renewed at the option of the borrower, and a part of what we call Steady Demand Loans, into Loans that when they come due cannot possibly have any claims on the Bank'. To this end they advised the executive committee to make purchases 'in the open market of Commercial paper and Collateral Loans'.[56]

Yet even if we grant, as the Shawmut evidence seems to suggest, that these new principles were indeed finding their way into everyday banking practice, we still need to assess the extent to which they actually shaped loan portfolios. Writing in the second decade of the twentieth century, the economist H.G. Moulton attacked the (by then) conventional wisdom of the practical banking literature by arguing that, theory notwithstanding, 'the distinction between commercial and investment operations is ignored in practice'. Moulton firmly believed that banks should play an active role in supporting manufacturing investment, and in order to demonstrate that such lending would not undermine the safety of the banking system, he undertook to show that a considerable portion of existing loans already financed fixed investment. Moulton conceded that banks decided whether to make unsecured loans by calculating the ratio of a firm's debt obligations to its quick assets. He also admitted that such loans were rarely granted for periods longer than six months. But he argued that many short-term loans were regularly renewed, and that once a loan was granted, banks had no control over the use to which the borrower put the funds. As a practical matter, the proceeds of a loan could be used as easily to pay for investments in plant and equipment as to finance goods in the stream of production. Based on his own (undescribed) 'investigations extending over a period of several years', Moulton claimed that as much as 20 per cent of the banking sector's unsecured commercial loans were used for investment purposes.[57]

Moulton's assertions are difficult to verify, because most of the bank records that are extant contain only scattered data on loans, with no information at all about their terms or the kinds of security that backed them up. There is, however, a brief run of complete loan records for the Suffolk National Bank in Boston.[58] Analysis of these records shows that 54 per cent of the bank's portfolio consisted of short-term loans based on personal security, and that it is unlikely that many of these loans could have supported investments in plant and equipment. Fully two-thirds (by value) were notes purchased on the commercial-paper market, that is, bought from individuals or firms that served neither as principals nor endorsers for the notes. Although many of the signatories on these loans were manufacturers, they were not themselves customers of the bank and hence could not expect their notes to be renewed at maturity. In fact, only 19 per cent of the bank's loan portfolio consisted of notes backed by personal security that were discounted for the benefit of customers who were signatories, and only 41 per cent of this amount involved manufacturing enterprises. Most of the bank's customers (accounting for 75 per cent of its personal loans and 88 per cent of its collateral loans) were brokers or distributors. In other words, the bulk of this important bank's business was commercial lending pure and simple.

It is possible, of course, that the Suffolk Bank was unusually specialised in the commercial lending business, and that the loan portfolios of other institutions would look quite different. But the (much less complete) evidence on loans that is available for other banks in Massachusetts and Rhode Island suggests otherwise. The problem with these records is that it is impossible to distinguish loans to regular customers from short-term commercial paper bought in the open market. But a proxy for this distinction can be constructed by assuming that all loans to local firms (that is, loans whose principals or endorsers were listed in the local city directories) were loans to customers, and that all other loans consisted of purchased commercial paper. Such a calculation reveals that loans to local customers who were manufacturers ranged from 0 to at most 20 per cent of the total sample, with most banks clustering between 14 and 20 per cent. There is no reason to assume, moreover, that all of the loans in this category supported investments in fixed capital. A large proportion undoubtedly financed bills receivable.[59]

Of course, other factors besides the reformers' campaign may have encouraged this shift toward short-term commercial loans. Past experience, for example, may have played a conditioning role. Whenever bankers previously had found themselves with more funds than their directors needed, they may have regarded the surplus as temporary and sought out short-term uses for the money. Habits once established may have affected lending behaviour later on. For example, the City Bank of Lynn, Massachusetts, tried to buy commercial paper in 1857, as did the Sowamset Bank in Warren, Rhode Island, in 1861.[60] But early banks also sought out a variety of other employments for their surplus funds. Some, like the Bank of Rhode Island in Newport, bought readily marketable securities.[61] Others, like Boston's Atlantic and Massachusetts Banks, became involved in western development. The Massachusetts Bank invested its funds directly in distant lands, while the Atlantic Bank loaned money to real-estate promoters, secured by mortgages on western property. Neither type of investment would have satisfied the criteria for sound banking as developed subsequently by the reformers.[62]

It is also possible that, in the eyes of conservative bankers, a sound enterprise by definition was one that borrowed for short-term purposes only. Men like William Goddard, president of the Providence National Bank, undoubtedly used their own firms as models for what they sought in their customers, and Goddard Brothers borrowed only in order to meet the extreme demand for capital that occurred during the autumn cotton-buying season.[63] It is likely that, from Goddard's point of view, a firm seeking long-term loans was one whose capital was not sufficient to conduct its ordinary business, and was therefore a poor credit risk. On this point it is interesting to note, however, that there was little or no discussion in the contemporary banking literature about what constituted safe borrowing from the customers' point of view. Banks were instructed to restrict their business to short-term commercial loans, not because firms that borrowed funds for longer periods of time were by nature weak and likely to repudiate their debts, but simply because sound banking practice required it.[64]

Another possibility is that banks shifted their portfolios toward short-term commercial loans because the demand for other types of loans had declined as a result of the growing availability of equity finance. While it is true that industrials were increasingly traded on the exchanges by the end of the century, access to the securities markets were for the most part restricted to large, well established firms, and especially to giant consolidations formed during the great merger wave at the turn of the century. For small- and medium-sized firms, particularly in new industries, sources of finance were largely the same as they had been several decades before.[65]

Finally, it is possible that bankers shifted their portfolios toward short-term commercial loans because this type of lending was highly profitable. For some well established banks like Goddard's Providence National, this was clearly the case. But while the Providence Bank earned dividends averaging eight per cent over the last two decades of the century, other banks with similar portfolios were less prosperous. Of the banks for which we have information on lending behaviour, only a couple performed as well as the Providence. Several of the others (Shoe & Leather National Bank in Boston, First National Bank of Warren, Rhode

Island, and the National Warren Bank) each paid dividends of half or less than half that amount during the 1890s.[66] In general, the last three decades of the nineteenth century were a period of declining profits for banks. Between 1871–75 and 1896–1900 the annual profit rate of national banks in New England fell 48 per cent. Over the same period of time, the yield on a broad index of New England municipal bonds fell only 39 per cent.[67]

VI

The available evidence thus suggests that, by the turn of the century, banks in New England were moving toward an increasingly specialised role in the economy, focusing on the provision of short-term loans to commercial borrowers and eschewing long-term relations with industrial enterprises. In this, they closely resembled their counterparts in Great Britain, but departed significantly from the practice of contemporary German institutions, which were deeply involved in financing manufacturing.

This contrast between British and German banking has generally been explained in terms of the so-called Gerschenkron hypothesis. In his famous essay, 'Economic Backwardness in Historical Perspective', Alexander Gerschenkron argued that banks needed to play a more active role in promoting industrialisation in relatively 'backward' nations, where capital resources and financial markets were not sufficiently developed to support industrial ventures on their own.[68] While there is undoubtedly some truth to this theory, the evolution of the banking system in nineteenth-century New England suggests that it may not offer a complete explanation for the divergent banking histories of these areas. Although the New England economy was relatively backward during the early part of the century, and although banks initially played an important role in financing industrial development, they had largely abandoned this function by the end of the century – in direct contrast to the German banks, where the connection with industry remained strong, as it continues to do until the present day.

As I have argued above, the change in the behaviour of New England banks resulted from a particular combination of circumstances: a tremendous expansion in the number of banks, and an equally dramatic rise in deposits as a source of lendable funds. The latter development increased the interdependence of the banking system, making each institution vulnerable to runs provoked by the unsound practices of its competitors. The former development made it difficult to regulate the lending practices of individual banks.

In order to remedy this situation, conservative bankers and their professional allies joined forces in the late nineteenth century to promote a set of lending rules that promised to limit the potential for abuse and, at the same time, make it easier for directors and stockholders to monitor the behaviour of their managers. They advocated short-term loans based on a borrower's quick assets, because such loans were believed to minimise judgement problems, and also because they reduced the likelihood that disastrous consequences would result from excessive borrowing by favoured parties.

It is beyond the scope of this paper to explore in any detailed way whether a similar combination of circumstances might have contributed to the emphasis on short-term loans in the British banking system. The secondary literature, however, is suggestive on this point. Recent research has shown that, until about the last third of the nineteenth century, British banks functioned much like their counterparts across the Atlantic. Provincial banks in particular often had close relationships with local manufacturers and provided them with accommodation loans that were repeatedly renewed. Interestingly, the heightened emphasis on short-term commercial paper during the latter part of the century followed a sharp expansion in the number of banks, the result of a liberalisation in the laws governing corporate charters. This expansion fragmented the financial system and provoked a wave of bank failures. Moreover, because banks by then were dependent on deposits as a source of funds, it threatened the survival, as well as the hegemony, of pre-existing banks. Older institutions attempted to distinguish themselves from newcomers by clinging to the principle of unlimited liability, but rather than protecting them, this strategy served only to increase their vulnerability, and they were forced to give it up.[69]

Ultimately, the major London banks were able to reassert control over the banking system through a series of mergers that reduced the number of banks to 40, the five largest of which controlled two-thirds of the system's total resources. Once these mergers had diminished the level of chaos in the industry, the pressure to specialise in short-term commercial loans seems to have abated. At any rate, British banks became heavily involved in industrial finance during the period after World War I, underwriting issues of new securities and extending overdrafts to manufacturing concerns, with little apparent concern that these advances be based on short-term convertible assets.[70]

The German case differed significantly from the British in that the concentration movement in banking largely preceded the growth of deposits as a source of lendable funds. Beginning in the 1870s large banks, especially those centred in Berlin, began to absorb smaller banks in the provinces and to create *interessengemeinschaften*, or groups of mutual interest, by (among other means) exchanging shares of stock with provincial institutions. These communities of interest extended the control of the Berlin banks into the countryside, limiting the provincial banks' independence of action, and effectively stabilising the banking system as a whole. There were relatively few failures after the early 1870s. During the 1920s, when deposit banking suddenly escalated in importance, these *interessengemeinschaften* frequently evolved into formal mergers. It has been estimated that by 1929, in one way or another, more than 63 per cent of the assets of all the nation's credit banks were under the control of Berlin's six institutions.[71] Hence the more active involvement of German banks in industrialisation may have been as much a consequence of the control that derived from the early concentration movement, as it was from the relative backwardness of the nation's economy.

It should be added that this level of dominance was denied to American banks during this same period. Although there was a wave of bank mergers at the end of the century, banks with national charters were prohibited from operating branches, and most states forbade branching within their own systems as well. Moreover, the political clout exercised by the nation's thousands of small bankers insured that this state of affairs would continue for some time.[72] Thus large New England banks were unable to achieve direct control over the hundreds of independent institutions with which they competed, and were forced to rely on more formalistic methods of discipline. Only the passage of federal deposit insurance legislation during the Great Depression – legislation which dramatically reduced the interdependence of the banking system – would free them from the need to measure loans against the standard of real commercial paper.

NOTES

I have greatly benefited from the comments and suggestions of an anonymous referee, Lance Davis, Louis Galambos, Geoffrey Jones, David Lamoreaux, John Landry, Edwin J. Perkins, Duncan M. Ross, Larry Schweikart, Kenneth Sokoloff, Jean Strouse, Richard Sylla, participants in the economic history seminars of the University of California-Los Angeles, Harvard University, and Columbia University, and members of the History Department Workshop at Brown University. Thanks too to my research assistant Andrew Morris and to the many helpful archivists and employees I encountered at the National Archives, the Harvard Business School's Baker Library, the Rhode Island Historical Society, the Fleet National Bank, Shawmut Bank, and the Bank of Boston. I am also grateful to the National Endowment for the Humanities, the American Council of Learned Societies, and the John Simon Guggenheim Foundation for the financial support that enabled me to take leave from teaching to pursue this research. This article is part of a study of banking in industrial New England (eastern Massachusetts, Rhode Island, southern New

Hampshire, and southern Maine – I excluded Connecticut because of its orientation toward New York) and hence retains the geographical focus of the larger project. The arguments I make, however, could easily be extended to the entire north-eastern quarter of the United States.

1. See N.R. Lamoreaux, 'Banks, Kinship, and Economic Development: The New England Case', *Journal of Economic History*, Vol. 46 (1986), pp. 647–67; B. Hammond, 'Long and Short Term Credit in Early American Banking', *Quarterly Journal of Economics*, Vol. 49 (1935), pp. 79–103; F. Redlich, *The Molding of American Banking: Men and Ideas* (New York, 1947), Pt. I, pp. 11–12; R. Sylla, 'American Banking and Growth in the Nineteenth Century: A Partial View of the Terrain', *Explorations in Economic History*, Vol. 9 (1971–72), pp. 197–227.
2. On the contrast between German and British banking see R. Tilly, *Financial Institutions and Industrialization in the Rhineland, 1815–1870* (Madison, WI, 1966); R. Cameron, *et al.*, *Banking in the Early Stages of Industrialization: A Study in Comparative Economic History* (New York, 1967); P.L. Cottrell, *Industrial Finance, 1830–1914: The Finance and Organization of English Manufacturing Industry* (1980), pp. 194–247; H.L. Engberg, *Mixed Banking and Economic Growth in Germany, 1850–1931* (New York, 1981); H. Pohl, 'Forms and Phases of Industry Finance up to the Second World War', *German Yearbook on Business History* (1984), pp. 75–94; M.H. Best and J. Humphries, 'The City and Industrial Decline', in B. Elbaum and W. Lazonick (eds.), *The Decline of the British Economy* (1986), pp. 223–39; W.P. Kennedy, *Industrial Structure, Capital Markets and the Origins of British Economic Decline* (Cambridge, 1987), pp. 110–23; S. Tolliday, *Business, Banking and Politics: The Case of British Steel, 1918–1939* (Cambridge, MA, 1987), pp. 169–88; R. Michie, 'Different in Name Only? The London Stock Exchange and Foreign Bourses, c. 1850–1914', in R.P.T. Davenport-Hines and G. Jones (eds.), *The End of Insularity: Essays in Comparative Business History* (1988), pp. 46–68; Y. Cassis, 'British Finance: Success and Controversy', in J.J. Van Helten and Y. Cassis (eds.), *Capitalism in a Mature Economy* (1990), pp. 1–22; Duncan M. Ross, 'The Clearing Banks and Industry: New Perspectives on the Inter-War Years', in Van Helten and Cassis, *Capitalism in a Mature Economy*, pp. 52–70.
3. Lamoreaux, 'Banks, Kinship, and Economic Development', pp. 647–67; Hammond, 'Long and Short Term Credit in Early American Banking'; Redlich, *The Molding of American Banking*, Pt. I, pp. 11, 31, 43; A.A. Beveridge, 'Local Lending Practice: Borrowers in a Small Northeastern Industrial City, 1832–1915', *Journal of Economic History*, Vol. 45 (1985), pp. 393–403.
4. R.E. Sylla, *The American Capital Market, 1846–1914: A Study of the Effects of Public Policy on Economic Development* (New York, 1975), pp. 251–2.
5. Rhode Island, General Assembly, *Report of the Committee to Inquire into the Expediency of Increasing the Banking Capital* (Providence, 1826), p. 24; N. Appleton, *An Examination of the Banking System of Massachusetts, in Reference to the Renewal of the Bank Charters* (Boston, 1831), pp. 19–20.
6. A Citizen of Boston, *A New System of Paper Money* (Boston, 1837), p. 3.
7. B. Hammond, *Banks and Politics in America from the Revolution to the Civil War* (Princeton, NJ, 1957), pp. 549–56; Redlich, *The Molding of American Banking*, Pt. I, pp. 67–81.
8. J.V. Fenstermaker, *The Development of American Commercial Banking, 1782–1837* (Kent, OH, 1965),. pp. 203–4, 207–8, 214–15, 226–7.
9. Rhode Island Historical Society Manuscript Collections, Farmers and Mechanics – Phenix Bank, Reports of Stockholders, 1833–34.
10. Rhode Island, General Assembly, *Acts and Resolves* (1831–45); N.W. Smith, 'A History of Commercial Banking in New Hampshire, 1792–1843' (unpublished Ph.D. thesis, University of Wisconsin, 1967), pp. 157–219; W.W. Chadbourne, 'A History of Banking in Maine, 1799–1930', *Maine Bulletin*, Vol. 39 (1936), pp. 69, 181–2; Massachusetts, General Court, 'List of Banks Chartered in Massachusetts', House Doc. 93 (1850), pp. 4–19.

11. Sylla, *The American Capital Market*, p.251; US, Comptroller of the Currency, *Annual Report* (1900), Vol.1, p.746.
12. US, Comptroller of the Currency, *Annual Report* (1885), pp.62–83. These balance sheets were not certified by auditors, but they were checked periodically by national bank examiners.
13. C.W. Calomiris and G. Gorton, 'The Origins of Banking Panics: Models, Facts, and Bank Regulation', unpublished paper.
14. *Bankers' Magazine*, Vol.38 (1884), pp.886, 901–2; Vol.39 (1884), p.45; Vol.42 (1887), p.83.
15. US, Comptroller of the Currency, *Annual Report* (1900), pp.502–11; O.M.W. Sprague, *History of Crises under the National Banking System* (Washington, DC, 1910).
16. See G. Gorton, 'Clearinghouses and the Origin of Central Banking in the United States', *Journal of Economic History*, Vol.45 (1985), pp.277–83. According to a manual put out by the Maverick National Bank (Boston, 1887), p.93, seven other New England cities had clearing houses by the late 1880s.
17. C.B. Patten, *The Methods and Machinery of Practical Banking* (7th ed. 1896), p.357. At the time of the Pacific National failure, Patten was cashier at Boston's State National Bank, a member of the Clearing House. On the admission policies of clearing houses, see also E. Carroll, Jr., *Principles and Practice of Finance: A Practical Guide for Bankers, Merchants, and Lawyers* (New York, 1895), pp.132–3.
18. Patten, *The Methods and Machinery of Practical Banking,* p.357.
19. This argument was made by A.S. Bolles in 'The Functions of Clearing Houses: The New York Clearing House Controversy', *Proceedings of the Convention of the American Bankers' Association* (1890), pp.127–31.
20. *Boston Evening Transcript* (2 Nov. 1891), pp.1–2, and (3 Nov. 1891), p.8.
21. Ibid.
22. *Bankers' Magazine*, Vol.37 (1882), p.445; A.R. Barrett, *Modern Banking Methods and Practical Bank Bookkeeping* (5th ed. 1907), p.289.
23. E.N. White, 'The Political Economy of Banking Regulation, 1864–1933', *Journal of Economic History*, Vol.42 (1982), pp.33–40; J.A. James, *Money and Capital Markets in Postbellum America* (Princeton, NJ, 1978), pp.36–40.
24. B. Rhodes, 'Introduction', in Patten, *The Methods and Machinery of Practical Banking*, p.iii. See also *Rhodes' Journal of Banking*, 13 (1886), pp.417–18.
25. *National Cyclopedia of American Biography*, Vol.10, p.416.
26. *Dictionary of American Biography*, Vol.10, p.477.
27. *Bankers' Magazine*, Vol.36 (1882), pp.733–5. See also Vol.37 (1883), p.656; Vol.38 (1884), p.963; and Vol.42 (1888), p.511; J.G. Cannon, 'An Ideal Bank', address delivered before the Institute of Accounts of New York City (1891), pp.5, 10, 18; Patten, *The Methods and Machinery of Practical Banking,* pp.266, 300–1; B.B. Comegys, 'How a Banker Should Treat his Dealers and the Public; Or, What Matter of Man Should a Banker Be', *Proceedings of the Twentieth Annual Convention of the American Bankers' Association* (1894), p.39. See also the fundamental principles of banking articulated by Hugh McCulloch, first Comptroller of the Currency, quoted in Barrett, *Modern Banking Methods*, p.305.
28. *Bankers' Magazine*, Vol.38 (1884), p.908; and Vol.39 (1884), pp.8, 35. See also Vol.39 (1884), p.243, and Vol.39 (1885), pp.483–7.
29. On this point, see especially Patten, *The Methods and Machinery of Practical Banking*, pp.272–3. See also Barrett, *Modern Banking Methods*, p.25; Comegys, 'How a Banker Should Treat his Dealers', pp.37–8; *Bankers' Magazine*, Vol.38 (1884), p.963.
30. Patten, *The Methods and Machinery of Practical Banking*, p.271.
31. Cannon, 'An Ideal Bank', p.18. See also E.T. Coman, 'The Requisites of a Good Loan', in W.H. Hull (ed.), *Practical Problems in Banking and Currency*, (New York, 1907), pp.73–5.
32. The phrase is Comptroller of the Currency Hugh McCulloch's. See Barrett, *Modern Banking Methods,* pp.305–6.
33. On the real-bills doctrine, see L.W. Mintz, *A History of Banking Theory in Great*

Britain and the United States (Chicago, 1945), pp. 206–10; and Sylla, 'American Banking and Growth in the Nineteenth Century', pp. 197–227. See also R.C. West, *Banking Reform and the Federal Reserve, 1863–1923* (Ithaca, NY, 1977), pp. 136–62.
34. J.B. Forgan, *A Good Note* (1903 ed. 1920), p. 8.
35. T.F. Woodlock, 'Banking Conditions in Wall Street', in Hull (ed.), *Practical Problems in Banking and Currency*, pp. 23–4.
36. The statute is quoted in G.M. Coffin, *Hand-Book for Bank Officers* (Washington, DC, 1896), p. 64.
37. Forgan, *A Good Note*, pp. 21–2. See also Comegys, 'How a Bankers Should Treat his Dealers', pp. 40–41.
38. On this point, see West, *Banking Reform and the Federal Reserve*, pp. 157–62. See also James, *Money and Capital Markets in Postbellum America*, pp. 55–9.
39. *Bankers' Magazine*, Vol. 38 (1884), p. 908.
40. Barrett, *Modern Banking Methods*, p. 184; Cannon, 'An Ideal Bank', pp. 6–7; Forgan, *A Good Note*, pp. 8–11.
41. J.G. Cannon, 'Bank Credits', in Hull (ed.), *Practical Problems in Banking and Currency*, pp. 44, 47. See also Forgan, *A Good Note*, pp. 8–10.
42. Forgan, *A Good Note*, pp. 8–10.
43. See Mintz, *A History of Banking Thought in Great Britain and the United States*, pp. 216–19. Even writers who insisted that short-term loans were necessary for liquidity recognised that this problem undermined the force of their argument, and they struggled to find other justifications for the policy. See, for example, the American Institute of Banking pamphlet entitled *Loans and Investments* (New York, 1916), pp. 14–15.
44. Coman, 'Requisites of a Good Loan', pp. 69–71.
45. Ibid., p. 66.
46. *Bankers' Magazine*, Vol. 57 (1898), p. 384.
47. Quoted in Barrett, *Modern Banking Methods*, p. 305.
48. In the early twentieth century banking professionals began to worry about this bias, and to argue that the strict 50 per cent rule should be modified in favour of a more flexible assessment of each individual borrower's credit position. Nevertheless, they continued to argue that banks should grant only short-term commercial loans. See, for example, Cannon, 'Bank Credits', pp. 49–50; and A.N. Hogg, *The Sixth Sense* (Philadelphia, 1915), p. 20.
49. This information was abstracted from the Reports of the National Bank Examiners to the US Comptroller of the Currency. The records of the Examination Division are stored at the National Archives in Washington, DC, Record Group 101.
50. Bank of Boston Archives, People's National Bank of Roxbury, Directors' and Stockholders' Minute Book, 1883–98; Atlantic National Bank of Boston, Directors' and Stockholders' Minute Book, 1877–1912; *A Century of Banking in Historic Charlestown* (Boston, 1925), pp. 25–6; N.S.B. Gras, *The Massachusetts First National Bank of Boston, 1784–1934* (Cambridge, MA, 1937), pp. 152–4, 159. Country banks were somewhat slower to professionalise than city banks. Popular histories published by the banks themselves suggest that the movement would not spread to the hinterlands until the second decade of the twentieth century.
51. Bank of Boston Archives, Shoe & Leather National Bank of Boston, Directors' and Stockholders' Minute Book, 1885–93, and Scrap Book, 1836–1901; Providence *Telegram* (8 Oct. 1901); F. Weston and F. Piggott, *The Passing Years, 1791 to 1966* (Providence, 1966), pp. 48, 135.
52. *Rhodes' Journal of Banking*, Vol. 12 (1885), pp. 131, 207; and Vol. 13 (1886), pp. 347–52. In addition, the American Bankers' Association devoted an increasing proportion of its program to practical banking matters. There was also a movement to form local Bankers' Institutes, 'voluntary association[s] of gentlemen engaged in banking, or otherwise interested in banking affairs, who organize for the purpose of advancing the interests as well of their profession generally as of themselves'. The above quotation is from *Rhodes Journal of Banking*, Vol. 12 (1885), pp. 184–5.
53. *Boston Evening Transcript* (3 Nov. 1891), p. 8.
54. Bank of Boston Archives, Boylston National Bank, Directors and Stockholders'

Minute Book, 1864–87, and Directors' and Stockholders' Minute Book, 1887–1909; Massachusetts National Bank, Directors' and Stockholders' Minute Book, 1865–83, and Directors' and Stockholders' Minute Book, 1883–1900; People's National Bank, Directors' and Stockholders' Minute Book, 1864–83, and Directors' and Stockholders' Minute Book, 1883–98.

55. This generalisation is based on my reading of minute books for a large number of banks in the region.
56. Shawmut National Bank Archives, National Shawmut Bank, Directors' Minute Book, 1898–1903, Report of the Committee to Examine the Loans and Securities of the Bank, April 23, 1903.
57. Moulton also argued that collateral loans to brokers and other intermediaries who dealt in the securities markets indirectly underwrote the investment activities of the firms that had issued the securities in the first place. This argument has some validity, but he assumed unrealistically that the amount of investment activity thus generated was fully equal to the value of these loans. H.G. Moulton, 'Commercial Banking and Capital Formation', *Journal of Political Economy*, vol. 26 (1918), pp. 638–63.
58. Harvard Graduate School of Business Administration, Baker Library, Mss. 781, Suffolk Bank, Boston, Massachusetts, Vol. 75, Discount Register, 1899–1902; Vol. 101, Discounted Notes Balance, 1900–1902; Vol. 102, Discount Ledger, 1901–1902. I analysed all loans granted in the months of January, April, July and October, 1901.
59. At least some information on loans is available for the following banks and years: Shoe & Leather National Bank, Boston, 1887; Monument National Bank of Charlestown, Boston, Massachusetts, 1905; National Bank of Rhode Island, Newport, 1888; First National Bank of Warren, Rhode Island, 1886; National Hope Bank, Warren, Rhode Island, 1889; National Warren Bank, Warren, Rhode Island, 1888 and 1898; National Niantic Bank, Westerly, Rhode Island, 1893; and First National Bank of Bristol, Rhode Island, 1898. See Shoe & Leather National Bank, Directors' and Stockholders' Minute Book, 1885–93; Baker Library, Mss. 781, Monument National Bank, loose sheets in Directors' Minute Book, 1892–1905. The following bank records are all located at the Fleet National Bank Archives: National Bank of Rhode Island, Directors' Minute Book, 1862–1902; First National Bank of Warren, Directors' and Stockholders' Minute Book, 1864–89; National Hope Bank, Directors' and Stockholders' Minute Book, 1873–92; National Warren Bank, Directors' and Stockholders' Minute Book, 1887–1899; National Niantic Bank, Directors' and Stockholders' Minute Book, 1892–1905; First National Bank of Bristol, Rhode Island, Directors' and Stockholders' Minute Book, 1865–1901.
60. *Semi-Centennial of the National City Bank of Lynn, Massachusetts* (Lynn, 1904), p. 37; Fleet National Bank Archives, Sowamset Bank of Warren, Rhode Island, Directors' and Stockholders' Minute Book, 1854–76, Directors' Meeting, April 12, 1860.
61. National Bank of Rhode Island, Newport, Rhode Island, Directors' Minute Book, 1862–1902, Directors' Meetings, March 26, 1863, and March 24, 1864.
62. See the numerous records of land sales as noted in Massachusetts National Bank, Boston, Directors' and Stockholders' Minute Book, 1865–83. In the case of the Atlantic Bank, after one of the western promoters failed, it took more than a decade for the bank finally to settle the business. In the interim, the bank actually managed commercial real estate holdings in St. Louis. See Atlantic National Bank, Boston, Stockholders' Minute Book, 1828–64, Stockholders' Meeting, Oct. 1, 1855, and Directors' and Stockholders' Minute Book, 1864–77, Stockholders' Meeting, Jan. 14, 1868.
63. See Rhode Island Historical Society Manuscript Collections, Brown & Ives Manufacturing Records, Goddard Brothers Diaries, MSS 9, Sub Group 10, Series D. See also J.B. Hedges, *The Browns of Providence Plantations: The Nineteenth Century* (Providence, 1968), esp. chapters 8 and 11.
64. The closest thing I have found to a criticism of long-term borrowing by customers is the following passage: 'It is to be presumed also that borrowers will use the proceeds of loans which they are to repay in a few months more wisely than might be the case if the payment were indefinitely deferred'. *Loans and Discounts* (Chicago, 1918), pp. 14–15.
65. See T.R. Navin and M.V. Sears, 'The Rise of a Market for Industrial Securities, 1887–

1902', *Business History Review*, Vol. 24 (1955), pp. 116–26. See also J.G. Martin, *A Century of Finance: Martin's History of the Boston Stock and Money Markets* (Boston, 1898).

66. Dividend rates were recorded in the directors' minute books for each of these banks. For locations of records, see above, note 59.
67. US, Comptroller of the Currency, *Annual Reports*; S. Homan, *A History of Interest Rates* (New Brunswick, NJ, 1963), p. 288.
68. A Gerschenkron, *Economic Backwardness in Historical Perspective: A Book of Essays* (New York, 1962), pp. 5–30.
69. See espcially Cottrell, *Industrial Finance*, pp. 194–247.
70. Cottrell, *Industrial Finance*, pp. 194–247; Tolliday, *Business, Banking and Politics*, pp. 174–85; Cassis, 'British Finance'; Ross, 'The Clearing Banks and Industry'.
71. Engberg, *Mixed Banking and Economic Growth in Germany,* pp. 43–83, 199; J. Riesser, *The German Great Banks and their Concentration in Connection with the Economic Development of Germany* (Washington, DC, 1911), pp. 602–80.
72. E.N. White, *The Regulation and Reform of the American Banking System, 1900–1929* (Princeton, NJ, 1983), pp. 156–65.

Long Term Contracts in the Swedish Bank-Orientated Financial System During the Inter-War Period

HANS SJÖGREN

Uppsala University

No social system can work which is based exclusively upon a network of free contracts between (legally) equal contracting parties and in which everyone is supposed to be guided by nothing except his own (short-run) utilitarian ends.

Joseph A. Schumpeter in Capitalism, Socialism and Democracy, (1987, first published 1943), pp. 423–4.

This essay deals with bank–industry relations in an historical perspective. It is well known that since the process of industrialisation began these relations have played an important role for the economic progress in most European countries. In the case of Sweden, which compared to England can be characterised as a late-comer in the industrial revolution, this relationship broadened and deepened during the industrial boom of the late 1890s. The fact that Sweden had the highest growth rate of per capita GNP of any European country between 1870 and 1914 has very often been explained by the existence of a well functioning financial system, with commercial banks as efficient prime movers.[1] The pattern of development was similar to that of Germany – another late-comer.[2] In both countries, the established bank-industry connections were vitally necessary for their dramatic industrial take-offs in the late nineteenth century.

From the 1910s, the traditional credit relationship between the bank and the firm was often supplemented by both share ownership and interlocking directorships. Consequently, by the early inter-war period, the banks had slipped into a close relationship with industry. This was partly caused by the demand for capital to finance industry in the 1910s, as well as by the deflationary crisis in the early 1920s, which forced banks to take over shares. During this crisis the wholesale price index decreased by 50–60 per cent at the same time as the cost of living index declined by more than 30 per cent. When the demand for industrial goods suddenly declined after the inflationary boom of 1914–20, the banks had to grant higher credit limits and financially reconstruct firms. In many indebted firms, collateral shares were transferred to the banks as protection for credit claims. As a result, the banks became owners of many enterprises and the capital market structure of Swedish large industry became dominated by the main commercial banks. The financial system had become highly bank-orientated.

A well known definition of a financial system is 'institutional arrangements designed to transfer savings from those who generate them to those who are willing to make use of them'.[3] These arrangements take place in a capital market (including a credit, a bond and a share market) and are ultimately determined by a certain legal framework (which is dictated by the state and operationalised by different government institutions). Financial systems in capitalist countries can be classified either as *market-orientated* or *bank-orientated*.[4] In a bank-orientated system the banks take more responsibility for corporate financing than in a market-orientated one. Therefore, the credit and owner relationships are much longer and more concentrated than in the latter. It is also significant for a bank-orientated system that banks in times of distress increase their involvement in indebted firms. Earlier research has also stressed the low level of external financing via the bond and the share market. Obviously, we will not find as many financial instruments in the bank-orientated system as in the market-orientated. Of course, in reality there are no perfectly 'pure' systems, and each country's economy contains a mixture of both. However, there are significant differences in the capital intermediation between countries like the United States, the United Kingdom, Germany, Japan and Sweden.

A company's relations with other actors and institutions within a certain financial system can be viewed as a set of various contracts. The credit and ownership contracts are two examples. It seems to be characteristic for a bank-orientated financial system that these two types of contracts are long-term. The *credit contract* is necessarily *incomplete* since it does not specify the parties' obligations under every conceivable contingency.[5] A bank can only partially anticipate the future behaviour of a borrower. To reduce the resulting risk, the bank will demand an element of control over the firm's behaviour through demanding more information, interlocking directors and/or partial ownership. Especially ownership can be used as a complement to the credit contract in the bank's attempt to retain control over situations that the contract cannot include.

Financial historians and economists have brought to light new evidence on the problems concerning financial systems and incomplete contracts (some of these are described in sections II and III). The aim of this essay is to highlight some of the characteristic features of a bank-orientated financial system in a small economy like Sweden, during the inter-war years. Furthermore, by complementing the broad financial story with various case studies on a micro-level, we can attain a much clearer understanding of these long-term relations.

To be more precise: what was the structure of these connections? How concentrated were they, and were they connected to performance variables and bank ownership in the indebted companies? Secondly, was their appearance and persistence correlated to slumps and/or booms? Thirdly, how did the institutional framework promote or inhibit development?

This essay begins with an overview of Swedish financial history (section II), which focuses on the characterisation of a bank-orientated financial system. In the following section (section III) the contract approach is presented. One important issue in the contemporary literature deals with potential banking control and how the different ways of contracting the dependent industrial enterprises are used. Section IV is concerned with an illustration of incomplete contracts: their scope and importance in inter-war Sweden.

II

Bank-Orientated and Market-Orientated Systems – in General and the Case of Sweden

The main differences between a bank-orientated and a market-orientated system are best observed when we look at them in operation in various countries. In the USA and UK the financial system early developed into specialised markets, wtih different institutions performing highly specialised functions.[6] There existed a large number of financial instruments as well as a high incidence of internal financing which provided the capital for industry independent of banks. Most banks in this market-orientated system concentrated on meeting the short-term needs of industry, while, at the same time, the state played a rather passive role.[7] In Japan and Sweden, both the state and the banks have been more integrated in the capital market. Government authorities not only regulated the market; they were also concerned 'to assist the country's industrial health and maintain its international competitiveness'.[8]

The general financial system established in Sweden in the middle of the nineteenth century, before the industrial boom, was influenced by the British deposit banking tradition, and therefore concentrated on short-term deposits rather than on corporate finance.[9] Some of the private bankers that founded banks were also interested in the functions and organisations fo the Crédit Mobilier and the banks in Belgium and Germany. The way in which these banks actively took part in industrial development through investment banking, holding companies, trusts and cartels was largely adopted by Swedish industrialists during the industrial 'take-off' in the late 1890s and the first decade of the twentieth century. Therefore, the financial system that emerged by the eve of the First World War was actually an amalgam of traditional deposit banking and universal banking, including corporate finance.

An important difference between British and Swedish commercial banks after 1912 was that the Swedish banks were allowed to acquire shares in joint-stock companies.[10] The banks' shareholding became legalised by the 1911 Banking Law. Even before that time, syndicates and issuing companies – directed by the banks – were deeply engaged in providing industrial companies with risk-bearing capital. The activities of the issuing companies were very often financed by the banks, with shares in the firms' portfolios as collaterals for loans.[11] Moreover, the members of the boards in those syndicates often acted in the interest of their respective bank. In that respect they frequently held shares in bank-allied companies.

The 1920s – a Strong Bank-Orientated System

When the deflationary crisis occurred in 1920–21, the effect of falling prices hit the share-issuing companies severely.[12] Repayments on loans were suspended and the collateral shares were transferred to the banks as protection for credit claims. Within a few years the banks suddenly became owners of key industries. To secure their loans the banks placed directors on the companies' boards, which increased their control over these companies. These directors played a monitoring role in the bank-directed industrial transformation of the 1920s. Moreover, in the mid-1920s 75 per cent of credit in the large companies sector was granted to more or less bank-owned enterprises.[13] This situation suggests a bank-orientated financial system with close relations between banks and industry.

In contrast to the Swedish case, British bankers hesitated to use their potential influence over firms. The combination of a high degree of internal financing and a lack of industrial expertise within banks left the British banks with few chances to intervene. And when they did get such an opportunity, they were very much afraid of getting too involved. One chairman of the National Provincial Bank characterised this type of bank behaviour with a metaphor: 'we often have the whip hand, but it is not always desirable for us to use it'.[14]

Such a passive attitude to industry was unfamiliar to the Swedish bankers. They might even have become too involved. A political debate arose in Sweden as to whether the banks should have the right to own shares in industry or not. The underlying question was to what extent the companies should be controlled by banks. It was pointed out by the Bank Committee of 1924 that 26 per cent of the enterprises in the large company sector were more or less controlled by banks, compared to three per cent in 1913.[15] The percentage share of enterprises that were considered independent fell from 91 to 66 per cent between 1913 and 1924.

The Bank Committee of 1924 discussed the question of bank ownership in industry at length, but it was not until after the collapse of the Kreuger group in 1932 that the banks' industrial holdings were sharply restricted. The importance of the Kreuger group débâcle for future developments cannot be overestimated. In 1930 this group controlled the four largest industrial enterprises in Sweden.[16] At this time, the group's operations were largely financed with foreign capital. Gradually, however, the Swedish banks, and finally even the Central Bank, had to give extensive financial support, because of the group's liquidity crisis. By the time of Ivar Kreuger's death in 1932 about 15 per cent of the total assets of Swedish banks were lent to this group.[17] The crash on the international stock market definitely led to the collapse of the Kreuger 'empire' and the shares were taken over by the banks as protection for credit claims.

The long-run intention of the Government Bill of 1933 was to break up the symbiotic bank–industry relationship. There were two main reasons for this policy. Firstly, since the banks were deeply engaged in industrial enterprises, an additional risk factor like shareholding, especially on a market with falling share prices, was unwanted. In case of bankruptcy the shareholding would become one further threat to the bank's solvency. Secondly, both international experiences (the collapse of the stock market and several bank liquidations in Europe) and national ones (the Kreuger collapse) produced severe liquidity crises for some banks, thereby threatening the deposits of households and the general public. The turbulence on the share market gave the state a direct reason to force the banks to change their attitude to collaterals.[18] To guarantee the depositors' money, restrictions were tightened, the state's former recommendations were converted into banking laws, and the role of the supervisory authority – the Bank Inspectorate – was confirmed.

The 1930s – a New Design for a Prolonged Bank-Orientated System

During the 1930s corporate finance was partially replaced by traditional retail banking. This was most obvious in the large companies, where internal financing started to exceed external. To some extent, a higher degree of bond financing compensated for the falling volume of short-term bank credits. In this way the financial system began to resemble a market-orientated one: high internal financing and financing via bonds instead of short-term loans. But that was not all. A well functioning share market is one of the main criteria of a market-orientated system, but after the crash on the stock market there were few opportunities to finance companies through share-issuing. In the case of borrowing, the small and medium-sized firms seemed to have generated prolonged relationships, often getting the banks to grant them high credit limits. It is therefore reasonable to believe that the demand for credit by entrepreneurs was as high as usual.[19] Obviously, there were elements from both a bank-orientated and a market-orientated system in the structure of the capital market during the 1930s. On the whole, however, it is more correct to characterise the 1930s as a bank-orientated decade. The reasons for this is to be found in the prolonged relationship between large companies and banks.

When the established bank–industry connections were disrupted by the Government Act in 1934, the banks designed a new means to enable them to continue their control over the companies. The fear of losing these firms as customers led to the foundation of several bank-allied investment companies, which were allowed to hold shares.[20] Three of the four largest banks created their own spheres in which the responsibility for the part of their business consisting of ownership secured by long-term contracts was transferred to the investment companies.[21] Therefore, despite a lower credit demand among large companies and more strict legal framework it is wrong to say that bank domination totally disappeared from the financial scene in the mid-1930s. The design of the new institutional arrangement definitely guaranteed a prolonged tight relationship.

III

Long-term Contracts

Between every borrower and the bank there exists a loan contract in order to diminish the risk the bank has taken in the credit relationship. To secure the credit granted by always keeping satisfactory collateral is one way to diminish the risk. By collecting information about the company and its branch, the banks get further signals from the market that are relevant for the evaluation of the credit contract.

But the loan contract also exists to make it easier for the company. The bank's guarantee of further tranches, a fixed interest rate for the loans, cash management and saving accounts for the workers are all important financial services for a company.

In a broader perspective, the existence of contracts can be viewed as the result of oligopolistic bank behaviour. The competition between different institutions on the capital market forces the banks to create groups of companies under their influence, often firms operating in the same branch of industry. In this process, long established contractual relationships play an important role in restricting competiton.

A contract, established on short-term credit, may be transformed into a long-term credit relationship in which the two actors – the bank and the customer – have to meet certain conditions written into the contract. Most of these conditions are renewed annually, such as the date of payment and the collaterals. This circumstance creates the possibility of a long-term credit relationship between the lender and the borrower.

Even if the quality of the relationship is not contractable this aspect also gains in importance for a relationship that is in progress.[22] Both high efficiency and a positive social atmosphere keeps down the price for the contract. The social context is also important for explaining why the relations become long-term. It seems as if moral codes, informal rules and customs all have a preservative effect on the relationship and, therefore, strongly contribute to prolonging the contract.[23]

The long-term credit contract can also be viewed from the point of view of transaction cost analysis.[24] How effectively the credit contract really can be organised depends on the level of the transaction costs. There are costs for 'drafting, negotiating and safe-guarding' an agreement, but also for implementing the contract, such as 'maladaption costs incurred when transactions drift out of alignment' (one way of safe-guarding the contract is to use ownership). From the point of view of the contractual parties – the bank and the firm – there is an incentive to keep these costs on a low level. To use short-term instead of long-term bank relationships is the same as to choose high transaction costs. With a long-term relationship the introductory costs would obviously disappear. Implicitly, the transaction cost analysis suggests a shift towards long-term contracts between banks and industry.

Who Controls Whom?

Questions such as who controls whom and under what circumstances the control shifts from the entrepreneur to the bank, or *vice versa*, are of great importance for the contracting approach. Theoretically, and in the short term, it seems as if industry was independent of the banks. Once the loan has been granted, the bank does not know what the borrower will do, or even if he is honest. Assuming that the borrower opts for a very risky project, then the lender can not, once having issued the loan, fully observe or control the operations of the borrower. In this case there is a problem of moral hazard.[25] The borrower has a opportunity to maximise his own utility to the detriment of the bank, because the firm does not have to bear the full responsibility for its actions, due to a incomplete or restricted contract with the bank. If the project fails, the bank may still continue in the medium or long term to extend new credit to the firm. Because of asymmetric information, there is a discrepancy between the marginal return from the company's project and the market interest rate. Therefore, in spite of failure, the bank will still, in the short term, have the same claims on the company as it had before the crisis (that is the same level of repayment and the same interest rate). Even when the failure is known to the bank, there can still exist an incentive to continue to give credits to the firm, as the only way to make it possible for the firm to make further repayments on loans is for the bank to grant new credits – in fact to throw good money after bad.

However, in a crisis, the creditor can put pressure on the debtor by dictating harsh conditions. Thus, the risk of lock-in effects and opportunism are obvious.[26] In cases of lock-in the creditor has closed alternative ways for solving the financial problems of a firm. In practice, the bank will try to prevent the indebted company from chosing another financier, and instead of helping the firm to reconstruct, the bank will no longer provide further financial support. Only a 'complete contract' could solve all problems due to these complications. Unfortunately, this does not exist. Instead, in a crisis the lender typically has a self-serving incentive to demand a higher interest rate or better collateral than would be efficient in a competitive market situation.

Viewing credit contracting in the long term, it seems as if banks control industry. First of all, the problems of asymmetric information and moral hazard do not overshadow the relationship any longer. Moreover, when most firms in the same industry have their credit from only one bank, we can assume that there is a bank-controlled industry (very often, the bank also endeavours to be the only creditor to the individual firm). In that case the bank wields great monopoly power. Moreover, if the relationships include shares in the companies and interlocking directors there is no doubt about the fact that the bank has the potential to control such companies. For example, the banks have great opportunities to enforce mergers amongst these firms. To what extent the potentialities of control are exploited or not depends on other variables, such as the economic performance of the company, and/or the relative strength of the managers.

Contracts and Performance

To map out the contracts we have to look at variables such as solvency, degree of ownership and concentration of credit relations, but also the informal way of contracting. This information helps us to interpret whether we have a bank-orientated or a market-orientated financial system. For instance, if the bank debt/equity ratio is high among firms (or the solvency is low), the bank ownership extensive and the credit relations concentrated (merely one or two main banks) it would imply a bank-orientated financial system.

A comparison of the bank-orientated and the market-orientated financial systems of six different capitalist countries during the 1980s has been done by Erik Berglöf.[27] Companies in countries with the former system (Germany, France, Japan and Sweden) had (1) generally higher debt/equity ratios, (2) more homogeneous, stable and concentrated credit relations than in the other countries (United States and United Kingdom). Besides, (3) the shareholding by banks was long-term and corporate take-overs were less usual in the first countries. Due to the incomplete contracting approach the last result is not surprising at all. In the market-orientated system it is more common that the control goes from one owner to another more frequently. It is comparable to the difference between firms having short-term relations with many banks instead of a few long-term connections with a small number of banks. With banks as risk-bearers a high ratio of debt/equity is normally accepted and can be managed by the reconstruction experts in the bank. To search for a new reconstructor – actually a new owner – would be superfluous.

In a comprehensive study of investment behaviour and industrial shareholding during the inter-war period done by Alice Teichova and Alois Mosser, the focus is partly on the Österreichische Creditanstalt (CA) as both shareholder and creditor.[28] There were about 120 large industrial clients that had well established long-term relations with the bank in the late 1920s. These close relationships concerned both large credits, ownership by the bank and interlocking directors. To secure its credits during the crisis in the early 1920s the CA, like the Swedish commercial banks, acquired shares in various large enterprises. As the new owner of key industries it used its monopoly power to reconstruct several companies, initiate mergers, and organise cartels.

The Swedish case of long-term contracts in the financial market has been investigated for one bank – Stockholms Enskilda Bank – by Håkan Lindgren.[29] It seems that the most common way to keep bank-directed control over industry was by having a minority ownership-interest in the companies. This gave the bank sufficient information and influence to dictate all the financial arrangements. There were two types of explicit contracts: the gentlemen's agreement and the formal contract. The first type was established by confidence and moral codes. It provided an important network of relationships between the contracting actors which is still an important component of the oligopolistic Swedish banking system.

The second type of contract emerged when the bank was in danger of losing the firm as a customer. When the bank sold its shares in a company a contract was signed to secure a continued relationship. These two types of agreements sometimes substituted for a more extensive ownership in the company or at least made this less important.

Unfortunately, the informal way of contracting customers has so far been ignored, especially by economists. The result above suggest institutional arrangements that are far removed from a strict market situation. Maybe 'the vision of a "pure" market or capitalist system which has driven out all vestiges of habit and tradition is both theoretically implausible and unrealizable in practice'.[30]

In the long run lenders and borrowers derive a more social, personal knowledge about each other. The lender gets an insight into the competence and capacity of the human capital of the firm, and the borrower knows what kind of services the bank can deliver. For instance, the bank can arrange a new board or at least suggest a change of some of the directors.

The larger Swedish banks regarded some of their customers as their own companies.[31] This attitude was most apparent in Stockholms Enskilda Bank and the control exercised by the 'Wallenberg group'. Several generations of the Swedish Wallenberg family have for more than a hundred years combined concentrated ownership with great entrepreneurial interest. The development of Swedish multinational enterprises based on Swedish innovations from the late nineteenth century is certainly one result of this policy.

It seems that if the lender believes in the company's future the credit contract will be prolonged. When prospects look bleak, the bank and the borrower discuss the problems together. The company gets support during a crisis until it has been reconstructed and, of course, even beyond that. Such is the general banking-policy in most large banks or where a well established relationship exists between a creditor and a company.

IV

Large Companies' Contracts in a Bank-Orientated System[32]

As a starting point for an illustration of some incomplete contracts we take the 15 largest manufacturing companies in Sweden in 1919.[33] Eleven of them had long-term contracts (defined as a relationship of five years of more). The aim is to follow the business of these eleven firms during the inter-war period. Between 1919 and 1939 two of them went into bankruptcy, while the others survived and grew.

Four variables are used to examine these relations: profit, solvency, concentration and volume of credits, and bank share holding. The effects of the deflationary crisis which hit all 11 companies led to the most important changes. The losses shown were great – in 1922 five of the 11 companies reported a loss amounting to more than seven per cent of their total balance. After that their performance stabilised on a profit level and during the 1930s the main trend of profits was slightly upward. Solvency, which was extremely high after the First World War, showed a falling tendency after the depression in the 1930s (this was partly caused by abolishing restrictions on depreciation and partly by new techniques of bookkeeping). Despite losses and falling solvency, the credit contracts in the companies were renewed every year.

In the early period it was common to have more than one credit contract (see Figure 1). Two firms had six different credit relationships while another company had ten. The number of credit contracts increased in times of crisis, for example in the beginning of the 1920s and the 1930s. In addition to the established one or two credit contracts, the enterprises had to get working capital from several 'new' banks for their survival.

This widespread credit structure successively disappeared during the inter-war period.[34] Most multi-bank relationships were replaced by a connection with one or two main banks. The same development has been observed for the bond market. Measured by number of loans, single bank underwriting increased relatively during the inter-war period, from 56 per cent 1926–35 to 70 per cent 1936–45.[35]

In the long term a strategic problem seems to have appeared when the firm had credit contracts with more than one bank. In that case no bank took sole responsibility for the company. When there existed a multi-bank situation, each bank had less information about the company than it would have had if it had been the sole creditor. On the other hand, a relationship including long-term credit contracts with one or two main banks seems to has been sufficient to provide enough financial support to companies during the crisis.

The length of a credit relation varied between five years and 20 (the whole inter-war period). It was even common that established one and/or two main credit contracts in 1919 continued during the entire period (four cases). During the deflationary crisis the banks granted higher credits. Some of the large companies were totally reconstructed by the banks after the depression. Through personal and financial engagement a majority of them could survive the deep crisis.

Finally, bank ownership was very often connected to credit contracts. In a clear majority of the companies the main credit bank also owned a large portion of shares. In some companies this ownership was combined with shares even from the second and the third main credit bank (it was

TABLE 1
MULTI-CREDIT CONTRACTS 1919–39

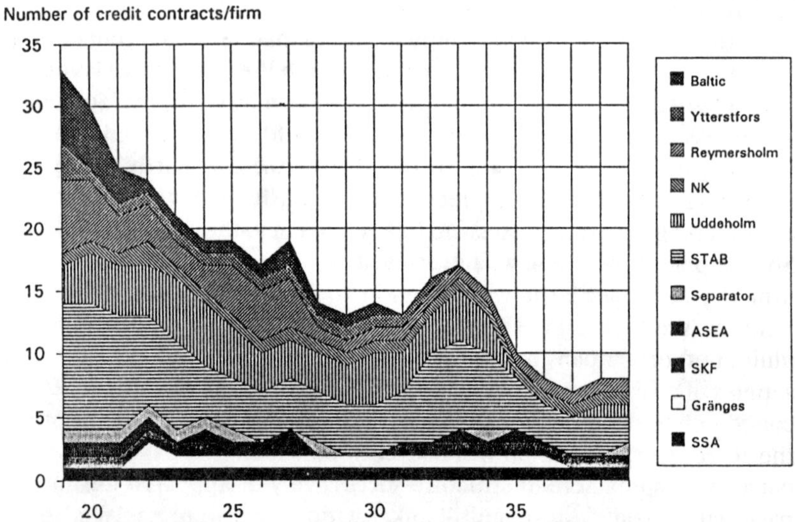

Source: National Archives, Bank Inspectorates Archives, The Register of Engagements, D VII, vol. 1–64.

very unusual that a non-credit bank had any shares at all). The trend here was towards a more concentrated ownership with only the main credit banks as shareholders in indebted firms.

Rescue Credits or Bankruptcy

The large company sector strongly increased its dependency on banks during the first half of the 1920s. Between 1918 and 1924 the proportion of the advances given to bank-owned companies in this sector increased from 22 to 72 per cent.[36] Two of the 11 companies above, Reymersholms Gamla Industri AB and Ytterstfors-Munksund, illustrate the consequences of many years of bank involvement. Ytterstfors-Munksund – a sawmill – first had two main bank relations but from 1921 Svenska Handelsbanken continued as the sole creditor.[37] When wood and pulp prices began to fall in the early 1920s the company experienced severe difficulties. In 1922 the loss was already 20 million Swedish crowns (£1.2 million). Increased 'rescue credits' were not able to save the situation. The problem was rather on a macro level since the Swedish wood industry needed to be structurally rationalised in order to become more competitive.

Svenska Handelsbanken's reliance on the management was extremely low and the bank refused to support the optimistic plans of the company. In a letter to the firm the bank's management expressed its lack of confidence:

> Regarding the extensive bank engagement, through large credits, the company calls for a capable board of directors, on which the bank could rely. As the new board does not satisfy this basic criterion we claim that either the credits are repaid or the company instals a more competent board acceptable by the bank.[38]

The company seemed to have been totally locked in by the bank. Shortly after the bank decided to cancel the credit contract in 1925, the firm went into bankruptcy.

This case exemplifies why banks sometimes want to write open, limited-term contracts instead of detailed ones concerning far-reaching support. In the short-term contract, the parties' obligations under every contingency are consciously left out. This principle can be derived from the attitude of the bank, which is to 'wait and see what happens'.[39] If the bank suddenly dislikes the activity of the firm, a short-term loan, compared to a detailed and far-reaching contract, can easily be revaluated or, as in the case of Ytterstfors-Munksund, cancelled.

Later on a new enterprise based on the assets from Ytterstfors-Munksund was founded – Munksund.[40] It was a result of negotiations initiated by directors from Svenska Handelsbanken. The business cycle was not beginning to move upwards, and the earlier effective concentration on the sulphate industry had become successful. After a bank-directed merger with the large SCA (Swedish Cellulose Co.) in 1933, which after the Kreuger crash was closely connected to Svenska Handelsbanken's sphere of industrial interest, the firm continued as a relatively profitable subsidiary company.

Reymersholms Gamla Industri AB, belonging to the chemical industry, was also hit by the deflationary crisis of 1920–21.[41] Losses and bank debts both accelerated, and in 1923 one of the three main creditors decided to break up the contract. The remaining bank relationships were divided between the two largest banks in that time – Svenska Handelsbanken and Skandinaviska Banken – in which Svenska Handelsbanken was the most important. In the financial reconstruction that followed, the share capital was depreciated from 33 to 3 million Swedish crowns (from £1.9 million to £0.2 million). At the same time equity capital was extended and to a large degree taken over by the bank in order to protect their claims. Svenska Handelsbanken became the majority owner.

Despite improvements in the business cycle in the late 1920s Reymersholms continued to be dependent on the bank. In 1928 the credits in Skandinavbanken were taken over by Handelsbanken.[42] In the new single bank relation the bank director at Handelsbanken played an important role in the second financial reconstruction of the firm in 1932–33. The bank stayed in the relationship even beyond the profitable years from the mid-1930s. When its ownership was threatened in 1934, due to the changing legal framework, the bank did not sell its shares in the market but to a holding company within its own bank-sphere – AB Regia.

It was characteristic of this type of relationship that the bank tried to strengthen its position without regard to the business cycle or the economic prospects. If the original motive with holding shares was to protect the bank's claims, the later motivation of the banks was certainly to dictate the company's future.

In the early 1920s the Swedish separator industry answered for more than half of the world production of separators.[43] Both Separator AB and Baltic were already multinationals with substantial manufacturing subsidiaries in the United States.[44] During the deflationary crisis the industry faced great difficulties. It needed to be concentrated. Separator bought the smaller Baltic and merged with a third company – Pump-separator. The concentration process was to a large extent managed by the banks.

The reason why Baltic, but not Separator, disappeared from the market was not only a question of size. It can also be explained from the view point of the credit structure. The companies' two different ways of organising their credit relations determined the degree of banking support they received. In Separator a one main-bank relationship existed during the whole inter-war period, even though there was a change in 1934 from Göteborgsbanken to Stockholms Enskilda Bank. The situation of Baltic was totally different. With ten different bank connections in 1918–21, the responsibility was dispersed between the various banks. Despite some 'rescue credits' provided by Skandinavbanken, which also had a long-term share holding in the company, Baltic could not survive the deflationary crisis.[45] The result of the multi-bank connection was that no one bank felt enough responsibility for the company to provide help at a critical time.

The foremost link between another multinational enterprise – ASEA – and Stockholms Enskilda Bank was on an individual base. An established personal network guaranteed the bank's continued control of the company.[46] From the turn of the century personal bonds between the managing directors made the relationship strong. During the deflationary crisis, the company had big losses and the credit limit was increased. Figures featuring years of high solvency did not represent the whole truth. In 1922 and 1923 when the formal solidity was 79 and 82 per cent respectively the losses amounted to nearly ten per cent of the total balance.[47] But the fact that the company already in 1924 was one of the largest depositors in the bank confirms its relative financial independence.[48]

There was no shareholding in this company by banks until the end of the 1920s, when the only creditor – Stockholms Enskilda Bank – broadened its engagement.[49] In the late 1920s there was international interest in ASEA which aimed at incorporating the firm into a cartel of the European high-voltage companies.[50] In this competitive situation the 'Wallenberg group' was pushed to make further agreements with the company. The personal links from the early period were complemented by both ownership, a more extensive credit contract and joint-venture projects in high-voltage industry.

The distinguished way in which the Wallenberg bank handled a multi-bank situation gives further evidence of the ambition to be 'the one and only'. This type of bank behaviour corresponds to the German 'Hausbank system'. When the Wallenberg bank's relations with its industrial clients were threatened, the bank reacted by increasing its share of ownership. If that was not enough, the bank would implement a merger, offering contracts in which all the business operations were proportionally divided between the bank and the next-largest creditor.[51] In this respect, ASEA was certainly one of the banks' own companies, supported and controlled by the different institutions within the powerful 'Wallenberg group'.

V

Conclusion

In this essay various characteristic features have been presented to shed some light on the Swedish financial system during the inter-war period, such as bank domination and long-term credit and owner relationships between firms and banks.

It appears that the so called bank-orientated system and the structure of these relations was made possible because of legal framework which existed. In this respect the right of banks to act as shareholders was the most important factor in giving the banks dominant position on the capital market.

However, the Swedish case does not fully fit in with the common view of a bank-orientated system. Because of the very active share-issuing companies, which were owned by the banks, there was especially in the 1910s a highly developed capital market. The industrial firms were, in opposition to the traditional view of a bank-orientated system, very often externally financed through the share market. Due to the fact that the banks dictated the rules for the share-issuing companies, as well as financing their operations, the development of industry was highly dependent on the behaviour of the banks.

Another notable exception from the common pattern deals with bond financing, which has been considered insignificant in a bank-orientated system. Especially in the late 1930s, bonds constituted a large part of the external financing among Swedish large enterprises.

The contract approach had proven to be a suitable analytical tool in an empirical study of bank–industry relations. Because of the incompleteness of the credit contract the banks in inter-war Sweden combined their credits with shareholding and personal links to achieve better control and information about the companies. In Sweden, as in most European countries (except the UK), this combination of mutural ties has been very characteristic and important for the prominent role of banks since the beginning of this century.

From the empirical study of the largest Swedish firms (in the last part of this paper) it seems that most enterprises had long-term relationships with banks, including both credit contracts and banks' ownership in their equity. Moreover, the relationships were often prolonged no matter how business cycles developed. This banking policy promoted an extensive division of industrial clients in a oligopolistic manner.

It was common among large scale companies to have one or two long-term credit contracts. This situation resembled the German case of 'Hausbank'. In periods of crisis the number of credit contracts temporarily increased, because the companies were forced to secure new financial sources to survive the depression. During such periods, if the financial problems of the industrial companies increased, the Hausbank offered rescue credits, which were followed by various forms of financial and industrial reconstruction assistance.

Close bank-industry relations remained part of the Swedish economy even after the inter-war period. When banks were prohibited from owning shares in joint-stock companies by the Government Act of 1934, they founded investment companies for the continued control of their own enterprises, in a oligopolistic manner. This development was similar to what happened in other European countries characterised by the bank-orientated financial system.[52] On the Continent of Europe, but also in Japan, the banks continued to play a prominent role in the economy after the Second World War.

Many of the results in this essay concerns an implicit critique of the neo-classical way of describing developments in the capital market. From our point of view institutional factors seem to be of much greater importance for the development of bank-industry connections than the pure economic factors. Surely, for the banks and the firms, the 'perfect' market was too hazardous for them to risk their relationship.

NOTES

This research is part of the Swedish Banking Project at the Department of Economic History at Uppsala University. The research programme focuses on the role of banks in the industrial transformation of Sweden during this century. The Project is part of an international project. Economic historians from England, Sweden, Hungary and Austria have already met in three workshops to discuss bank–industry relations and do comparisons between different countries. I would like to thank not only the members of the Swedish project – Ragnhild Lundström, Håkan Lindgren, Mats Larsson, Jan Ottoson and Kristina Björkegren – but also Lynn Karlsson and my 'international supervisor' Alice Teichova for all their good advice and linguistic help with this paper.

1. See for example L.G. Sandberg, 'Banking and Economic Growth in Sweden before World War I', *Journal of Economic History,* Vol. XXXVIII, No. 3 (1978).
2. For a brief summary of the German case, see A. Teichova, 'Rivals and Partners', *Uppsala Papers in Economic History*, Working Paper No. 1, (1988), pp. 6–8.
3. T.M. Rybczynski, 'Industrial Finance System in Europe, U.S. and Japan', *Journal of Economic Behavior and Organization*, Vol. 5 (1984), p. 276.
4. For a more detailed definition, see Rybczynski, 'Industrial Finance System'. See also E. Berglöf, 'Capital Structure as a Mechanism of Control; A Comparison of Financial Systems', in M. Aoki, B. Gustafsson and O.E. Williamson (eds.), *The Firm as a Nexus of Treaties* (1990), pp. 244–50; and Y.-S. Hu, 'Industrial Banking and Special Credit Institutions; A Comparative Study', *Policy Studies Institute*, No. 632 (Oct. 1984).
5. B. Holmström and J. Tirole, 'The Theory of the Firm', in R. Schmalensee and R.D. Willig (eds.), *Handbook of Industrial Organisation*, Vol. 1 (1989), pp. 120–3.
6. Rybszynski, 'Industrial Finance System'; Berglöf, 'Capital Structure'.
7. With a longer historical perspective this is not the whole truth. Despite a tradition of both a high degree of internal financing and a low demand for credits it was not unusual that even the British firms during the second half of the eighteenth century and the inter-war period had long-term relations with commercial banks. See P.L. Cottrell, *Industrial Finance, 1830–1914* (1979), pp. 210–44 and D.M. Ross, 'The Clearing Banks and the Finance of British Industry, 1930–1959' (unpublished Ph.D. thesis, London School of Economics, 1990), pp. 245–8.
8. Hu, 'Industrial Banking', p. 1.
9. See G.B. Nilsson, *Banker i brytningstid* (Stockholm, 1981), pp. 329–33 and 339.
10. Before 1912, as well as after that time, there was also a possibility for the banks to take over shares as protection for their claims in times of bankruptcy. See H. Lindgren, 'Banking Group Investments in Swedish Industry', *Uppsala Papers in Economic History*, Research Report No. 15 (1987), pp. 7–8.
11. National Archives (hereafter NA), Stockholm, Kommittéarkiv, Komm. nr. 83, 1917 års bankkommitté, bilaga 3 (Orienterings-Promemoria) and Betänkande nr 5. See also R. Lundström, 'Banks and Early Swedish Multinationls', in Teichova, M. Lévy-Leboyer and H. Nussbaum (eds.), *Multinational Enterprise in Historical Perspective* (Cambridge, 1986), pp. 202–3.
12. In Sweden the deflationary crisis of 1920 hit industry harder than the depression of the early 1930s. In 1922 the rate of unemployment reached 35 per cent. Five small and medium-sized banks were reconstructed after they went bankrupt. Two large banks – Skandinavbanken and Handelsbanken – were also badly hit by the financial crises. For further comments, see R. Lundström, 'Banks and Early Swedish Multinationals', pp. 203–5 and 210.
13. M. Larsson and H. Lindgren, 'Risktagandets Gränser', in C.G. Thunman and K. Eriksson (eds.), *Bankmarknader i förvandling* (Lund, 1990), p. 156.

14. S. Tolliday, *Business, Banking and Politics: The Case of British Steel, 1918–1939* (1987), p. 179.
15. R. Lundström, 'Banks and Early Swedish Multinationals', p. 204; NA, Kommittéarkiv, 1924 års bankkommitté, Kommuniké.
16. A lot of research has been done on the 'Kreuger Empire'. See K.G. Hildebrand, *Expansion, Crisis, Reconstruction, 1917–1939 – The Swedish Match Company, 1917–1939: Studies in Business Internationalisation* (Stockholm, 1985) and H. Lindgren, 'The Kreuger Crash of 1932: In Memory of a Financial Genius, or Was He a Simple Swindler?', *Scandinavian Economic History Review*, Vol. XXX, No. 3 (1982).
17. J. Glete, *Kreugerkoncernen och krisen på svensk aktiemarknad* (Stockholm 1981), p. 610, (includes an English summary).
18. Larsson and Lindgren, 'Risktagandets Gränser', pp. 150–2.
19. H. Sjögren, 'Credit Connections in the Interwar Period' in P. L. Cottrell, H. Lindgren and A. Teichova (eds.), *European Industry and Banking, 1920–39: A Review of Bank–Industry Relations* (Leicester 1991, forthcoming).
20. It was not until the 1940s that all the shares in the banks were completely sold out or transferred to the investment companies. See H. Lindgren, 'Longterm Contracts in Financial Markets: Bank–Industry Connections in Sweden, Illustrated by the Operations of Stockholms Enskilda Bank, 1900–70', in M. Aoki, B. Gustafsson and O.E. Williamson (eds.), *The Firm as a Nexus of Treaties* (1990), p. 269.
21. The established structure mentioned here was still prominent in the 1980s. Two sharp bankspheres were discernible – the Wallenberg group and Svenska Handelsbanken/Industrivärden. In 1985 the two spheres had respectively 24 and 15 per cent of the Swedish industrial employment. See H. Lindgren, 'Affärsbankerna – Näringslivets herrar eller tjänare?', *Pecvnia* (skrifter i myn toch penninghistoriska ämnen utgivna av Kungl. Myntkabinettet, Stockholm), Vol. 1 (1990), p. 27.
22. J. Farrell and C. Shapiro, 'Optimal Contracts with LockIn', *American Economic Review* (March 1989), pp. 51–66.
23. See G.M. Hodgson, *Economics and Institutions* (Cambridge, 1989), pp. 157–61.
24. O.E. Williamson, *The Economic Institutions of Capitalism* (New York, 1985), pp. 20–21.
25. For a brief summary of the study of credit rationing, which includes a discussion of problems such a moral hazard and asymmetric information, see P. Crawford, 'International Lending, Longterm Credit Relationships, and Dynamic Contract Theory', *Princeton Studies in International Finance*, No. 59 (March 1987). See also Y. Kotowitz, 'Moral Hazard' and A. Postlewaite, 'Asymmetric Information', in J. Eatwell, M. Milgate and P. Newman (eds.), *Allocation, Information and Markets* (1989).
26. See Williamson, *Economic Institutions*, pp. 47–9 and Farrell and Shapiro, 'Optimal Contracts with LockIn', pp. 51–52.
27. Berglöf, 'Capital Structure'.
28. A. Mosser and A. Teichova, 'Investment Behaviour of Industrial jointstock companies and industrial shareholding by the Österreichishe Creditanstalt: Inducement or Obstacle to Renewal and Change in Industry in Interwar Austria', in H. James, H. Lindgren and A. Teichova (eds.), *The Role of Banks in the Interwar Economy* (Cambridge, 1991).
29. Lindgren, 'Longterm Contracts', pp. 278–80.
30. Hodgson, *Economics and Institutions*, p. 160.
31. Lundström, 'Banks and Early Swedish Multinationals', pp. 213–4.
32. The results in this subsection are based on three sources: NA; Bank Inspectorates Archives, D VII aa and F I ab; and *Swedish Jointstock Companies, Yearbooks 1919–1939.*
33. The criterion used is share capital. Turnover figures are not accessible for the total number of jointstock companies. It is also useless to choose value of shares as a criterion for 1919, since the volume of transactions on the Stock Exchange was very low during the First World War, even for the large listed joint stock companies.
34. A wave of mergers hit the banking sector during the 1920s, caused mainly by a stricter banking law demanding a higher portion of reserves. Several small banks also

experienced problems during the crisis. Since the large companies did not have credit relations to the small banks the concentration of the credit structure within the enterprises was not a consequence of this merger wave. The merger wave was contrasted with an increasing number of new bank offices – from 269 offices in 1900 to 1,410 in the late 1920s. See L.E. Thunholm, *Svenskt Kreditväsen*, (1971), p. 42.

35. H. Lindgren, 'Commercial Banks as Intermediaries in the Swedish Bond Market, 1924–1945' in K. Ullenhag (ed.), *'Hundred Flowers Bloom': Essays in Honour of Bo Gustafsson* (Uppsala, 1991).
36. K.G. Hildebrand, *I omvandlingens tjänst. Svenska Handelsbanken, 1871–1955* (Stockholm 1971), p. 239.
37. Ibid., pp. 268–76. See also G. Dyverfeldt, *Norrbottnisk sågverksindustri, 1900–1925: AB YtterstforsMunksund och dess föregångare* (*Uppsala Studies in Economic History 11*) (Uppsala, 1974).
38. NA, Bank Inspectorates Archives, F I ab, vol. 46, appendix 118.
39. O. Hart, 'Incomplete Contracts', in J. Eatwell and M. Milgate and P. Newman (eds.), *Allocation, Information and Markets* (1989), p. 166.
40. Hildebrand, *I omvandlingens tjänst*, pp. 276–88.
41. Ibid., pp. 307–15; NA, Bank Inspectorates Archives, F I ab, vol. 44.
42. NA, Bank Inspectorates Archives, F I ab, vol. 50.
43. M. Fritz, *Ett världsföretag växer fram*, II (1983), p. 85.
44. Lundström, 'Banks and Early Swedish Multinationals', p. 211. See also R. Lundström, 'Swedish Multinational Growth before 1930', in P. Hertner and G. Jones (eds.) *Multinationals: Theory and History* (Aldershot, 1986), pp. 138–9.
45. E. Söderlund, *Skandinaviska Banken i det svenska bankväsendets historia 1914–1939*, II (Uppsala, 1978), p. 425.
46. H. Lindgren, *Bank, investmentbolag, bankirfirma* (1987), p. 431; Lindgren, 'Longterm Contracts', p. 281.
47. Lundström, 'Banks and Early Swedish Multinationals', p. 211; J. Glete, *ASEA under hundra år* (1983), p. 80.
48. Lindgren, *Bank, investmentbolag, bankirfirma*, p. 431.
49. That is partly true. Before the period for this empirical study, between 1903 and 1911, the bank was one of the shareholders in the company.
50. Glete, *ASEA*, pp. 100–102.
51. Lindgren, *Bank, investmentbolag, bankirfirma*, p. 480.
52. Rybszynski, 'Industrial Finance System'. See also G. Vanthemsche, 'State, Banks and Industry in Belgium and the Netherlands, 1918–1939', in James *et al.*, *The Role of Banks in the Interwar Economy*. Especially in Belgium there were great similarities with developments in Sweden.

Banks, Institutional Constraints and the Limits of Central Banking: Monetary Policy in Britain and West Germany, 1950–52

TILL GEIGER and DUNCAN M. ROSS
University of Aberdeen
and Victoria University of Wellington

The primary role of monetary policy is today widely held to be the stabilisation of the price level, whether this is achieved through a series of rules or by the discretionary policy of the authorities.[1] But monetary policy is imposed through an institutional framework, the nature of which may have a decisive impact on its formulation and effective implementation. This paper focuses on a similar inflationary episode in two countries, one of which followed a monetary policy vested in an independent central banking system, while the other pursued the strategy of joint government–central bank responsibility for the conduct of policy. It considers the relationship between the institutional structure of the monetary and banking system and the effectiveness of policy in the light of the inflationary pressures in Britain and the Federal Republic of Germany as a result of the Korean War. Attention will be focused on the respective economies prior to the war, the inflationary problems associated with the outbreak of hostilities, the policies adopted in both countries to constrain domestic demand and the relative success achieved. We argue that the crucial factor in determining the success of monetary policy was not the degree of independence of the central bank,[2] but the strength of the policy transmission mechanisms and the ability of the authorities to force the banking system to comply with their chosen policy. This lesson was learned in Germany in this period. It was not learned in Britain.

The British and West German economies on the eve of the Korean War

In the period immediately prior to the outbreak of the Korean War, both the British and West German economies were experiencing rapid growth and their balance of payments positions, though far from healthy, were showing signs of improvement. There were, however, serious problems in both countries – in Britain shortages of industrial materials was the major difficulty, while in Germany a large pool of under-utilised resources constituted a political problem for the government.

During the war years and in the post-1945 period, the greatest fear of British policy makers had been that the economy would repeat the inflationary boom and recession experience of 1918–19; direct controls were maintained in the post-war period in order to smooth the expected fluctuations in demand. In the monetary sphere, Dalton attempted to drive long-term interest rates down to 2.5 per cent in order to keep the costs of reconstruction as low as possible. This policy became untenable, however, with the series of crises in 1946–47 and monetary policy thereafter played little part in constraining domestic demand. Fiscal policy and the pursuit of budgetary surpluses were used to mop up some of the excess demand in the economy, while direct controls over allocation of many materials remained in force. The problem of shortages, which arose both from the rapid rate of industrial growth (industrial production had exceeded pre-war levels by 1947) and the inability to pay for imports from the United States, remained the most serious economic problem.

The German situation was different. In that country, much of the government's internal debt had been removed by the currency reform of 1948 and the new Deutsche Mark provided a sound base for growth. In the last quarter of 1949 industrial production reached its 1936 level and by 1950 Germany had also largely re-established its position in intra-European trade. Milward has suggested that 'the actual level of intra-Western European trade in 1947 would have been 24.5 per cent higher had West German trade been at its normal pre-war level, 18.4 per cent higher in 1948, 13.1 per cent higher in 1949, 4.5 per cent higher in 1950 and ... 4.1 per cent higher in 1951'.[3] Despite this rapid expansion, the influx of refugees from the East meant that unemployment in West Germany reached record levels in the winter of 1949/50, although serious skill shortages remained in many areas. Fearing the inflationary consequences, the government held out against pressure from the Social Democrats and the Allied High Commissioners to institute expansionary employment creation programmes, but was eventually forced to reconsider. A first set of measures was largely ineffectual and the second programme, announced in March 1950, came too late to stimulate economic activity before the outbreak of the Korean War.[4]

There were similarities between the two countries in this period. Shortages of steel and coal hampered recovery. In addition the level of inventories held by industry had been run down to low levels. In Britain, the increase in world raw material prices in the first half of 1950 was reflected in a larger than expected rise in import prices (17 per cent as against 5 per cent for export prices). Thus firms preferred to rely on their current levels of stocks and were reluctant to buy raw materials at what they perceived as inflated prices.[5] In Germany a similar reluctance to undertake this kind of investment was evident, and by June 1950 inventories in both countries had been run down to levels insufficient to meet the increased demand arising from the outbreak of hostilities.[6] This had important repercussions for the banking system and monetary policy in that in both countries the predominant source of finance for investment in industrial stocks was short-term bank borrowing.

Banking Systems After the War

The banking and monetary systems in both countries underwent important changes in the period immediately after the war. The institutional structures which were created in the two countries reflected different views on the importance of central bank independence and the transmission mechanism of monetary policy. Whereas in Britain it was expected that by bringing the Bank of England under government control it could be used to regulate the economy, in Germany a different perspective held sway. In that country the occupying authorities were in a position to create an entirely new set of banking and monetary institutions, and they were explicitly modelled on the Federal Reserve System in the United States. Monetary policy was therefore to be pursued independently of government. By the time of the outbreak of the Korean War, however, serious weaknesses in the ability of both systems to control the level of inflation in the economy had become apparent.

In Britain, the Labour government's decision to nationalise the Bank of England gave it nominal power to issue directives relating to the level of money and credit in the economy. Such directives could only, however, be issued to the Bank of England, which acted as an intermediary between the government and the clearing banks, passing on the former's wishes to the latter. There are two points to make about this situation. The first is that it was not expected to make much difference to the conduct of monetary policy. The debate in the House of Commons on the Bank of England Bill consisted largely of statements from the Labour benches that a simple formalisation of the position as it had existed for 20 years was taking place and that there was no reason to oppose it; and from the Conservative side that it would change very little and that the Bill arose from irrelevant ideological vindictiveness.[7] In practice these forecasts proved to be accurate; Cairncross has pointed out that the Bank of England Act effected 'little discernible change in the relationship between the Bank and the Government (nor indeed in any other Bank relationships)'.[8]

The second point of interest to note about the institutional relationships established relates to the position of the Bank of England between the government and the clearing banks. The Bank acted not only as intermediary between policy formulation and the institutions which it targetted, but also as a buffer. Douglas Jay's appointment as Economic

Secretary to the Treasury in December 1947 signalled the beginning of a series of attempts to impose a ceiling on the level of bank advances, which were considered one of the main engines of domestic inflation.[9] On each occasion, however, the Bank of England's officials argued vehemently that such a move would jeopardise the smooth workings of the banking system.[10] They exerted pressure in the opposite direction, insisting that more traditional methods, such as reductions in government expenditure or increases in Bank Rate, were the only ways to control the growth of the money supply.[11] Although this response greatly frustrated those in Whitehall, while bank advances continued to rise throughout 1949 and 1950 the Bank's view prevailed. Robert Hall [the Director of the Economic Section] noted that on this issue 'we were defeated by the Bank'. Gaitskell urged him to 'write a paper and if necessary have a clash with Cobbold [Governor of the Bank of England] and accept his resignation if he offered it'.[12]

In addition to the problems of ensuring Bank of England compliance with its policy goals, the government had also to enlist the support of the clearing banks themselves. Given that lending is the most profitable aspect of a bank's business, however, they were naturally reluctant voluntarily to curtail their activities in that direction. It is clear therefore, that although nationalisation of the Bank of England gave the government greater nominal powers over the monetary system, institutional inertia and imperfect policy transmission channels meant that its ability to control the banking system was significantly less than total.

The German financial system underwent a much more radical restructuring after 1945, although it, too, displayed a crucial inability to restrain inflationary lending by the banking sector. The main goal of the occupying powers in creating a new set of financial institutions was to denazify and curb the power of the German universal banks. The three remaining large Berlin banks (Deutsche Bank, Dresdner Bank, Commerzbank) were split up into 30 regional successor banks in 1947/48. A wide range of restrictions were placed on these institutions, the most important of which was that they could only offer their services in one state. This placed them at a disadvantage against well-established regional private banks, municipal savings institutions (*Sparkassen*) and credit co-operatives (*Kreditgenossenschaften*). In addition, the successor institutions were further handicapped by the fact that they held a significant proportion of their assets in low-interest bearing (3 per cent) equalisation claims, with which they had been compensated for their holdings of pre-war government debt.[13]

The second important aspect of this restructuring was the insulation of the central bank from the government and the replacement of the Reichsbank with a two-tier central banking system modelled on the Federal

Reserve in the United States.[14] In each of the new German states (*Länder*) a central bank (*Landeszentralbank*) was formed. The relationship between these *Landeszentralbanken* (LZB) and the *Bank deutscher Länder* (BdL), the federal central bank, was a precarious one. The BdL was governed by the *Zentralbankrat* (ZBR) (central bank council) which was made up of the 11 presidents of the LZBs (who were appointed by their respective state governments), a chairman (Karl Bernard) and the executive director of the BdL (Wilhelm Vocke). Monetary policy was formulated by the executive director together with the ZBR. The Executive Director and the BdL directorate were responsible for the implementation of ZBR decisions, but they had to rely on the LZBs to carry out day-to-day operations. Bill discounting, inter-state clearing and giro-transfers were the most important parts of their business and within their state they were jointly responsible for bank supervision with the state government. The ZBR could fix minimum reserve requirements and discount rates.[15] Its power, therefore, rested on its authority to regulate directly the local banking systems and their relationship with the LZBs, rather than indirectly by altering conditions and rules of operation of the LZBs themselves.[16] This was to prove important in defining the nature and extent of the BdL's ability to influence monetary conditions. The Allied Banking Commission (ABC) supervised this system until the Federal government asserted sovereignty over it in July 1951, although its independence from government control remained untouched.[17]

After the currency reform in July 1948, seeking to stabilise the currency, the BdL followed a fairly restrictive monetary policy. This involved the raising of minimum reserve requirements, imposition of a ceiling on bank lending and restrictions on the level of discounts and acceptances. The deflationary policy, however, was felt to be constraining growth, and it attracted mounting criticism. During 1949 the BdL gradually eased monetary conditions, abandoning the credit limit in March, lowering the discount rate in July and the minimum reserve requirement in September.[18]

The loosening of monetary conditions, combined with partial liberalisation of foreign trade, quickly resulted in a rapid growth of imports and monetary policy was tightened once more from November 1949. This was frustrated, however, by a similar institutional inertia on the part of the LZBs to that which had contributed to the unwillingness of the British clearing banks to reduce their lending. Keen to provide credit in their local states, they ignored policy which they themselves had set in Frankfurt and discounted bills to their respective banking systems almost without limit. Some banks discounted up to 30 times their capital – a situation which clearly ran contrary to the aims of ZBR policy and which illustrates the limits to the BdL's ability to control the monetary system.

The institutional arrangements which existed in Britain and the Federal Republic in this period contained different perceptions of the nature of monetary control and therefore of ideal government – central bank – banking system relationships. To some extent these differeneces reflected continuity between pre- and post-war arrangements in Britain and a decisive change, imposed by the allied powers, in Germany. What is important for the current discussion, however, is that serious weaknesses in the ability to both sets of monetary institutions to control inflationary pressure had been made clearly apparent even before the shock of the Korean War.

The Korean War and responses to the crisis

With the outbreak of the Korean War both countries faced a new array of challenges. The North Korean invasion led to panic purchases of raw materials in the industrial sector, strategic restocking in many countries and large increases in defence expenditure.[19] The result of these factors was a major upward shift in raw material prices which found most European economies unprepared. The dramatic change in the terms of trade plunged most of them into severe balance of payments difficulties in the first 18 months of the conflict.[20]

In the Federal Republic, the impact was almost immediate and the ensuing balance of payments crisis threatened the stability of the European Payments Union and, in turn, Western European recovery. In contrast the immediate impact of the crisis on Britain was less severe, since, in the short term, that country was insulated from the worst effects of the shift in world prices by the increased export receipts of the sterling area.

TABLE 1

CURRENT BALANCE OF PAYMENTS OF THE UNITED KINGDOM AND WEST GERMANY, 1947–51 ($m)

	1947	1948	1949	1950	1951
UK	−1510	50	310	770	−1430
W. Germany	650	−1120	−1060	−640	130

Source: United Nations Economic Commission for Europe, *Economic Survey of Europe Since the War: A Reappraisal of Problems and Prospects* (Geneva 1953) Table XL, p. 249.

Table 1 indicates that while the crisis demanded decisive measures from the West German economic policy makers, there was little need for a tightening of policy in Britain.

The beginning of the war coincided with the creation of the European Payments Union and further steps towards liberalisation of intra-European trade. These had the effect of limiting the tools which were available to both the British and West German governments to combat the inflow of expensive raw materials. Import controls, especially, became more difficult to impose, although they were used to some extent in both countries. Other policy options, therefore, had to bear the brunt of the anti-inflationary drive. Monetary policy and, in particular, attempts to control the level of bank lending was the method adopted.

In West Germany the raw material price increases were compounded by a wave of panic buying and there was some disagreement and indecision about how to respond. The rising price level was observed with some alarm by the BdL directorate and in an attempt to stop this feeding through into the money supply, some tightening of monetary policy was contemplated.[21] No immediate action was agreed upon, however, beyond a request from the BdL to the LZBs that they ask the banks in their states not to finance further private sector inventory investment.[22] Erhard and the government took the opposite view. During a meeting with representatives from industry, ministers Blücher and Erhard insisted that higher raw material prices were unlikely to lead to inflation. Confident that industry held sufficient inventories of materials, they felt that rather than tightening monetary policy the time had come to encourage the export of manufactured goods.[23] As one observer laconically commented, given higher raw material prices and the prospect of large scale rearmament abroad, the government would have done well to limit the impact on the West German economy.[24]

This period of indecision lasted until the end of September 1950. In the ZBR meeting on 6/7 September 1950 the President of the LZB Bremen, Tepe, suggested a lowering of the discount rate. This was rejected, Vocke arguing that any easing of monetary policy would lead to a significant expansion of credit. In the end the ZBR decided that no further action was necessary as long as bank lending continued to grow within reason.[25]

The BdL's cautious, but determined, stance found critical support. In several commentaries, the government was accused of compounding the crisis by its failure to curtail expansionary expenditure in connection with the second programme to combat unemployment. Massive borrowing by the public sector, it was argued, would defeat the efforts of the central bank to contain the inflationary potential of rising raw material prices. Renewed inflation could only lead to the reintroduction of controls which would in turn stifle the economy.[26]

Throughout September signs of renewed shortages and bottlenecks appeared.[27] While industrialists tried to stock up on raw materials, consumers continued their panic buying spree.[28] The latter was fuelled by the increase in spending power created by a retrospective reduction in income tax in June 1950. While in normal circumstances the tax refunds would have been saved, in this situation consumers started to reduce their savings,[29] which aggravated the precarious liquidity position of most banks. Booming demand and rising import prices led to a rapid deterioration in the balance of payments. By the middle of September it became clear that West Germany would exhaust its quota within the EPU before the end of October if imports continued to grow at their present rate.[30]

As the crisis unfolded, both the BdL and the government were forced into action. To slow down the expansion of short-term credit, the BdL imposed a 50 per cent increase in minimum reserve requirements for commercial banks, effective from October 1.[31] It was clear, however, that the increase in minimum reserve requirements would not achieve the desired effect unless the discounting of bills was also restricted.[32] Accordingly, from 13 October, the LZBs were instructed to limit their rediscounting of bankers' acceptance to the level of the previous day.[33] This measure coincided with the decision of the *Interministerieller Einfuhrausschuss* (interdepartmental import committee) to annul all outstanding import licences overnight and impose a 50 per cent advance deposit requirement on all new licences for imports from OEEC countries.[34] The government felt that these measures would be sufficient and Erhard rejected demands of the American High Commission for the control and rationing of scarce resources.[35]

Over the following two weeks the ZBR discussed the possibility of raising interest rates. Adenauer and his Finance Minister Schäffer were opposed to such a step, while only Erhard was in favour.[36] After a meeting in the Chancellory in Bonn, the ZBR decided to defy the Chancellor and raise discount rate from 4 to 6 per cent and the rate on loans made against security from 5 to 7 per cent.[37] Two days later the BdL asked the LZBs to reduce their holdings of bills of exchange by 10 per cent, this target to be achieved by 31 January 1951.[38] This was a controversial move, and the banks complained that the restrictions – especially relating to the minimum reserve requirement – hit them unduly hard.[39]

Since the currency reform in 1948, the banking system had financed the import boom by borrowing from the Central Bank. Although this had begun to tail off in the first half of 1950, the price shock associated with the war, compounded by widespread dissaving on the part of the public, exerted pressure of their liquidity positon. The objective of the measures – except the increase in the interest rates – imposed in September and October was to reduce the banks' ability to expand their short-term lending. As West Germany lacked a functioning money and capital market, the only source for additional funds for the banks was the central banking system. This dependence of the banks was seen by the BdL officials as the major obstacle to the full implementation of the restrictive policy measures since, if they refused to provide the funds needed by the banks, the stability of the banking system could clearly be endangered.[40]

In this context the relative failure of the advance deposit requirement is of particular interest. To a large extent these were financed by increased short-term bank lending, which suggests that this restrictive measure actually induced banks to increase their lending and consequently their demand for funds from the central banking system.[41] Additionally, banks responded to the restrictive measures of the BdL by expanding longer term lending.[42]

TABLE 2

STRUCTURE OF WEST GERMAN BANK LENDING TO NON-BANKS IN MILLION DM

	Short-term advances	Promissory Notes	Medium-term Credits	Long-term Credits
1950				
August	7,649.0	4,135.4	815.1	3,669.8
September	8,200.1	4,176.8	853.5	4,019.3
October	8,669.1	4,311.4	897.8	4,424.8
November	8,787.5	4,484.1	922.5	4,751.8
December	8,458.6	5,065.5	962.0	5,148.3
1951				
January	8,548.6	5,156.9	992.3	5,395.8
February	8,703.5	5,384.2	1,042.8	5,630.9
March	8,154.4	5,335.6	1,167.2	5,916.5
April	7,849.0	5,330.3	1,227.6	6,201.8
May	7,924.1	5,283.6	1,268.3	6,407.9
June	7,887.0	5,660.9	1,340.7	6,647.9
July	7,928.0	5,933.6	1,370.0	6,859.3
August	8,065.3	6,108.6	1,396.9	7,158.8
September	8,557.9	6,181.8	1,439.4	7,391.4

Source: BdL, *Monatsberichte*, October 1951.

As Table 2 shows, the level of short-term advances by the banks started to fall from February 1951. The levels of long-term lending and promissory note discounts rose, however. The balance of payments crisis showed no sign of abating and the question of tightening monetary policy was raised,[43] particularly as the Federal government seemed reluctant to adopt any further restrictive measures and continued to issue a large number of import licenses.[44] Eventually, the ZBR adopted a number of balance sheet restrictions. These 'guidelines' sought to establish parameters for a number of operating ratios, the most important of which was that advances could not exceed a certain (variable) percentage of the capital and reserves of the bank. Under these guidelines it was envisaged that many private banks would have to reduce their lending to conform with the credit restrictions.[45] These measures were strengthened after the Federal government suspended trade liberalisation within the EPU on 22 February.[46] This decision by the government prompted the ZBR to restrict short-term lending even further, and it requested that the banks reduce their short-term lending by DM 1,000 million, to be achieved in the three months to the end of May 1951. To back up these administrative controls on the level of credit in the economy the BdL activated its most powerful threat – the withdrawal of all central banking discount facilities.[47]

As can be seen from Table 2, the reductions in lending were never quite achieved. To some extent, this was due to the fact that for a number of reasons West Germany's balance of payments problem became less pressing. Suspension of trade liberalisation curtailed imports from EPU countries[48] and at the same time the terms of trade started to shift significantly in Germany's favour from March 1951. These factors contributed to a West German payments surplus with the EPU after March 1951 and as a direct consequence banks profited from the influx of funds from abroad.[49] These developments reduced the need to enforce the controls over bank lending, and after a drop in the volume of short-term advances in March and April the rate of growth recovered. It is not clear, therefore, that the reduction in inflationary pressure was solely due to the tightening of monetary conditions.

In addition, the crisis exposed a number of weaknesses in the dual nature of the West German central banking system. As in 1949, the monetary policy set by the ZBR was not always rigorously enforced by the LZBs or their local banking system.[50] It is clear, for example, that the banks were converting many short-term advances into medium and long-term loans.[51] At local level LZB branch directors seemed to discount bills almost indiscriminately,[52] a throwback to the old Reichsbank practice of discounting any bills which met the minimum requirements of the bank. This allowed the banks to expand their lending without restrictions as long as business could 'produce' bills of exchange.[53] Another difficulty was that for the first few months after October 1950, the decision by the LZB in Berlin to raise neither the minimum reserve requirement nor the interest rate provided banks with a loophole through which they could avoid the restrictions imposed in the Federal Republic.[54]

By the summer of 1951 the threat of inflation had largely receded. Nevertheless, the restrictions were maintained and discussions within the BdL centred on how to close the loopholes in the system of monetary control which the Korean episode had identified.[55] The new minimum reserve requirement and the imposition of rediscount ceilings, buttressed by the threat of withdrawal of access to central bank funds, were ratified by the ZBR in October 1951.[56] These measures pulled the banks into the central banking system and at the same time extended the powers of sanction which the BdL could use over those deemed to be lending to excess. They represented, then, a clear attempt to enhance the effectiveness of monetary policy in restraining inflationary growth of credit.[57]

This control over the banking and monetary system had of course been approached in a different way in Britain. Nationalisation, the Labour Party hoped, would greatly increase the responsiveness of the banking system to government policy and by benign co-operation would prevent a repetition of the experience of the inter-war years when monetary policy was perceived as having added to economic dislocation.[58] This proved not to be the case. The experience of the government in attempting to control inflationary pressure in 1949–50, and perhaps even more so of the BdL in 1950–51, indicated that even had the Bank of England and the government been in complete agreement over policy, successful execution was by no means guaranteed. The oligopolistic nature of the banking system in Britain was very different from the fragmented and competitive situation in Germany, but the extent to which the Bank of England could enforce compliance with policy remained unknown. It is interesting, therefore, that during the inflationary crisis in Britain in 1951, a joint approach of quantitative monetary restriction and qualitative guidelines on bank lending was used.

As the economic repercussions of the Korean War started to make themselves felt, the government, rather than using monetary policy, turned to selective tightening of controls.[59] Gaitskell's budget in 1951 tried to limit the impact of increased demand brought about by the expansion of defence expenditure by raising taxes and reducing food subsidies – the policy of 'disinflation through rising prices'.[60] The clearing banks were requested to exercise vigilance over their lending and they responded by stressing to their branch managers the need to control the growth of inflationary advances, and by jointly raising the rate they charged for this accommodation by 0.5 per cent.[61]

The government also attempted to control and direct investment flows through the operations of such bodies as the Capital Issues Committee (CIC) and the National Investment Board,[62] although these were of only minor assistance in curtailing domestic demand. *The Economic Survey for 1951* contained the assumption that the drop in exports and the higher raw material prices would absorb the current account surplus, and it allowed for a small balance of payments deficit to cover the expenses for strategic stockpiling.[63] This was especially necessary as both industrialists and the government delayed their restocking expenditure until after prices had increased significantly.[64] The massive private sector investment in inventories which began to build up from the beginning of 1951 was financed to a large extent by an increase in bank borrowing.[65] An analysis of Midland Bank advances in May 1951 confirmed this trend. The report indicated that while the effect of higher raw material prices had fed through to higher borrowing levels, especially where 'stocks and work in progress represent a substantial part of total assets', rearmament had not yet led to an increase in advances to defence contractors.[66]

Over the summer of 1951 the balance of payments, not only of Britain but of the whole of the sterling area, deteriorated rapidly.[67] The government, however, continued to resist very strong pressure from the Bank of England to tighten monetary policy and raise short-term interest rates.[68] By the time of the election in October, the government had come under severe criticism for the limited scope of its policy. Per Jacobssen (head of the Bank for International Settlements) found the Chancellor's strategy incoherent and heavily flawed.[69] The *Economist* had published a series of articles debating the need for a tighter monetary policy in May 1951,[70] while in July of that year, The *Banker* argued that the 'tarnished weapons of monetary orthodoxy ... could make a significant contribution to anti-inflation efforts as a whole'.[71]

Within the Treasury, also, the arguments were being strongly made that the point had been reached where technical measures were needed to reinforce official guidelines on monetary policy,[72] and the new Chancellor did not disappoint. On 7 November 1951, Butler announced a series of measures designed to restore confidence in sterling, bolster the exchange rate and reduce the balance of payments deficit. Bank Rate was raised from 2 to 2.5 per cent and a short-term funding operation was launched in an attempt to reduce floating debt in the hands of the clearing banks. The previous government had borrowed in the market for short-term money at a low and fixed rate which had been made possible by the Bank of England's willingness by buy unlimited amounts of Treasury Bills at 0.5 per cent. This constantly available flow of cash to the banking system made the control of credit extremely difficult. In an attempt to turn off this tap of funds, the Bank announced a short-term rate of 2 per cent at which advances to the discount market would be made against Treasury Bills.

The thrust of this policy, in a fashion similar to that pursued in Germany, was clearly to impose some quantitative control over the level of bank deposits, and a target of 30 per cent liquidity ratio was established at the same time. The fundamental difference between the two countries, however, lay in the added burden brought about by the war itself. Monetary policy is essentially a blunt weapon, in that interest rates and bank liquidity ratios have indiscriminate effects over the whole range of borrowers. Given that in Britain the government sought to encourage lending in particular directions to stimulate armaments and export industries, while seeking to contain domestic inflation and pressure on the balance of payments, the direction of bank lending was in many ways of greater importance than the aggregate level. The *Economic Survey for 1952* noted that as part of the strengthening of monetary policy, qualitative controls were continued and intensified.[73] In April 1951 a directive had been issued to the Capital Issues Committee which specifically singled out projects essential for defence production as one area in which finance was to be freely available.[74] As part of the package of restrictions in October, the CIC was asked for greater stringency in the appraisal of all investment projects and the new memorandum of guidance set out very clearly the sectors for which funds could be raised. The Chancellor sent a new request to the Bank of England, asking that the banks pay close attention to the priorities set out in the CIC directive. This combination of quantitative tightening of monetary conditions and qualitative attempts to influence the direction of lending the investment in the economy is the most distinctive feature of British antiinflationary policy in this period.

These measures were further reinforced in the budget of March 1952, in which Bank Rate was raised to 4 per cent and hirepurchase lending was singled out by the government as being especially harmful to the domestic inflationary situation. The general request to the banks to ensure that lending accorded with government policy was reiterated. Longterm interest rates rose considerably as a result of the effects of this budget on top of the November measures, and a considerable easing of inflationary pressure was evident in the economy from the second quarter of 1952. The volume of personal consumption expenditure fell, unemployment showed signs of rising and bank advances to industry declined markedly over the following six months. The balance of payments improved sharply and pressure on the reserves of gold and dollars eased.[75]

As had been the case in Germany, the British policy measures were given a considerable amount of credit for dealing with the inflationary problems brought about by the Korean War. The *Economic Survey for 1953*, for example, was congratulatory in tone and noted that 'changes in the economy during 1952 were broadly in line with the main objectives of government policy'.[76] The extent to which this credit is deserved is open to debate, however. It is clear that the initial shock of the Korean boom was largely over by the installation of the new government at the end of 1951. The most significant factor in the return to surplus of the balance of payments was the reversal of the terms of trade and the fall in import prices throughout 1952.[77] The positive role of monetary policy in constraining demand in this period is more difficult to discern. It seems likely that the funding operation of November 1951 squeezed bank liquidity levels, but not to the extent that they were forced to reduce loans to any great extent. That bank advances grew only slowly throughout 1952 was due more to the reduction in import prices – and therefore requests for funding – than the squeeze on bank assets. The requests to the banks to restrain lending probably added to the recession from the middle of 1952, but the reduction in consumer expenditure had a greater impact there also.[78] The impression remains of a monetary policy made irrelevant by more important and dramatic shifts elsewhere in the economy.

Conclusion

This analysis of the impact of the Korean War on the British and West German economies, and the responses of the respective governments, says much about the institutional structures of the banking and monetary systems in both countries, and the relationship between those structures and the effectiveness of the anti-inflationary policies. The most obvious comparison is that in both countries a tighter policy was implemented only after the worst of the crisis was over. In their response to the crisis the BdL first attempted to restrict credit through an array of traditional measures. Only when these failed to achieve the desired results did they resort to tougher forms of credit restrictions: first through the banking guidelines and then through imposition of a reduction in bank lending with the threat of a withdrawal of central bank discounting facilities. It is probable, however, that these measures came too late to have any real impact on the level of inflation – although they did contribute to the stabilisation of the economy from the second quarter of 1951.

In Britain, the policy options open to the monetary authorities were more limited due to the necessity of encouraging production in specific sectors. This meant that in addition to technical measures designed to squeeze the clearing banks' assets – the forced funding operation, the interest rate rises and the institution of a target (not statutory) liquidity ratio of 30 per cent – the government sought to influence the direction of bank lending. Rather than assist in stabilisation, however, it seems that the measures adopted in Britain came as the economy started to adjust to the period of overstocking associated with the increased armaments expenditure, and may have accelerated the onset of a minor recession. In both countries, the major factor in the turn-around of the balance of payments in 1951–52 was the shift in the terms of trade.

The inflationary problems, the policies adopted and the outcomes of those policies were, to a significant extent, similar in the two countries here studied. The channels of policy communication and transmission were, however, notably different – as were the lessons learned in each country. In the German case, the BdL was able to formulate monetary policy independently and, ultimately, against the wishes of the government. Comparison with Britain in this period is instructive on this point. There, the Bank of England saw its role as protector of the banking system from the worst effects of government interference and restriction. Throughout the period of the Labour government it advocated the implementation of an orthodox monetary policy and resisted the imposition of a ceiling on bank advances. The Bank of England was therefore able to exert a degree of *de facto* independence. The result of the disagreement and need for compromise between the Bank and the government was a serious weakening in the authorities' ability to contain inflationary pressure during the period of high import prices in 1951.

In Germany, also, considerable weakness in the policy channels became evident. These were caused in the first place by the dual nature of the central bank system and by the inability of the BdL to enforce compliance with its monetary strategy on the LZBs and secondly by the nature of the German banking system itself. The banking system in the Federal Republic in this period was highly competitive. Given the desolate state of the capital market, the banks constituted the major source of funding for industry and they therefore had a powerful incentive to circumvent restrictions on their operation. The lesson for the BdL was that strong central control of the monetary system – adequately buttressed by the powerful threat of the withdrawal of discounting facilities – was necessary if it was to have a meaningful role in restraining inflation.[79]

In Britain, this lesson was not learned. The absence of a strong monetary authority able to impose its desired policy (regardless of whether that be an orthodox monetary squeeze or a ceiling on bank advances) clearly delayed the implementation of an effective anti-inflation policy. The path of the economy in 1951–52 owed little to the measures which were eventually introduced. The government, however, had a different perception of the events of 1952 and proclaimed that restrictions had been successful. It therefore failed to identify the debilitating weaknesses in the relationship between the various institutions and saw no need to overhaul the monetary policy mechanism. This failure had important repercussions during subsequent inflationary episodes. In 1955, for example, when inflationary pressure once more became very strong, the government turned to the combination of a tightening of monetary conditions and requests to the banks regarding their credit allocation decisions which they considered to have worked so well in 1951–52. This time, however, the banks took evasive action by selling off their investments – in many cases at a significant loss – in order to continue lending. With no change in the external conditions as there had been in 1952, the policy failed to check monetary growth and the Chancellor was forced to exert considerable direct pressure on the banks.[80]

The lesson of the Korean inflation in Britain and West Germany is not that an independent central bank (whether that independence is *de facto* or *de jure*) is more able to combat inflationary pressure than one which is government-controlled. Rather, it is that a strong and clear-cut policy transmission mechanism will be much more effective than one which is subject to disagreement, debate and compromise. Dow and Saville have recently suggested that, over the long run, monetary policy is essentially of little use in the fight against inflation.[81] In periods of stress, however, the ability to take decisive action and enforce (at least temporary) compliance from the banking system can be of crucial importance in averting a crisis.[82] The evidence in this paper suggests that where this mechanism is weak, the policy will have little chance of success.

NOTES

We would like to thank Edwin Green, Clive Lee, Dieter Lindenlaub, Neil Quigley, the participants in Professor Griffiths' research seminar at the European University Institute and the Economic History Seminar at the Victoria University of Wellington and an anonymous referee for helpful comments on earlier draft of this paper. We are grateful to the archivists of all the collections cited for assistance, to the holders of copyright material for permission to consult their records and to Mr Grosskopf and the Bank of International Settlements for their generosity.

1. See, for example, C.A.E. Goodhart, *Money, Information and Uncertainty* (2nd ed. 1989), Ch. XV. Dow and Saville have recently questioned whether monetary policy can have any meaningful long-term impact on inflation. J.C.R. Dow and I. Saville, *A Critique of Monetary Policy* (Oxford, 1988).
2. For a review of some of the literature and the issues on this point, see J. Woolley, 'Central Banks and Inflation', in L. Lindberg and C. Maier (eds.), *The Politics of Inflation and Stagnation* (Washington, 1985).
3. A.S. Milward, *The Reconstruction of Western Europe, 1945–51* (1984), p. 355 and 359–61.
4. W. Abelhauser, *Wirtschaftsgeschichte der Bundesrepublik Deutschland, 1945–1980* (Frankfurt, 1983), pp. 63–8; H.R. Adamsen, *Investitionshilfe für die Ruhr: Verbände und Soziale Marktwirtschaft*, 1948–1952 (Wuppertal, 1981), pp. 56–77; L. Erhard, *Prosperity through Competition* (1958), pp. 33–5. See also the meetings of the Allied High Commissioners with Adenauer: Wortprotokoll der Sitzung vom 16 Februar 1950 in Auswärtiges Amt. *Akten zur Auswärtigen Politik der Bundesrepublik Deutschland* (hereafter AAPBD), Vol. 1, pp. 102–17 and Wortprotokoll der Sitzung vom 2 März 1950 in AAPD, Vol. 1, pp. 118–42. See also Record of a Conversation with the Secretary of State, 15 March 1950, in *Documents of British Policy Overseas* (hereafter DBPO) series 2, Vol. 2 (1950), pp. 21–6.
5. J. Mitchell, *Britain in Crisis, 1951* (1963), pp. 60–1.
6. Erhard, *Prosperity through Competition*, pp. 40.
7. Hansard (Commons), 415, 29 Oct. 1945, cols. 43–158.
8. A. Cairncross, 'The Bank of England: Relationships with the Government, the Civil

Service and Parliament', in G. Toniolo (ed.), *Central Banks' Independence in Historical Perspective* (Berlin, 1988), p. 50.

9. His first sally in this direction was made even before his appointment; PRO, T233/481, 'Interest Rates, Credit Inflation and Budget Surplus', Jay to Cripps, 5 Nov. 1947.
10. Bank of England Archives (hereafter BoE), C40/685, Catto to Cripps, 15 Dec. 1948.
11. PRO, T233/481, Bank Deposits and Inflation; aide-memoire by Sir Kenneth Peppiat, 28 Jan. 1948.
12. Diary entry, 29 Sept. 1949, in A. Cairncross (ed.), *The Robert Hall Diaries, 1947–53* (1989), p. 88.
13. M. Pohl, 'The Dismemberment and Reconstruction of Germany's Big Banks, 1945–1957' in *Studies in Economic and Monetary Problems and on Banking History* (Mainz, 1988) p. 343–53; K.E. Born, *International Banking in the 19th and 20th Centuries* (Leamington Spa, 1983), pp. 312–3; J. Lanner, 'Changes in the Structure of the German Banking System', *Economica*, new series, Vol. 18 (1951), pp. 169–83.
14. V. Hentschel, 'Die Enstehung des Bundesbankgesetzes, 1949–1957: Politische Kontroversen und Konflikte', *Bankhistorisches Archiv* (1988), pp. 5–7.
15. Hentschel, 'Bundesbankgesetz', pp. 5–7.
16. R.E. Emmer, 'West German Monetary Policy, 1948–54', *Journal of Political Economy*, Vol. 63 (1955), pp. 52–69.
17. A provisional act was passed by the Bundestag in July 1951. Hentschel, 'Bundesbankgesetz', pp. 17–19.
18. Abelhauser, *Wirtschaftsgeschichte*, pp. 66–7.
19. M. Hogan, *The Marshall Plan: America, Britain and Reconstruction of Western Europe, 1947–52* (Cambridge, 1987) pp. 354–5. On the harmful effects of the British raw material stockpiling programme, see L. Pliatzky, *Getting and Spending: Public Expenditure, Employment and Inflation* (Oxford, 1982), pp. 13–14.
20. Hogan, *The Marshall Plan*, p. 393.
21. Archiv der Landzentralbank in Baden – Würtemburg (hereafter LZB), 61.2.37, Pfleiderer to Vocke, 5 Aug. 1950.
22. Historisches Archiv der Deutschen Bundesbank (hereafter HA), 2045, Sitzung des Direktoriums der Bank deutscher Länder, 3 Aug. 1950.
23. Erhard to Vocke, 2 Aug. 1950, in Ludwig-Erhard-Stiftung (ed.), *Die Korea-Krise als ordnungspolitische Herausforderung der Deutschen Wirtschaftspolitik: Texte und Dokumente* (Stuttgart, 1986), pp. 183–4.
24. LZB, 09.105, Platow-Brief, 5 Aug. 1950.
25. HA, 30, Protokoll über die 68. Sitzung des Zentralbankrats, 6/7 Sept. 1980; see also the verbatim record of the discussion, HA, 30.
26. E. Welter, 'Der Damm hält', *Frankfurter Allgemeine Zeitung*, 2 Sept. 1950; E. Welter, 'Die Kraft zur Anpassung', *Frankfurter Allgemeine Zeitung*, 16 Sept. 1950; E. Welter, 'Bollwerk Bundesrepublik', *Frankfurter Allgemeine Zeitung*, 23 Sept. 1950; LZB, 09.105, Anlage zum Platowbrief, *Platow Brief*, 23 Sept. 1950.
27. Adamsen, *Investionshilfe für die Ruhr*, pp. 84–98; O. Emminger, *D-Mark, Dollar, Währungskrisen: Erinnerungen eines ehemaligen Bundesbankpräsidenten* (Stuttgart, 1986), p. 48.
28. M. Schmitt, Aussenwirtschaftsprobleme der Bundesrepublik während der Korea-Krise', in Ludwig-Erhard-Stiftung, *Korea-Krise*, pp. 57–8.
29. 'Die Umsatzentwicklung im Einzelhandel seit Ausbruch des Korea-Krieges', *Wirtschaft und Statistik*, neue folge, Vol. 3 (1951), Textband, pp. 206–8; R. Hauf, *Von der Armenkasse zum Universal-Kreditinstitut: 125 Jahre Kreis- und Stadtsparkasse Neu-Ulm* (Neu Ulm, 1985), pp. 174–5.
30. Bundesarchiv (hereafter BA), 146/464, von Mangoldt to Blücher, 16 Sept. 1950.
31. The requirements on demand deposits were raised from 10 to 15 per cent and on time and savings deposits from 8 to 12 per cent. H. Schlesinger, 'Geldpolitik in der Phase des Wiederaufbaus (1950–58)', in Deutsche Bundesbank (ed.), *Währung und Wirtschaft in Deutschland, 1876–1975* (Frankfurt, 1976), pp. 567–8.
32. LZB, 61.2.37, Sandler-Weidmann, 28 Sept. 1950.
33. HA, 31, Protokoll über die ausserordentliche Sitzung des Zentralbankrats in Bonn im

Bundeskanzleramt, 13 Oct. 1950.

34. Schmitt, 'Aussenwirtschaftsprobleme', p. 58–9; HA, 32, Protokoll über die 71. Sitzung des Zentralbankrats, 18/19 Oct. 1950.
35. Extract from minutes of a meeting between Erhard and the Wirtschaftsausschuss der Allierten Hohen Kommission, 20 Oct. 1950, in Ludwig-Erhard-Stiftung, *Korea-Krise*, pp. 197–8. See also BA, 146/464, Podeyn-Blücher, 31 Oct. 1950.
36. BA, 146/499 note by Blücher, 25 Oct. 1950; BoE, OV34/35, Macdonald to Rootham, 31 Oct. 1950.
37. HA, 32, Protokoll über die 72. Sitzung des Zentralbankrats in Bonn im Bundeskanzleramt, 26 Oct. 1950. See also W. Vocke, *Memoiren* (Stuttgart 1973), pp. 154–5; Emminger *D-Mark, Dollar, Währungskrisen*, pp. 53–7.
38. For a discussion of these measures see Emmer, 'West German Monetary Policy', pp. 61–4.
39. Arbeitsgemeinschaft der Verbände des privaten Bankgewerbes-Bernard, 6 Nov. 1950; LZB, 109.06, Auszug aus einem Schreiben der Frankfurter Privatbankiers-Vorstand der LZB Hessen, 11 Nov. 1950; LZB, Protokolle Bankenrat und sonstige Sitzungen, 1947–51, Besprechung mit Vertretern der Kreditinstitut von Württemberg-Baden, 27 Nov. 1950; LZB, Freiburg 368, Hinte to Paule, 10 Oct, 1950.
40. HA, 3390, Wrede to Vocke, 7 Nov. 1950; HA, 3148, Kreditvolumen und Refinanzierungsbedarf', note by Schmidt, 7 Nov. 1950.
41. On the willingness of banks to finance the advance deposits, see for example: HA, 10449, Betr.: Einfuhrverfahren Bardepot', Anweisung No. 5, BdL-Vorstände der LZBs, 23 Dec. 1950; HA, 5407, Vorstand der LZB für Württemberg und Hohenzollern-Auslandsabteilung BdL, 5 Dec. 1950; 5407; BdL, *Monatsberichte*, March 1951, p. 6. See also LZB, 09.64, note for Pfleiderer, 7 May 1951; H. Schlesinger, 'Geldpolitik', pp. 570–1; E.A. Birnbaum and M.A. Quareshi, 'Advance Deposit Requirements for Imports', *International Monetary Fund Staff Papers*, Vol. 8 (1960), pp. 115–25.
42. E. Dürr, *Wirkungsanalyse der monetären Konjunkturpolitik* (Frankfurt 1960), pp. 139–40.
43. BA, 146/473, 'Vermerk betr: Defizit in der Europäischen Zahlungsunion', 16 Jan. 1951; LZB, 09.106, 'Die Wirkung einer Mindestreserveerhöhung auf die Banken', note by Wolf (undated).
44. BA, 146/473, 'Vermerk betr: Defizit in der Europäischen Zahlungsunion', 16 Jan. 1951; HA, 2015, Blücher to Vocke, 23 Jan. 1951; Vocke to Blücher, 27 Jan. 1951.
45. In the first instance the measure was restricted to this sector. Later the Sparkassen and the Kreditgenossenschaften were included. HA, 38, Protokoll über die 84. Sitzung des Zentralbankrats, 31 Jan. 1951.
46. 132. Kabinettssitzung der Bundesregierung, ausserhalb der Tagesordnung: 'Wirtschafts- und Devisenlage', Kurzprotokoll, 27 Feb. 1951, in Ludwig-Erhard-Stiftung, *Korea-Krise*, pp. 278–81.
47. HA, 39, Protokoll über die 86. und 87. Sitzung des Zentralbankrats, 24 and 28 Feb./1 March 1951.
48. Milward, *Reconstruction of Western Europe*, pp. 432–3.
49. Dürr, *Monetären Konjunkturpolitik*, p. 141.
50. HA, 41, Protokoll über die 90. Sitzung des Zentralbankrats, 29 March 1951.
51. LZB, 61.2.37, Auszug aus Vermerk über die Besprechung mit der Badischen Bank über die neuen Kreditrichtlinien, 7 Feb. 1951.
52. LZB, 61.2.37, Vorstand, LZB Württemberg-Baden-Hauptstelle/Zweigstellen, 27 Sept. 1950; Sandler-Weidmann, 28 Sept. 1950; LZB, 61.58/1, Ergebnis einer Besprechung mit den ersten Direktoren der Haupstellen am 22 Nov. 1950, 4 Dec. 1950.
53. HA, 3148, 'Vorschlag zur Verschärfung der Kreditrestriktionen', note by Wolf, 19 Feb. 1951; HA, 41, Protokoll der 90. Sitzung des Zentralbankrats der Bank deutscher Länder, 29 March 1951.
54. The LZB Berlin was just an associate member of the BdL system, because of the special status of Berlin; LZB, 61.2.37 Vocke to Pfleiderer, 6 Dec. 1950; Vocke to Bernard, 22 Jan. 1951.

55. LZB, 09.106, Schmidt to Pfleiderer, 6 Sept. 1951, attached note by Schmidt, 'Kreditpolitik am Scheideweg', 4 Sept. 1951.
56. Schlesinger, 'Geldpolitik', pp. 130–1.
57. K.J. Ehlen, *Filialgrossbanken: Entwicklung und Stellung im deutschen Kreditsystem* (Stuttgart, 1960), pp. 50–9.
58. For an example of this kind of argument, see the speech by Ernest Davies on the Bank of England Bill; Hansard (Commons), 415, 29 Oct. 1945, col. 60.
59. *Economic Survey for 1951*, (Cmnd. 8195, P.p. 1950–51), para. 24.
60. J.C.R. Dow, *The Management of the British Economy, 1945–60*, (Cambridge, 1965), p. 243.
61. Quoted in BoE, C40/687, note of CEO meeting, Committee of London Clearing Bankers, 16 July 1951.
62. Dow, *Managment of the British Economy*, p. 243.
63. *Economic Survey for 1951*, para. 93.
64. A. Cairncross, *Years of Recovery: British Economic Policy, 1945–51* (1985), pp. 234–5.
65. Dow, *Management of the British Economy*, pp. 237–8.
66. Midland Group Archives, Management Committee Files, Box ACC 200/3, notes on the Results of the Classification of Advances, May 1951.
67. Dow, *Management of the British Economy*, p. 62; Cairncross, *Years of Recovery*, pp. 229–30; M.F.G. Scott 'The Balance of Payments Crisis', in G.D.N. Worswick and P.H. Ady (eds.), *The British Economy in the Nineteen-Fifties* (Oxford, 1962), pp. 213–5.
68. BoE, G1/71, Governor's Notes, 3 July 1951; 31 August 1951.
69. BoE, OV9/503, Jacobssen to Niemeyer, 28 April 1951.
70. *Economist*, 5, 12, 19 May 1951.
71. *Banker*, July 1951.
72. PRO, T233/1684, 'Credit Policy', Trend to Eady, 25 Oct. 1951.
73. *Economic Survey for 1952* (Cmnd. 8509 P.P. 1951–52), paras. 108–10.
74. T. Geiger, 'The Next War is Bound to Come: Defence Production Policy, the Ministry of Defence and Defence Contractors, 1945–1957', in A. Gorst, L. Johnman and S. Lucas (eds.), *Contemporary British History, 1931–61: Adjusting to Consensus* (1991) provides evidence of bank lending to aircraft manufacturers.
75. F. Paish, *Studies in an Inflationary Economy: The United Kingdom*, 1948–61 (1966), p. 145.
76. *Economic Survey for 1953* (Cmnd. 8800, P.P. 1952–53), para. 59.
77. Cairncross, *Years of Recovery*, p. 229.
78. Dow, *Management of the British Economy*, pp. 73–5.
79. For a similar realization of the need for strength in a two-tier central banking system see N. Thygesen, 'Decentralization and Accountability Within the Central Bank: Any Lessons from the US Experience for the Potential Organization of a European Central Banking Institution?', in P. De Grauwe and T. Peeters (eds.), *The ECU and European Monetary Integration* (Basingstoke, 1989).
80. A detailed analysis of these policies throughout the 1950s is contained in D.M. Ross, 'The Clearing Banks and the Finance of British Industry, 1930–1959' (unpublished Ph.D. thesis, University of London, 1990), Ch. 4.
81. Dow and Saville, *A Critique of Monetary Policy*.
82. C. Allsopp has suggested that the 1970s indicate that the inflationary potential of external price shocks is more likely to be contained if central banks immediately adopt deflationary policies even at the risk of a recession; 'Inflation' in A. Boltho (ed.), *European Economy: Growth and Crisis* (Oxford, 1982).

The British Overseas Banks and Development Finance in Africa after 1945

FRANCES BOSTOCK
University of Reading

This essay examines the entry into medium- and long-term development finance in Africa by British overseas banks after the Second World War. There is a substantial literature on the origins of these banks, to which Professor Cottrell's contribution to this collection has added a further dimension.[1] Much less attention has been given to their subsequent evolution in the twentieth century and, indeed, it has tended to be assumed that they faded away along with the Empire.[2] In fact, the British overseas banks retained large multinational branch networks. According to one recent estimate, British overseas banks had some 3,710 foreign branches in 1970 – far more than those owned by banks of any other country.[3]

In much of the literature a stereotyped view of the policies of the British overseas banks persists. In Africa, Asia and Latin America, they are seen as being largely concerned with foreign trade finance and exchange banking, with strong links to expatriate business and very limited links to the indigenous economy. The reality is more complex. It is clear that considerable product innovation occurred over the twentieth century as banks adjusted their strategies to changing political and economic realities in the host economies within which they operated. Kate Phylaktis has examined this process in Cyprus, where the largest British overseas bank in the 1930s, Barclays (DCO), became involved in lending to agricultural co-operatives.[4] However, the organisational structure of British overseas banks, and their limited organisational capability, appear to have handicapped the process of product innovation after 1945.[5]

This study is a further contribution to the debate on the ability of the British banks to respond to changing economic and political realities. British overseas banks had first established branches in East, West and Central Africa in the 1890s. Their branch networks expanded in these colonial territories in the inter-war period, but their business continued to be focused largely on the needs of the colonial governments and the expatriate settlers or trading companies. After 1945, circumstances changed. Self-government and independence did not come to British colonial Africa until the 1960s, but in the lead-up there was considerable pressure on the banks to become more closely involved with the local economies. The upshot was the creation by several of the banks of development corporations, or institutions specialising in the provision of medium- and long-term finance, which were quite similar in some respects to the Industrial and Commercial Finance Corporation (ICFC) created in Britain in 1945. This study examines the origins of these corporations, before turning to a brief evaluation of their success.

II

A number of British overseas banks had branches in British colonial Africa after the Second World War. Table 1 lists the banks, their total assets and deposits, and the number of their branches in East and West Africa, in 1951, together with comparative assets and deposits data on two UK domestic banks.

TABLE 1

BRITISH BANKS IN COLONIAL AFRICA IN 1951

Institution	Total Assets (£m)	Total Deposits (£m)	Branches in East Africa	Branches in West Africa
Barclays DCO	504.4	442.9	25	19
Standard	325.6	268.2	25	–
National Bank of India	147.3	133.0	20	–
Bank of British West Africa	66.3	52.7	–	34
Lloyds Bank	1,367.2	1,169.6	–	–
Midland Bank	1,468.0	1,392.0	–	–

The most important institution was Barclays (DCO). This multi-regional bank had been created in 1926, with a branch network spanning the West Indies; most of Africa, including Egypt and the Sudan; Palestine; and the Mediterranean. It was partly owned and wholly controlled by Barclays, one the largest domestic banks.[6] The other three banks were not directly controlled by domestic banks. They were, in the British tradition of banking, specialists in particular geographical areas – the Bank of British West Africa (BBWA) in West Africa, the Standard Bank of South Africa in East, Central and Southern Africa, and the National Bank of India in India and East (and later Central) Africa.

In 1945 the stereotyped picture of the British overseas banks in colonial Africa was largely true. Unlike the situation in Latin America and Asia, they were still the principal (in many cases the only) modern commercial banking institutions operating in Britain's African colonies. Their role was the traditional one of British overseas banking: the finance of external trade, to facilitate which they collected local deposits and extended short-term credit against suitable security. In effect this meant that their lending was almost entirely focused on the needs of the expatriate trading companies, merchants and plantation owners, although they also acted as bankers to the colonial governments and as currency board agents. Their portfolio of local loans was relatively small, and considerations of liquidity led to a policy of sending a high proportion of their funds to London for employment. There were no central banks in British colonial Africa, merely London-based currency boards, and consequently no available liquid earning assets and no securities or security markets. On the other hand, the currency board system made it simple for the banks to invest their surplus funds in the London money market.[7] In addition, they were reluctant to engage in medium- or long-term lending, to extend credit to peasant agriculturalists, or to involve themselves in mortgage lending. One reason for this was the caution bred by traditional attitudes to the specialised nature of bank lending. Another was the absence in the underdeveloped economies in which the banks operated of suitable security for this sort of lending: in general the only asset possessed by the indigenous population was land, a form of security disliked by British banks at the best of times because it was not easily marketable and even more disliked in British colonial Africa because of complex land tenure systems among the indigenous populations.

In West Africa at least, the banks recognised the limitations of their traditional role and tried to enlist Colonial Office support for the formation of financial intermediaries to undertake the kind of lending which they themselves could not justify. As early as 1905, the Bank of British West Africa (BBWA) suggested to the Colonial Secretary that an agricultural mortgage corporation should be established, and offered to help form and finance such a corporation in co-operation with the Colonial Office (which in effect meant the Colonial Office being prepared to issue appropriate guarantees). Although the Colonial Secretary promised to consult the governments concerned, nothing was done and the idea was dropped. In 1914, BBWA approached the Colonial Office again, and this time a memorandum on the bank's scheme was sent to Nigeria, only to be rejected by the Colonial Governor, Lord Lugard, land tenure difficulties being the major obstacle cited. By 1938, both BBWA and Barclays (DCO) were still professing their willingness to participate in the formation of an agricultural banking intermediary if the overriding obstacle of adequate security could be overcome.[8]

The Colonial Office was as wary of the notion of establishing an agricultural bank in West Africa in 1938 as before the First World War,[9] despite the fact that by that time there were two government-sponsored Land Banks operating elsewhere in British colonial Africa: the Land & Agricultural Banks of Southern Rhodesia and Kenya, established in 1924 and 1931 respectively. The difference was that both the existing Land & Agricultural Banks were operating in settler economies, serving the needs of white farmers well versed in the imperatives of land mortgage lending.

During the Second World War, as Britain's dependence on its colonies for essential foodstuffs and raw materials grew along with the sterling balances of those colonies and their potential importance as a market for British capital goods, colonial investment became an important issue.[10] Major decisions were made by the Treasury, but the debate on how the issue should be tackled was largely centred in the Colonial Office. In 1942 a Colonial Research Committee was formed to look into the problem, and a year later the Colonial Economic Advisory Committee (CEAC) was set up to advise the Secretary of State on matters of general economic policy, especially with regard to programmes of economic development. Its membership was broadly based (including academics, administrators, businessmen, representatives of the trades unions and the Fabian Society, and two directors of British overseas banks – Sir William Goodenough, vice-chairman of Barclays (DCO) and Sir John Hay of Mercantile), reflecting government's wish to involve fully the private sector.[11] In his opening address to the Committee, the Colonial Secretary referred to 'the necessity of some kind of partnership between Government and private enterprise in colonial development'.[12]

While the Colonial Office was anxious to consult the private sector, and especially to tap the knowledge of the banks operating in the colonies about current investment levels and potential, officials were suspicious of private enterprise. In the case of the banks, there was growing criticism within the Colonial Office over the way that deposits gathered in the British colonies were being exported to the London money markets rather than re-invested in the colonies.[13] Ironically, the information on which a number of these criticisms were based was supplied to Colonial Office officials by the banks themselves in 1944.[14] Statistics provided by Barclays (DCO), for example, showed that in March 1939 the overall rate of its advances to deposits overseas was roughly 30 per cent. However, this covered wide variations in individual territories, from 129 per cent in Uganda, 64 per cent in Kenya and 88 per cent in Northern Rhodesia, to 14 per cent in Nigeria and five per cent in the Gold Coast. By the end of 1943, these percentages had plummeted, ranging from 14 per cent in Uganda for the three British banks there to three per cent in Gold Coast (two banks), Nigeria (two British banks and a local one) and Northern Rhodesia (two banks).[15] In contrast, the level of the banks' liquid resources in London had risen. While there was general acceptance of the fact that the wartime figures were distorted in so far as there was very much more money about and fewer outlets for it than before the war,[16] they highlighted an unsatisfactory situation. The problem for the banks (especially during the war) was that as banks of deposit in territories where they were often the only financial institutions they found themselves on the one hand receiving funds which were not usually deposited with commercial banks, and on the other having few suitable outlets for these funds if the rules of British banking orthodoxy were to be observed, and the safety of depositors' funds regarded.[17]

The problem generated both a public and a private sector response. The Colonial Office's deliberations resulted in the eventual formation of the Colonial (from 1963, Commonwealth) Development Corporation (CDC), established as an instrument for pump-priming to attract private investment to the colonies. Its purpose was described as being to investigate, formulate and carry out projects for developing the resources of colonial territories, with a view to expansion of production of foodstuffs and raw materials, or for other agricultural, industrial or trade development. Fundamental to this was that it should operate as a commercial organisation and engage in remunerative enterprises.[18]

Incorporated in January 1948 under the chairmanship of Lord Trefgarne, CDC's capital resources consisted of Exchequer loans amounting to £110 million, £100 million of which were long-term and £10 million short-term. This debenture capital, on which interest was payable, was to be a cause of irritation to CDC's second chairman, Lord Reith, who complained that while the Corporation was constituted to operate commercially, its 'financial circumstances and conditions are at variance with commercial practice and purpose'.[19]

Meanwhile, Barclays (DCO) had already taken steps of its own to generate ideas. In September 1942 an internal essay competition open to all members of staff was launched on the subject of 'The Bank in Relation to Post-War Colonial Development', with monetary prizes being offered for the best contributions. The issue of medium- and long-term lending and the need to identify local investment opportunities were topics addressed by a number of competitors, aware of the need for the bank to increase its stake in the overseas territories in which it was represented.[20]

The essay competition stimulated thought and discussion on topics outside the usual domain of a commercial deposit bank, and DCO's sponsorship of it argued a readiness to consider fresh approaches to the problems of development finance.

Thus it was that early in 1944 DCO took the old notion of sponsoring an agricultural credit institution for the colonies a step further. It put forward to the Colonial Office a specific plan for the setting up of a centralised institution responsible for capital investment in agriculture, indicating that it would be willing to subscribe to such an institution. In October of the same year, Julian Crossley of DCO reminded Colonial Office officials that these proposals had been mooted, and said that he saw no reason why the scope of the institution should be limited to assisting agriculture – it might equally well cover the development of local industry.[21] However, although the DCO plan was welcomed, it became clear that the idea of such a centralised investment institution was still no more than a topic for discussion within the Colonial Office, and might well remain so for some time to come. DCO therefore decided to go ahead on its own with the formation of a wholly-owned subsidiary to undertake medium- and long-term lending in the colonies, though on the understanding that there would be 'no over-lapping of function' with any official agency which might be established.[22] By November 1944 a draft constitution for a development bank with an authorised capital of £5 million was in place, and consultations with the Colonial Office, the Bank of England, the Treasury and the Board of Trade began.

Colonial Office officials were enthusiastic over DCO's plans, but objections were raised by the Bank of England, Treasury and Board of Trade. The Bank of England and Treasury preferred to see all the British overseas banks co-operating in such a development institution. They favoured a scheme whereby separate development banks would be established for each colonial territory, with all the British commercial banks operating in a territory combining to form that territory's institution.[23] There were several underlying reasons for this opposition to the Barclays' proposal. The Bank of England had been against the involvement of British clearing banks in overseas banking in the first place, on grounds of risk. There was still support for this official policy; and yet further involvement, especially in risky lending, was not looked upon with favour.[24] Moreover, the Bank of England from at least the early twentieth century had had a general preference for collusive agreements in all dimensions of British banking. It disliked the very idea of competition, and distrusted the instability that product innovation could bring.[25] As always, Treasury officials were worried about the impact on sterling of the proposal, afraid that any funds spent by the development corporation might be disruptive to the macro-economic policies being pursued.[26]

Despite these objections, Barclays (DCO) remained undeterred. During 1945, it patiently – and ultimately successfully – argued its case. Within a few months the Bank of England had withdrawn its objections. By the end of the year Treasury endorsement was indicated when approval was obtained from the Capital Issues Committee (appointed at the beginning of the war, when capital issues were prohibited except with Treasury consent, to advise the Treasury on the exercise of its power) for £1 million of the £5 million authorised capital of the new subsidiary to be issued at a 50 per cent premium. However, DCO also had to make compromises, agreeing, for example, to give an undertaking to the Colonial Office:

> to the effect that the Corporation will pay special regard to questions of government policy and will work in the closest touch with the Colonial Office and the Colonial Governments and will co-operate closely with the officials chiefly concerned, both in London and overseas.[27]

The Barclays Overseas Development Corporation (BODC) was incorporated on 10 January 1946, as a wholly-owned subsidiary of Barclays (DCO). The Corporation had its own Board of Directors under the chairmanship of Geoffrey Cockayne Gibbs, who was also a vice-chairman of DCO. Julian Crossley, deputy-chairman of DCO and one of the principal architects of BODC, became deputy-chairman, and initially there were three other directors. It had been hoped to appoint a London School of Economics professor, Arnold Plant, to the Board. He had good connections with the newly elected Labour government and was, in the words of Julian Crossley, 'one of the few who has survived the London School of Economics background with an unwarped mind and outlook', but Plant's appointment was vetoed by the University.[28] A London manager was appointed to the Corporation, and all propositions had to be submitted to London for approval. However, the London administration was otherwise kept to a basic minimum, and, overseas, BODC operated through DCO's existing branches which acted as its agents.

DCO's initiative in setting up a wholly-owned development corporation was soon emulated by two of the other British overseas banks operating in Africa – Standard Bank of South Africa and National Bank of India. The Standard Bank Finance & Development Corporation (SBFDC) came into existence in March 1947 and the National Bank of India Finance & Development Corporation (NBFDC) was registered in November 1948.[29] These latter institutions were, however, conceived on a smaller scale than the BODC in terms of the area they covered and their capitalisation. Both started with an authorised capital of £500,000 (fully issued in the case of Standard's Corporation, and £250,000 issued in the case of National Bank of India's Corporation), and, unlike BODC whose sphere of operation from the start covered all the territories in which Barclays (DCO) was represented, they largely confined their operations to East Africa where their parent banks were strongly competitive with Barclays (DCO).

The National Bank and Standard followed Barclays DCO more out of fear of competition than any genuine conversion to the cause of 'developing banking'. National Bank's chairman later recalled that NBFDC 'had been established in order to provide long-term finance as a means of protecting the banking business against the competition of Development Corporations established by Barclays DCO and the Standard Bank'.[30]

Standard's Corporation also got off to an unenthusiastic start, only being registered to do business in East Africa at first. It operated there as part of Standard Bank, without any separate management or staff but with a local advisory board of directors. Standard tried to persuade Barclays to form a 'rates agreement' for the development corporations – on the lines of the extensive collusive agreements in operation in the commercial banking domain in East Africa – but had a frosty reception from the larger bank.[31] In 1961, SBFDC was registered in Rhodesia, and thereafter its sphere of operations was widened to include all the African territories in which Standard Bank, and then BBWA (from 1965 part of the Standard Group), were represented.[32] The Corporation was reorganised in April 1966, and strengthened administratively 'to make it a more effective instrument for channelling medium and long term funds to development projects in Africa'. It became a separate entity within the Standard Group, based in London and, under the control of a newly-appointed managing director, responsible to a reconstituted SBFDC Board.[33]

Interestingly, while inter-bank competition in East Africa led to Standard and the National Bank of India following DCO's example, this did not happen in West Africa where DCO was in competition with the Bank of British West Africa. Instead of setting up a finance and development subsidiary, BBWA chose to enter the field of medium- and long-term lending directly. In January 1947, in view of the Nigerian government's tentative request that BBWA should contemplate a long-term development loan in the region of £3 million, the bank's board held a special meeting to consider the whole question of long-term lending and discuss the issue with the representatives of BBWA's shareholder banks, 'as the granting of long term facilities of such large figures represented a new departure in the Bank's policy'. They decided that a representative should be sent out to Nigeria to indicate the bank's favourable response to the prospect of granting the development loan, and also to discuss with government the bank's decision to involve itself in 'the new departure of long term Commercial or suchlike Loans similar to what is being done by Barclays Overseas Development Corporation'.[34]

Given the customary antipathy of commercial banks towards involving themselves in long-term lending, especially in developing economies, it seems surprising that BBWA should choose to involve itself in direct lending of this kind instead of setting up a subsidiary like that of Barclays (DCO). The reason for this decision remains unclear. However, the establishment of a statutory development board in Nigeria in 1946 (replaced by regional boards in 1949 after rather disappointing results) and of a local Co-operative Bank in the Gold Coast in 1944 must have influenced BBWA's thinking.[35] It seems likely that BBWA's pre-war willingness to help finance intermediary financial institutions was simply put into operation post-war when these intermediaries began to appear. In October 1946, for example, BBWA provided facilities for the newly-formed Gold Coast Co-operative Bank, to assist it to finance the seasonal cocoa crop.[36] Also, BBWA's traditional role as government banker in Nigeria and Ghana meant that the colonial governments and native administrations in West Africa naturally turned to it directly for developmental loans.[37] The question of establishing a special subsidiary to undertake these kinds of lending just did not arise.

Obviously, as in East Africa, the establishment of BODC provided an immediate stimulus for BBWA's 'new departure' into medium- and long-term lending, and indeed the competition provided by BODC continued to spur BBWA on: for example, in March 1948 when approving a loan of £66,000 for a 15-year period to the Accra Town Council for the purchase of new motor buses, BBWA's directors were animated by the fact that BODC had already provided the Town Council with a £40,000 loan for the same purpose and that if BBWA did not advance the £66,000 now required 'the Council would automatically place the business with Barclays Overseas Development Corporation'.[38]

When the officially-sponsored CDC came into being in 1948, BODC and SBFDC were already in existence and NBFDC was soon to be established, and at first there was some anxiety that the bank corporations and the government-funded corporation would be competitive. The Treasury's attitude towards a loan BODC had referred to it for sanction reflected this anxiety. Sanction was refused for this loan, arranged with the colonial government of Tanganyika for the erection of a canning factory, on the grounds that the project was more suited to the newly established CDC. The Colonial Office had to step in: it was pointed out to the Treasury that not only had 'the whole business ... been worked out with the Government of Tanganyika and Barclays before the C.D.C. existed', but that 'what the Treasury were trying to do in relation to Barclays seemed to be contrary to assurances which had been given to Parliament about the C.D.C. in relation to private enterprise'.[39]

In fact, there was never any intention that the bank development corporations and CDC should compete. Their roles were as different as the resources at their command. The bank corporations were, in essence, simply finance corporations, designed to experiment with the sort of lending that British commercial banking orthodoxy found difficult to contemplate. CDC was conceived on a much larger and broader scale, to foster and exploit colonial resources. In particular, it was expected to undertake projects itself where necessary; to initiate and act as principal,[40] a role never envisaged for the bank development corporations. Julian Crossley, by this time chairman of Barclays (DCO), was quite clear that the work of the government and bank corporations would be 'complementary rather than competitive'. 'We', he said, 'look forward confidently to much fruitful co-operation with the new Corporation'.[41]

TThe Standard and National Bank Finance & Development Corporations did not seem to evoke the same concern as BODC. Not only were they smaller and more limited in their scope, but, perhaps more importantly, they did not have the same intimate relationship with the Colonial Office. Colonial Office officials remained for some years very aware of this special relationship, which had grown out of the fact that BODC was the first in the field. When BODC was set up, 'considerable emphasis was laid by the Secretary of State on the desirability of constant consultation between the Corporation and the Colonial Office'. Moreover, sanction for the issue of BODC's initial capital was obtained from the Capital Issues Committee on the understanding that the Treasury expected the Colonial Office 'to keep a fair tab on what the Corporation are doing'.[42] Barclays (DCO) was equally conscious of the close connection. Announcing the formation of BODC, DCO's Chairman told his share-holders that the Corporation would 'welcome any suitable opportunities which may arise to co-operate with the appropriate Government Departments in the furtherance of development schemes which the Authorities may desire to encourage'.[43]

III

The three bank development corporations in Africa got off to relatively slow starts. To a certain extent this was because of the general economic difficulties in the immediate post-war years, when materials were scarce, transport difficult, and all loans of more than £50,000 had to be submitted to the Capital Issues Committee for approval. In addition, the field the development corporations were entering was a new one, and much preparation and organisation was necessary. Staffed by British bankers, they were also very cautious. BODC's guiding principle (and that of the other development corporations) came to be that any funds provided should be used for what it called 'genuine development purposes', and 'not merely to finance the transfer of ownership or to repay existing creditors, unless such operations reflect a subordinate measure of reconstruction in a scheme for further development'. Moreover, the Corporation did not expect, or consider it a sound policy, that it would bear the whole, or a disproportionately large share, of any medium- or long-term capital risk: applicants were generally expected to be in a position to contribute their share of their capital requirements, or to have enlisted reasonable financial support before approaching BODC.[44]

At the end of its first nine months, BODC had approved loans amounting to no more than £500,000, and none of these had yet been drawn upon.[45] From 1948, BODC's progress was much more rapid. By September of that year, its loans and investments amounted to £1.1 million, covering 58 projects in 17 territories in Africa and elsewhere, and its capital and reserves had risen to £3 million.[46] Moreover, the Corporation was beginning to stand on its own feet. It had made a small net profit (£12,992), over and above the loss carried forward from the previous year, and it was not being subsidised by DCO except in so far as it was not paying an agency fee for the use of DCO's branches.[47]

At this stage, the sort of projects BODC favoured in Africa appeared to be mainly agricultural or small-scale industrial. In the three months November 1948 to February 1949, new business undertaken ranged from an experiment to promote small businesses in the Gold Coast in partnership with the Gold Coast government (WA £12,000), to agricultural loans to individual (expatriate) farmers in Kenya (two at £12,000 each), an agricultural loan to a Tanganyikan sisal estate (£25,000), an agricultural loan (£25,000) to a Southern Rhodesian farming enterprise, and a loan to the English Press Ltd. in Kenya to acquire new premises for its printing works (£20,000).[48]

Table 2 gives a profile of BODC's lending in 1951 and 1958, breaking down the total number of loans by region, category of development, amount of loan, and period of loan. Unfortunately it is not possible to separate out the projects in Africa and other areas, except by region, but the general pattern is clear. The number of projects in each of the four classification categories was 212 for 1951 and 398 for 1958, and the amounts committed totalled £5,252,139 and £11,049,730 respectively.

The modest scale of its lending – and judicious selection of projects – enabled BODC to make commercial profits, and in 1952 the Corporation paid its first dividend, of three per cent. A year later, the dividend was increased to four per cent, and BODC was able to maintain payments at this level for the remainder of the 1950s despite making transfers to reserves from profits and increasing its capital. By 1956, BODC had a

TABLE 2
PROFILE OF BODC LENDING IN SEPTEMBER 1951 AND 1958

	1951			1958		
Classification	No.	Amount £'000	%	No.	Amount £'000	%
By Region						
East Africa	70	1,332	25.4	124	3,337	30.2
West Africa	13	588	11.2	23	1,046	9.5
Rhodesia/Nyasaland	15	732	14.2	60	2,378	21.5
West Indies	83	1,754	33.4	100	2,366	21.4
Other	31	846	15.8	91	1,923	17.4
By Development						
Agriculture/Forestry	49	1,339	25.3	52	2,042	18.5
Industrial	31	1,345	25.6	56	2,309	20.9
Building Development	61	1,278	24.3	147	2,521	22.8
Commercial	31	479	9.1	102	3,570	32.3
Other	40	821	15.6	41	608	5.5
By Amount						
£5,000 and Under	48	155	2.9	103	283	2.5
£5,000–£25,000	111	1,445	27.5	187	2,429	22.0
£25,000–£50,000	28	1,038	19.8	59	2,197	19.9
£50,000–£100,000	19	1,412	26.9	30	2,073	36.8
By Period						
5 Years and Under	50	999	19.0	181	2,641	23.9
6 to 10 Years	104	2,033	38.7	183	5,485	49.6
10 to 15 Years	39	1,407	26.8	19	936	8.5
Over 15 Years	12	453	8.6	13	1,029	9.3
Undated	7	360	6.9	12	958	8.7

Source: Barclays Bank Archives, and BODC Reports and Accounts.

paid-up capital of £6 million, and had lent and invested almost £14 million in the British territories in which it operated, of which £6.4 million had been repaid. Expansion continued. By 1958, BODC had lent and invested over £18 million and, as Table 2 illustrates, BODC's current commitments in that year amounted to more than £11 million. As in 1951, most of this financial assistance had been given to relatively small companies and firms which found it difficult to get accommodation from anywhere else, and by far the largest number of advances were below £50,000 and repayable within 10 years. However, while most loans in 1951, as well as most of the total amount lent, were going to projects in the areas of agriculture and forestry and of industry, by 1958 most loans were for building developments and the largest proportion of the money lent was for commercial projects. By 1958, too, lending to East Africa far outstripped that in any other region in or out of Africa, while the proportion of money lent to the Rhodesias and Nyasaland had also risen substantially. On the other hand, the proportion of total lending committed in West Africa had fallen.[49]

During the 1960s, BODC suffered a slow-down in the rate of repayment of its loans, and consequently of its profit growth. Unsettled conditions and political changes in Africa contributed largely to this, and by 1967 the Corporation was having to announce that it was making provision for loss on loans to Nigeria, Tanzania, and so on. Moreover, as a UK resident company it was not permitted to re-lend or remit funds which were accumulating in rebel Rhodesia.[50] Nevertheless, by the end of the decade the Corporation had provided a total of over £40 million of development finance since its inception in 1946 (a major proportion of which was in Africa as the figures quoted above indicate). The kind of projects undertaken was beginning to change by the end of the 1960s. A significant amount of BODC's funds was by then in hotels and tourism, and there was a move away from fixed interest to equity investments. Smaller development projects were being financed locally, many of them by 'mortgage lending institutions set up by our Parent Bank', and most new business consisted of providing finance for larger development projects, often in association with other development institutions.[51]

The development corporations of Standard and the National Bank remained modest affairs. By 1959, SBFDC's current loan and investment commitments had reached £1,883,852. The level of these commitments increased a little during the 1960s, and by the end of the decade, by which time the Corporation had expanded from its original East African locus, total loans current amounted to over £3 million.[52] Projects in which SBFDC was involved ranged from participation in a livestock scheme in Uganda in conjunction with the World Bank and other commercial banks, to setting up a project in Ghana in conjunction with the Ghanaian government to encourage commercial farming among Ghanaians, and loans totalling some £500,000 to the industrial sector in Tanzania covering such undertakings as the purchase of machinery, the erection of shops, offices and workshops, and the construction of an hotel. In addition, the Corporation was providing financial assistance for a number of official development projects in Tanzania, including the Kilombero Sugar Scheme, the Hale Hydro-Electric Scheme and the Makonde Water Project. By 1967, it had also invested in two of the largest textile mills in Uganda, one of which was owned by the government-sponsored Uganda Development Corporation and the other by Asian business interests, and (in conjunction with CDC and others) in the first locally-owned cotton mill in Kenya.[53]

The National Bank of India's development corporation was at first smaller than both its rivals. Essentially the parent bank (National and Grindlays from 1958) had no intention of expanding its business beyond the minimum. As its chairman commented in 1966, the Corporation's lending had been restricted 'to projects which were a means of defending existing business'.[54] Only in the mid-1960s was this policy reversed. In 1967, NBFDC's capital, which had risen by then to £1 million, was increased to £2 million, which made it double the size of SBFDC, and a more assertive strategy was adopted.[55]

In West Africa, where BODC's lending level continued to be substantially lower than in East or Central Africa, the Bank of British West Africa's direct involvement in medium- and long-term lending increased substantially between the end of the 1940s and 1965 when the bank was acquired by Standard. BBWA's historian observes that 'seen from the centre, the most significant change of policy was a massive shift of the Bank's resources from the London money market to West Africa' during this period, and ascribes this development partly to the decline in the value of British government securities post-war, leading to investment losses which counterbalanced the 'obvious risks of investing more heavily and for longer periods in West Africa'.[56] He quotes some typical investments which illustrated this trend: BBWA's investment in Gold Coast government Treasury Bills from 1954, to a limit from 1957 of up to £2 million; a £10,000 investment in ordinary shares in a company formed to build and operate an hotel in Lagos; participation to the extent of £1 million for a ten-year period in a local Nigerian railway loan issue in 1958; the subscription of £50,000 to the capital of the re-launched Nigeria Development Corporation in 1959, and participation in the series of development loans launched in Nigeria in subsequent years; and participation to the extent of £500,000 in the £5 millions of new finance supplied by a London syndicate of banks when the government of Ghana took over the mines in 1961.[57]

BBWA's long-term lending seemed largely to be concentrated on government developmental and infrastructural projects such as roads, railways, development corporations, and so on; the financing of local municipal projects such the purchase and operation of buses; and the provision of finance for such large private sector infrastructural projects as the construction of bulk oil storage plants and distribution centres in Nigeria, and the construction of the Volta Dam in Ghana.[58]

This article cannot offer a comprehensive critique of the performance of the development corporations or of BBWA's alternative direct lending strategies, but a number of points can be made. To start with, in terms of colonial development needs, what the banks provided was on a relatively small scale. Also, the pattern of BODC's regional lending in Africa, together with the terms and conditions imposed, made it quite evident that lending to Africans was on a relatively minor scale: both the number of projects undertaken in West Africa and their value was less than in either East or Central Africa where the banks were able to direct their lending, to a much greater extent, to the non-indigenous sector of the economy. On the whole, lending to Africans tended to be undertaken through the provision of finance by the parent banks to government development institutions, to government-sponsored development projects, or to co-operatives, although there were obviously some exceptions.[59]

Moreover, some of the projects promoted by the development corporations were of dubious developmental value. An illustration of such a project was BODC's loan to the Accra Club in early 1949, which, as a Colonial Office official observed, 'only doubtfully comes within the category of priorities for Colonial development'. On the other hand, he admitted, 'the fact that the Corporation are financing the rebuilding of the Club House ... relieves the Government of a certain amount of embarrassment, in that, while I think they admit the need for a Club House, they are unable to assist in financing it so long as it maintains discriminatory rules regarding entry'.[60] In 1955, the same official observed that it should be remembered that BODC and the other bank corporations were, after all, to all intents and purposes merely profit-making banking enterprises. BODC, he said, 'quite happily lends for the construction of cinemas no doubt on the grounds that they contribute to raising the standard of life'.[61]

On the other hand, their performance, if modest, takes on a better light if viewed in contrast with that of the state-run CDC. D.J. Morgan's official history of colonial development makes it clear that CDC's early years were little short of a disaster. A succession of varied projects, the majority of which were directly operated and managed by CDC, were launched too rapidly in a number of territories, without sufficient preliminary investigation (no feasibility studies or market surveys were undertaken, for example) or pilot schemes. Often management was inefficient. As a result, no fewer than 15 schemes had been abandoned by 1953, with the consequent write-off of capital, nine of which were in Africa (where the projects ranged from fisheries in West Africa and Nyasaland to a camel and sheep abattoir in British Somaliland). Moreover, much of CDC's remaining committed capital was tied up in schemes which were not expected to make a profit, and which had been undertaken because of pressure exerted by colonial governments.[62]

There were three basic reasons for this poor early performance, all of which were largely avoided by bank development corporations. Firstly, CDC had inordinately high overheads. In part, this was due to the size of its establishment; its UK staff in 1952 totalled 248, and its overseas staff 114, and total administrative costs were £457,642. This was a reflection of the complex functional rather than geographical organisational system set up under Lord Trefgarne.[63] The bank development corporations, in contrast, had relatively low overheads. They were able to operate through the branch systems of their parent banks, and thus to minimize the size of their own establishments. In 1952, for example, BODC only had a staff of nine in London, and four of its own representatives overseas. The other two bank development corporations were even smaller.

Secondly, CDC had a problem in defining its role. Given the fact that it functioned as an initiator and principal, it was not quite clear, as the Colonial Secretary minuted in November 1951, whether the Corporation was 'designated to be an investment, finance, or operating company'. In his opinion, it was desirable for CDC 'to emerge more as a finance, or investment, house with wide powers to help the local management rather than an operating company in the first instance'.[64] On the other hand, sometimes development opportunities occurred in circumstances where investment *and* operation or direction by CDC was the only way to get a project off the ground (a good example in Africa was the Swaziland Irrigation Scheme).[65] The bank development corporations did not face this ambiguity of role and function; they were simply financial enablers, and on a smaller scale and with more limited resources than CDC.

Thirdly, the CDC, particularly in its early years, made poor choices of projects. Its brief was so broad, and the pressures to forge ahead as fast as possible to develop colonial resources so intense, that there was a tendency to go 'in the direction of development almost for the sake of development'.[66] As a result, essential preliminary investigations were not carried out and 'many of the canons which govern commercial enterprises were ignored'.[67] The bank development corporations, for their part, were able to filter and sift through projects brought to them by potential borrowers, many of whom were already customers of, or at least known to, their parent banks, and choose those projects whose viability had been established. Mistakes were still made, especially in the early years, but not such expensive ones.

IV

The greater commitment of the British overseas banks to development financing in Africa post-1945 demonstrated, as did Barclays (DCO)'s involvement in financing agricultural co-operatives in Cyprus in the 1930s,[68] that they had sufficient flexibility to respond to changing host country conditions. The development corporations were one attempt to respond to the credit requirements of developing economies. BBWA's direct medium- and long-term lending, often to financial institutions established by local governments, was another variation. There was clearly a limit to their flexibility, however. Barclays (DCO) was basically the only bank seriously interested in the development corporation initiative. As the largest British overseas bank, with firm links with a major UK domestic bank, it had the resources and ability to act more entrepreneurially. Standard and National Bank were relatively unenthusiastic followers, at least until the 1960s, more concerned to prevent loss of market share than anything else. Moreover, the fact that the development corporations were commercial organisations which had to make a profit limited the kind of projects they were able to fund, although at least they avoided some of the mistakes of the public sector CDC.

The developmental impact of the bank development corporations is hard to assess. Certainly their contribution to solving Africa's development problems was minimal. However, they represented an advance over the previous short-term credit policies of the British overseas banks, and filled a gap in the financial structure of the British colonies in Africa at a time when there was a considerable and unsatisfied demand for small and medium-term finance in the private sector as well as for larger longer-term development finance. In recognising the 'propriety', in the words of African monetary and banking analysts Newlyn and Rowan, of allocating a certain proportion of their funds to the financing of longer term projects, the British overseas banks were performing a very necessary service, and their development subsidiaries were 'notable attempts to utilize the excess short-term funds of the banking systems to satisfy the excess medium-term demands which are characteristic of young economies'.[69]

The specialist development corporations are perhaps best seen as a transitory phenomenon. As the gap in the financial structure of the colonial and post-colonial economies was increasingly filled by a range of financial intermediaries, local and international, they changed the focus of their lending to meet the residual needs, until eventually, in the 1970s and 1980s, they were either subsumed into merchant banking subsidiaries, or themselves functioned as merchant banks. They had largely served their purpose. Conceived from the start as a quasi-political answer to the contemporary criticism that the overseas banks should be doing more to aid development and invest in their host economies, and never having been seen as a major source of profit, their parent banks were not averse to the development corporations' evolution into the more specialist institutions their increasingly sophisticated host economies required. Moreover, from the point of view of these host economies, they had become, in their original guise, redundant. On the one hand, local governments had assumed the major role in development financing. On the other, the onset of political independence and the establishment of central banks led rapidly to the localisation of the British overseas banks, and their adaptation to the imperatives of a locally-regulated financial environment.

NOTES

I am grateful to the Nuffield Foundation, whose grant SOC/181 (1986) made the research on which this article is based possible. I would also like to thank ANZ, Barclays and Standard Chartered plc for permission to cite material from their archives. Geoffrey Jones and an anonymous referee made helpful comments on an earlier draft.

1. P.L. Cottrell, 'The Coalescence of a Cluster of Corporate International Banks, 1855–1875', in this volume; A.J.S. Baster, *The Imperial Banks* (1929); idem, *The International Banks* (1934); F.H.H. King, *The Hongkong Bank in Late Imperial China, 1964–1902 (The History of the Hongkong and Shanghai Banking Corporation*, Vol. 1) (Cambridge, 1987); G. Jones, *Banking and Empire in Iran* (*The History of The British Bank of the Middle East* Vol. 1) (Cambridge, 1986); S.J. Butlin, *Australia and New Zealand Bank* (1961); C. Mackenzie, *Realms of Silver* (1954); J.A. Henry, *The First Hundred Years of the Standard Bank* (1963).
2. S. Strange, *Sterling and British Policy* (1971), p. 166.
3. G. Jones, 'Banks as Multinationals', in G. Jones (ed.), *Banks as Multinationals* (1990), p. 31.
4. K. Phylaktis, 'Banking in a British Colony: Cyprus 1878–1959', in *Business History*, Vol. XXX (1988), p. 425.
5. G. Jones, 'Competitive Advantages in British Multinational Banking', in Jones, *Banks as Multinationals*, p. 50.
6. J. Crossley and J. Blandford, *The DCO Story* (1975); Jones, 'Competitive Advantages', pp. 35–6.
7. See, for example, W.T. Newlyn, *Money in an African Context*, (Studies in African Economics; Nairobi, 1967), Ch. 4.
8. PRO, CO852/135/1, minute by Sir H. Moore, 28 Oct. 1938.
9. Ibid., minute by Sir H. Moore, 2 Nov. 1938: the difficulties for the banks of granting long-term advances without recognisable mortgage or other security was pointed out, the implication being that the necessary government guarantees would not be forthcoming.
10. See for example, PRO, CO852/554/7, Treasury memo of Jan. 1944, and minute by W.A. Lewis, 2 Feb. 1944.
11. A full list of members may be found in PRO, CO 852/510/29.
12. PRO, CO852/510/30, Sept. 1943.
13. See, for example, PRO, CO 852/554/1, minutes by W.A. Lewis, 1 June 1944 and 16 Aug. 1944, and by G.P.W. Lamb, 5 June 1944.
14. Ibid., J. Fisher to S. Caine, 15 May 1944, enclosing banking statistics.
15. Percentages derived from statistics for Barclays DCO (March 1939) and all reporting banks for Sept./Dec. 1943 in Ibid.
16. Ibid., minute by A. Emanuel, 5 Oct. 1944, reporting a meeting between various officials and Julian Crossley of Barclays DCO.
17. See, for example, Newlyn, *Money in an African Context*, Ch. 4.
18. PRO, CO852/1579, Information on existing avenues of loan finance for development being compiled for colonial government finance officers, 1955; see also, for the history of CDC, D.J. Morgan, *The Official History of Colonial Development* (1980), Vols. 1–5.
19. Morgan, *Colonial Development*, Vol. 4, p. 99.
20. Crossley and Blandford, *DCO Story*, p. 140; Barclays Bank (D.C. and O.), *A Bank in Battledress* (private circulation, 1948), p. 153.
21. PRO, CO852/554/1, minute by A. Emanuel, 5 Oct. 1944.
22. Barclays Bank Archives (hereafter, BBA), 38/209, Sir Julian Crossley Diaries, 23 Nov. 1944.

23. Ibid., 30 Nov. 1944, 26 Feb. 1945, 11 April 1945.
24. Ibid., 27 Dec. 1944; Jones, 'Competitive Advantages', p. 47.
25. G. Jones, 'Competition and Competitiveness in British Banking 1918–1971', in G. Jones and M. Kirby (eds.), *Competitiveness and the State* (Manchester, 1991).
26. BBA, 38/209, Sir Julian Crossley Diaries, 16 Feb. 1944; Bank of England Archives, G1/157, File of Barclays Development Co., Memorandum of O.E. Niemeyer, 6 Dec. 1944.
27. PRO, CO852/1049/3, Circular Telegram from Secretary of State for the Colonies to the various Colonial Governments, 27 April 1946.
28. BBA, 38/209, Sir Julian Crossley Diaries, 15 Oct. 1945.
29. Standard Bank of South Africa, Report and Accounts for the year ended March 1947, Chairman's Statement; National Bank of India, Report and Accounts for the year ended December 1948, Chairman's Statement.
30. Grindlays Bank Archives, ANZ, Meeting of Directors of the National and Grindlays Finance and Development Corporation Ltd., 11 Oct. 1966; G. Tyson, *100 Years of Banking in Asia and Africa* (1963), pp. 191–2.
31. BBA, 38/209, Sir Julian Crossley Diaries, 19 Nov. 1947.
32. Standard Chartered Archives (hereafter SCA), The Standard Bank Group, *London Newsletter*, No. 2, Sept. 1968, pp. 14–15.
33. Standard Bank, Annual Reports and Accounts for 1966 and 1967, Chairman's Statement.
34. SCA, BAC S/90, BBWA History Files, Fry's Digests of BBWA Board Minutes, private board minute of 29 Jan. 1947; Richard Fry, *Bankers in West Africa*, (1976), p. 168.
35. W.T. Newlyn and D.C. Rowan, *Money and Banking in British Colonial Africa* (Oxford, 1954), pp. 127–8; E.E. Jucker-Fleetwood, *Money and Finance in Africa* (1964), pp. 156–7.
36. SCA, BAC S/90, BBWA History Files, Fry's Digests of BBWA Board Minutes, minute of 9 Oct. 1946.
37. Ibid., private board minutes of 29 Jan. and 26 March 1947.
38. Ibid., board minute of 10 March 1948.
39. PRO, CO852/1049/3, minute by K.E. Robinson, 3 June 1948; see also, minutes by R.W. Newsam and R. Newton of 26 and 28 April 1948 respectively.
40. PRO, CO852/1579, Information on Existing Avenues of Loan Finance for Development being Compiled for Colonial Government Finance Officers, 1955.
41. Barclays Bank (D.C. and O.) 22nd Ordinary General Meeting, 19 Dec. 1947, Chairman's Statement.
42. PRO, CO 852/1049/3, minute by A. Emanuel, 1 Feb. 1949.
43. Ibid., circular letter from W.G. Goodenough to Barclays (DCO) shareholders, 17 Dec. 1945.
44. PRO, CO852/1579, Information on Existing Avenues of Loan Finance for Development being Compiled for Colonial Government Finance Officers, 1955: BODC; SCA, The Standard Bank Group, *London Newsletter*, No. 2, Sept. 1968, pp. 14–15.
45. Barclays Bank (D.C. and O.) 21st Ordinary General Meeting, 20 Dec. 1946, Chairman's Statement.
46. Barclays Overseas Development Corporation, Statements of Accounts, Directors' Report, to be presented at the Barclays (D.C. and O.) 23rd Ordinary General Meeting, 14 Dec. 1948.
47. Barclays Bank (D.C. and O.) 23rd Ordinary General Meeting 1948, Chairman's Statement.
48. PRO, CO852/1049/3, BODC, List of New Business arranged since the List given in Letter of 4 Nov. 1948.
49. Barclays Overseas Development Corporation, Reports and Accounts.
50. Barclays (D.C. and O.), Annual Reports and Accounts, especially 1967.
51. Ibid., 1969 and 1970.
52. Standard Bank Finance and Development Corporation, Balance Sheets, appended to Standard Bank of South Africa Reports and Accounts.
53. Standard Bank, Reports and Accounts for the year ended March 1968, Chairman's Statement. SCA, Tanzania Box, Nationalisation of Banks File, letter to President

Nyerere, 21 Feb. 1967, detailing SBFDC's liabilities and commitments in Tanzania; East Africa Box, memo to H.R. Reed from Standard Bank Economic Dept., 29 Sept. 1967.

54. Grindlays Bank Archives, ANZ, Meeting of Directors of the National and Grindlays Finance and Development Corporation Ltd., 11 Oct. 1966.
55. National Bank of India (subsequently National & Grindlays Bank), Reports of the Directors and Balance Sheets.
56. Fry, *Bankers*, p. 234.
57. Ibid., pp. 234–5.
58. SCA, BAC S/90, BBWA History Files, Fry's Digests of BBWA Board Minutes post 1945, passim.
59. PRO, CO852/1049/3, Lists of Projects undertaken by BODC.
60. Ibid., minute by A. Emanuel, 1 Feb. 1949.
61. PRO, CO852/1579, minute by A. Emanuel, 31 Aug. 1955.
62. Morgan, *Colonial Development*, Vol. 4, pp. 92–5, 220.
63. Ibid., pp. 96–8.
64. Ibid., Vol. 2, pp. 368–9.
65. Ibid., Vol. 4, p. 194.
66. Ibid., Vol. 2, p. 367.
67. Ibid., Vol. 4, p. 100: comment by Colonial Secretary in the House of Commons on 17 July 1953.
68. Phylaktis, 'Banking in a British Colony', p. 425.
69. Newlyn and Rowan, *Money and Banking*, pp. 138–40.

The House of Morgan Redivivus?: The Abortive Morgan International 1972–73

KATHLEEN BURK
University College, London

In 1984 the Office of Fair Trading forced the International Stock Exchange in London to end certain restrictive practices. One result was a renewed interest by foreign institutions in the possibilities of London, and a number bought equity in, or the whole of, British-owned financial institutions. Notable by their absence in this market were the American Morgan banks, J. P. Morgan & Co. and Morgan Stanley. It is impossible to know for certain why the Americans remained aloof, but strong corporate pride and confidence in their ability to continue playing a major role in London without native help must have influenced any internal discussion. For Morgan Grenfell, the situation was slightly more complicated. They knew that they did not relish foreign ownership nor even foreign influence, and they knew this because most of the main decision-makers still in the bank in the mid-1980s had been forced to decide on just this issue in the early 1970s. Cultural differences had proved too great, and sheer British – and even European – nationalism too strong to allow an Anglo-American merger. Only the need to fight off Japanese and French predators in 1988 forced them into a German one, with the Deutsche Bank.

During the first decades of the twentieth century the House of Morgan was, by common consent, the most powerful international banking house in the world. Possessing both capital and expertise, and with allied banks in New York City, London and Paris, it was pre-eminently the bank to which governments, great corporations and utilities turned when they needed to raise funds. The American Banking Act of 1933, however, required the separation of investment and commercial banking; the consequences were, first, the separation of Morgan Grenfell from J.P. Morgan & Co., and second, the carving out of Morgan Stanley from the latter. By 1936, therefore, the House of Morgan was no longer a single entity, and the three banks began to go their separate ways.

They concentrated on their domestic markets until the 1960s, when the return of currency convertibility in Europe, the activities of multinational corporations and the development of the Eurodollar market again stimulated the growth of international banking. They increasingly looked beyond their home markets and thereby re-discovered the attractions of co-operation. There were several joint ventures, and this led them by the early 1970s to consider whether the banks might not best serve their clients, as they put it, by uniting once again for international business. The upshot was an attempt to build on the existence of the 'Morgan family' and establish a Morgan International to exploit the possibilities. But conflicts of interest – and the refusal of Morgan Grenfell and the Bank of England to countenance the loss of the London bank's independence – doomed the attempt, and the eventual result was that the banks formally and finally separated.

I

The House of Morgan had its beginnings in 1838 when the American dry goods merchant, George Peabody, bought a supply of steel pens and foolscap paper, and a cashbox, and opened a counting-house at 31 Moorgate in the City of London. In 1854 he took as his partner another American, J. S. Morgan; by 1864, when Peabody retired from the bank, it was the leading American house in London. The bank now became J. S. Morgan & Co., and made its reputation as a banker to governments – and a great deal of money – by raising a loan for the besieged French government in 1870. By the time the bank became Morgan Grenfell in 1910, when the Englishman E. C. Grenfell became the senior resident partner, it was one of the five or six leading merchant banks in London.

During the last decades of the century, the London bank established close relationships with banks in New York and Paris. The son of J. S. Morgan, J. Pierpont Morgan, was asked by the senior partner of Drexel & Co. of Philadelphia and New York to join their firm as a senior partner. Thus was established in 1870 Drexel, Morgan & Co. of New York City, which in 1890, with the retirement of the senior Drexel, became J. P. Morgan & Co. At the same time Pierpont Morgan became a partner in Drexel, Harjes & Co. in Paris; this became Morgan, Harjes & Co. in 1890 as well.[1]

Over the subsequent 50 years, the House of Morgan came to dominate international merchant and investment banking. J. P. Morgan & Co. held by far the predominant position in the US, and could almost at will call on the resources of American finance; Morgan Grenfell was one of the most important merchant banks in London, and had some claim to being considered the predominant international issuing house there, as well as a pioneer in domestic corporate finance; Morgan Harjes et Cie, while less important in Paris than either J. P. Morgan & Co. in New York or Morgan Grenfell in London, nevertheless was a prominent underwriting house and provided a link with another important European capital market. The three banks were strong independently, but infinitely stronger taken together, a point which all partners acknowledged. Furthermore, the links between the partners, and particularly between J. P. Morgan Jr. and E. C. Grenfell, were strong and intimate, a situation which made the enforced break between the firms after 1933 a personal blow to many of the partners.

The Depression had brought hundreds of banking failures in the US, and a study by the Federal Reserve ascribed many of them, probably wrongly, to speculative investments by the banks in low grade bonds. Congress concluded from this that banks must be prevented from taking such risks, and must therefore make a choice: they could either be commercial banks, taking deposits and making loans, or they could be investment banks, issuing securities; they could not do both.[2] With the passing of the Banking Act of 1933 (the Glass-Steagall Act), then, J. P. Morgan & Co. had to choose, and the partners opted to remain a commercial bank rather than a securities house. This had repercussions both in London and in New York.

It affected London because the choice was applicable outside as well as inside the USA. The American partners were advised that it would be improper for them to continue as the principal shareholders and executive officers of a British bank with unlimited liability, an important part of whose business was issuing and underwriting, since they were prevented from engaging in this business in the USA. It was decided that the only way to maintain the close association between the two houses was to convert Morgan Grenfell into a limited liability company, thereby removing the risk which worried Congress. This was done, and thereafter J. P. Morgan & Co. held one-third of the management shares. The closeness remained for the remainder of the decade, since it was found to be legally permissible for J. P. Morgan Jr to remain a member of the board. But by 1943 both he and Grenfell were dead, and the close personal relations between London and New York necessarily began to fade, while the business relationship was abruptly curtailed by the war.[3]

The change in New York was even more far-reaching. The firm postponed a decision for more than a year, although eschewing the issuing of securities, while it agonised over what to do. In the end J. P. Morgan & Co. remained a commercial bank, announcing in September 1935 that several members of the Morgan Bond Department would leave to form a securities house, to be called Morgan Stanley. The latter was seen by Wall Street as inheriting the authority of the parent firm – certainly most of the start-up capital was provided by Morgan partners – and in its first year of operation Morgan Stanley handled $1 billion in issues, or a quarter of the year's total in the American money market. By the late 1930s, many of J.P. Morgan & Co.'s banking clients had come to Morgan Stanley for securities work, and it was clearly one of the major Wall Street players.[4]

By the time of the Second World War, then, although the two New York banks and the London bank were beginning to travel on separate paths, links were still close and would remain so for some years. Indeed, the immediate post-war period saw attempts between Morgan Grenfell and J.P. Morgan to try and work together abroad by means of joint ventures, but with no very great success. Both banks were working under some restraint, in particular a distinct lack of capital.

Morgan Grenfell were labouring under the heavier restrictions. Except for a short period of six weeks during July–August 1947, sterling was inconvertible until 1959, when restrictions were lifted on current, but not capital, account. Thus any loans or investments abroad had to be agreed to by the Treasury, which normally required that money for such investments be found abroad. This tended to limit what Morgan Grenfell could do. For example, in 1949 they joined with two other English firms, Lazard Brothers and Consolidated Zinc, to raise money in Australia in order to establish the first issuing house there. To expand, they had to take on Australian partners, and this lessened control considerably, as well as diluting earnings, and eventually Morgan Grenfell sold their share.[5] They had an analogous experience in Canada when, at the suggestion of J.P. Morgan & Co., with whom they were discussing ways of setting up business there, Morgan Grenfell and Baring Brothers joined with a finance and issuing house in Toronto to set up a new house. But again, expansion had to come from Canadian resources, and in addition, the Canadian government pushed for such businesses to be turned over to Canadians. The Morgan Grenfell shareholding drifted down, and they eventually sold out.[6]

J.P. Morgan & Co. were in a much better position to expand abroad. For one thing, they already had a one-third shareholding in Morgan Grenfell, as well as the wholly-owned Morgan et Compagnie in Paris (the name had been changed from Morgan Harjes et Cie in 1926, with the death of the senior French partner Herman Harjes). But they felt constrained by a lack of capital, and what they had to lend was easily disposed of in the USA. But this all changed in 1959, when J.P. Morgan & Co. merged with the rich but lazy Guaranty Trust Co., a bank four times its own size, with whom they had always had close business and personal relations. The new Morgan Guaranty was the world's largest wholesale bank, with over $4 billion in deposits. (It also presented a new threat to Morgan Grenfell in its own market, since Guaranty Trust had had a thriving London office since the turn of the century.)[7]

The establishment of the new bank more or less coincided with changes in the international economic environment which encouraged overseas expansion. 'In the 1950s', as one writer has put it, 'so long as America was rich and other countries poor, bright young Morgan bankers avoided international banking'.[8] By 1960 the climate had changed, with convertibility for the European currencies, and the accelerated thrust overseas by American multinational corporations. Furthermore, the 1960s saw the rapid growth of the new Eurodollar market, fed by American spending abroad, both governmental and private, and encouraged by decisions made by the government for domestic reasons. One was 'Regulation Q', dating from the 1930s,[9] by which the Federal Reserve limited the amount of interest US banks could pay on deposits. One response was for London banks in particular to bid for American dollars by offering higher rates of interest, and then to re-lend the dollars back to American companies to use abroad. Another limitation was that banks in the USA were forbidden to pay interest on deposits held under 30 days; in 1961 was invented the 'negotiable certificate of deposit' that matured in more than 30 days, and in this way banks could pay interest. Furthermore, CDs could be traded, and their use revolutionised the way commercial banks, such as Morgan Guaranty, could operate. Now they could sell CDs wholesale worldwide to finance their lending, rather than be constrained by the domestic money market.

The 1960s, then, saw a vista of accelerated business opportunities outside of the USA, particularly in Europe, combined with a rapidly growing pool of money, a situation which both Morgan Guaranty and Morgan Grenfell were keen to exploit. In November 1960 J.E.C. Collins, a partner in Morgan Grenfell, met Julian Allen, Morgan Guaranty's Vice President of European Affairs. The idea was to establish an investment bank – a *banque d'affaires* – in Paris. Morgan et Cie had incorporated in 1945, and now as Morgan Guaranty Paris it was not allowed, because of the Glass-Steagall Act, to participate in underwriting, formerly the Paris office's most profitable business. Therefore, Morgan Guaranty now wanted to establish a new organisation, in which its international subsidiary, Morgan Guaranty International Finance Corporation, would have a large minority interest, but in which the major shareholding would be held by European banks.

Morgan Grenfell, too, were keen on the idea, but first there was a hurdle to be vaulted: the Bank of England. In normal circumstances Morgans would have received their agreement, since the proposed investment in the EEC was the type of thing the Bank wanted to see; but in October 1961 current exchange control regulations would not permit it, so Morgan Grenfell had to bide their time until conditions changed.[10] In January 1962 they tried again, asking permission to subscribe for a 30 per cent interest in a new *banque d'affaires*, Morgan et Cie S.A. The other shareholders were to be Morgan Guaranty International Finance Corporation, with a 40 per cent shareholding, and two Dutch banks, each with 15 per cent. This time the Bank was a bit more helpful: permission was granted, as long as the money was found by borrowing outside the Scheduled Territories (essentially the sterling area), on terms which would not require repayment until exchange controls permitted funds to be remitted from the UK. The funds were loaned to Morgan Grenfell by Morgan Guaranty, although in the end Morgan Grenfell held only 15 per cent of the shares, with the two Dutch banks holding 15 per cent and Morgan Guaranty International holding the other 70 per cent.[11]

By 1963 Morgan et Cie S.A. were open for business. According to Morgan Guaranty, 'the new company should attempt to improve methods of distributing stocks in Europe, patterned, where applicable, on American practice. It would be desirable to introduce into the company some first-quality young American investment banking talent'.[12] The men they put in did not recognise, or chose not to recognise, national demarcation lines, and as a consequence they came into conflict with German banks and the Swiss government.[13] Indeed, the conflict with Deutsche Bank apparently so undermined Morgan Guaranty's confidence that they did not return to Euromarket issues for more than a decade.[14] This was the only major set-back, however, and in the three-and-a-half years of Morgan et Cie's independent existence they participated in and sometimes co-managed over a hundred issues in various currencies, including a score of Eurodollar issues. There was a surge of such issues in the autumn of 1965, after the imposition by the US government of the voluntary foreign credit restraint programme in early 1965, which was intended to limit the outflow of capital from the US in order to help the American balance of payment deficit.

The rapid growth of this business piqued the interest of Morgan Stanley. By far the most insular of the Morgan banks, until 1966 they lacked a single European office, when they secretly set up a joint venture with Banca d'Italia. Indeed, they had twice refused the chance to take a share in Morgan et Cie, in 1963 and March 1966; but when the opportunity came again later in the year, they changed their mind. The US authorities had ruled that Morgan et Cie could not take part in a number of proposed operations, a major obstacle being the Trust Indentures Act of 1939, which prevented Morgan et Cie from underwriting the securities, even in Paris, of any company for which the Morgan Guaranty Trust acted as a trustee. This, of course, was no small problem, since the Morgan Guaranty trust department acted for a substantial number of American companies. Negotiations with Morgan Stanley therefore received new life, and in due course a new company was set up in Paris, called Morgan et Cie International S.A. (MECI). This was to be two-thirds owned by

Morgan Stanley and one-third by Morgan et Cie; Morgan Grenfell's share in the new company would thus be five per cent.[15] From January 1967, then, MECI was essentially under the control of Morgan Stanley, who soon brought in their own team to run it. Fortunately for them, their advent coincided with a Eurobond boom, and MECI developed into a powerful Eurobond issuing house.[16]

Morgan Stanley's growing success in Paris happened to coincide with a change at the top in the bank in New York, when Robert Baldwin became the chief executive in 1970. Aggressive and ruthless, he encouraged the shedding of traditions and the cultivation of a hungry search for business. Morgan Grenfell, too, had recently acquired a new chief executive, when Sir John Stevens joined the bank from the Bank of England in 1967. Stevens emphasised the need to divert significant resources into overseas developments as part of his drive to increase the banking side of Morgan Grenfell, and in particular he believed that the London bank should look on Europe as its future home market.[17] Both banks, then, believed that they might have something to gain from co-operation in international markets, and in January 1972 embarked on very secret negotiations to that end – secret from all but a few in their own banks, and, in the first eight months, secret especially from Morgan Guaranty.

II

On 16 and 17 January 1972, Sir John Stevens and three managing directors of Morgan Grenfell, Kenneth Barrington, Philip Chappell and Christopher Reeves, met four partners of Morgan Stanley, Sam Payne, Frank Petito, Bill Sword and Jack Evans. In view of the fact that Morgan Stanley were reviewing their business, one result of which might be that MECI (their Eurobond house) would transfer their office from Paris to London, it is probable that the initiative came from them. The purpose of the meeting was to consider possible areas of co-operation, which might even include some form of share exchange.[18] A week later, 33 of the 34 Morgan Stanley partners had what was termed a 'planning Friday', in which they discussed long-term strategy. Bill Sword then telephoned Barrington to tell him that 'they were unanimous that the Morgan "family" had a unique opportunity to provide some form of international financial service to meet the needs of worldwide business and were very enthusiastic to continue exploring it with [Morgan Grenfell]. They were very conscious of the possible complications if they acquired a major involvement in an accepting house business and this would be one of the aspects that they would have to look at most closely'.[19]

The 'complication' to which they referred was the fact that the Bank of England forbade a foreign bank to own more than 15 per cent of an accepting house;[20] a special exemption was made for Morgan Guaranty's one-third ownership of Morgan Grenfell, since it pre-dated the rules, but Morgan Stanley would be another matter. Indeed, after this obeisance to the rule in the early stages of the negotiations, Morgan Stanley acted as if it were not an insuperable obstacle; they seemed to believe that although Morgan Grenfell might lose membership in the Accepting Houses Committee, no real damage would result. In the end, this was one of the rocks on which the negotiations would founder.

Another rock would be Morgan Stanley's drive for control. This emerges in Chappell's early assessment of Morgan Stanley: 'the overriding impression is one of developing business with a limited range of foreign and US corporations and governments. They have not been, on their own admission, innovative – but when their business relationship has been threatened by more aggressive houses developing a new area of business they have moved in in strength and done more business with more expertise than their competitors: MECI is a prime example ... They have the same attitude as us in controlling from the beginning to the last signature the whole course of a deal ... The overwhelming impression is one of a group which combines expertise with energy (the travel bill must be enormous) and flair, and which is looking for a new style, partly because of a change in senior management [presumably a reference to Baldwin] and partly because the world gets smaller. They do obviously appreciate many of the different things that we do, as well as seeing London as a place where they must be adequately represented'.[21]

There was, however, no sense of urgency in the early talks. As Stevens predicted in mid-February, 'I sense that our talks with Morgan Stanley will continue to lumber for some time', primarily because no one really knew what they wanted from them. Stevens visited Morgan Stanley on 10 and 11 February 1972, and realised that the 'problems lie in finding common ground between our respective objectives. Morgan Stanley want to concentrate on multinational corporations and stable foreign governments and to take such an interest in Morgan Grenfell as will enable them to offer a better service to such clients. From this it follows that our corporate finance department is the most interesting to them. They would prefer to split us into two units, if this did not weaken our overall standing. They regard MECI as the ideal model and would aim at a majority holding in us if practicable'. They also apparently agreed that in business getting, Morgan Grenfell was more ingenious, relying on new ideas and good information, while Morgan Stanley was more inclined to follow the bulldozer approach following on the heels of someone else's idea. According to Stevens, 'they do not claim to be innovators'. Significantly, they decided that there was a fruitful future for combined Morgan Grenfell/Morgan Stanley operations – that the Morgan family was a better unit than any other, such as a multinational corporation – but that any such arrangement had to fit in Morgan Guaranty and MECI.[22]

A fortnight later Stevens had dinner in New York with Sam Payne, Bill Sword and Sheppard Poor (the head of MECI). He later wrote that 'the only progress I can report is that my repeated insistence that (a) the Bank of England will not allow MS to take a large share in MG and (b) that MG would be weakened by splitting off its Corporate Finance activities into an MECI Limited are beginning to have some effect'. Yet ideas were beginning to emerge. Granted that 'Bill Sword continues to evangelise on the virtues of an MECI Limited mostly owned by MS and run by MG which will astonish the world', others in Morgan Stanley were looking at alternatives. At the dinner 'Shep Poor in particular threw out the idea of a Morgan International Ltd. located in e.g. Bermuda[23] which pooled the planning and the expertise of the members of the Morgan family. This concept I supported. All three continued to strike me as being genuinely interested to find a workable formula within the Morgan family'.[24] Although various ideas would be mooted over the following 15 months, discussion would return to the idea of a Morgan International – and Morgan Stanley would never shake loose from the conviction that whatever resulted from the talks, they should if possible control it.

It was only in August 1972 that Morgan Guaranty really joined in the talks. Stevens and Chappell went to New York and met Ellmore (Pat) Patterson (chairman), Walter Page (president) and Lew Preston (head of international banking) of Morgan Guaranty on 10 August: 'The meeting was very friendly. We got the impression that the full scope of our talks with MS was only beginning to dawn on them, and that they had imagined previously that they were being asked to bless some bilateral MG/MS arrangement rather than contribute to a general Morgan family exercise. They showed considerable interest in the larger operation'.[25] The code name for the discussions now became 'Triangle'.

Over the subsequent months there were visits back and forth, and Morgan Stanley and Morgan Guaranty men pored over Morgan Grenfell's books, trying to fathom just how a merchant bank did business. Ideas were proposed and discarded, although one to which Morgan Stanley stubbornly clung was that it could take a 50 per cent shareholding in Morgan Grenfell, and even the insistence of the Bank of England that it would not countenance the idea failed to convince.[26] By January 1973, however, the Morgan Stanley and Morgan Grenfell negotiators agreed that the possibility of setting up a 'Morgan International', which would handle the Morgan family's securities business outside the USA (and possibly outside the UK also), should be examined in greater detail.[27]

Back in February 1972, Stevens had predicted that 'our talks with MS will continue to lumber for some time at the end of which we may be faced with a situation that requires rapid thinking and decisions';[28] in March 1973 pressure was suddenly put on Morgan Grenfell. On 16 March Stevens 'spoke to Lew Preston [of Morgan Guaranty] on the telephone. He told me it looked as if MGT and Morgan Stanley were going to agree to set up Morgan International and, in his view, it would be a great pity if MG were not associated. When I reminded him that we had had nothing in writing setting out their ideas he promised that he would send a copy of the proposed plan. The 'Proposal for Discussion', dated 20 April 1973, arrived at Morgan Grenfell on 1 May, and the following afternoon the Morgan Grenfell Holdings Board met to consider it.

It was proposed that the three firms establish a new company, Morgan International, to conduct various activities outside the USA and Canada. Morgan Grenfell would continue its UK capital markets business and Morgan et Cie International would continue its international issue business. Morgan International would be owned 45 per cent each by Morgan Guaranty and Morgan Stanley and 10 per cent by Morgan Grenfell, and would increasingly be the focal point for the international non-commercial banking business of the three. Morgan Grenfell would continue as a UK firm, but instead of the 31.67 per cent shareholding by Morgan Guaranty, there would be substituted a 50 per cent shareholding by Morgan International. MECI would continue as a *banque d'affaires*, coming under the 100 per cent ownership of Morgan International.[29]

There is very little contemporary evidence that any member of the Holdings Board backed the plan as it stood, regardless of whatever feeling there might have been on the general advisability of some sort of joint venture with the two American cousins. The written reaction of David Bendall, who had joined the bank in 1971 from the Foreign Office to help Stevens develop the international side, was perhaps more trenchant than most, probably fuelled by the fact that he was a keen Europeanist. He pointed out that Morgan Grenfell were being asked to surrender not only currently profitable business, such as Eurobonds and project finance, but also future business in Europe, Asia, and so on. In return they would receive only 10 per cent (and for UK shareholders a net five per cent) of Morgan International's equity and profits. On the other hand, Morgan Guaranty and Morgan Stanley were giving up very little. Morgan Stanley, for example, were not willing to surrender their profitable Eurobond business in MECI, and the two in effect were only surrendering future possibilities. Further, Morgan International would clearly by American-dominated, and it was inconceivable that a British bank should develop its relations and business with other European countries under an American flag. In sum, 'this is a breath-takingly one-sided deal, favourable to MGT in particular, since they would have a very cheap entry to international investment banking. Meanwhile, MG will be bottled up for good in the UK. Europe is not the *foreign* market for MG but our future domestic market'.[30]

The scheme, in short, caused 'considerable ill-feeling'[31] in Morgan Grenfell; as one member of the bank later recalled, 'the Morgan Stanley boys were the real go-ahead graspers. You could see a mile off they were just there for the grab. They were assuming they would be entitled to boss the thing and lead it'.[32] The corporate finance directors were especially angry, and threatened to resign *en bloc* if the proposals were implemented.[33]

It transpired that the shape of the proposal resulted from the failure of the two American banks to agree. Morgan Guaranty were primarily concerned about investment management: 'they have reached a size in the USA (twice that of their nearest competitor) which meant that they are unlikely to be able to grow by any significant amount and they therefore wish to concentrate their efforts overseas. To this end they would like to see a unification of investment expertise'. Morgan Guaranty already had nearly 600 people in London, and stated that they would expect to control any joint company which dealt with investment management in London; the initial contribution of managed funds was likely to be Morgan Guaranty $500 million, Morgan Stanley $20 million and Morgan Grenfell $1.3 billion. Such a joint company would be the vehicle for world-wide activities in investment analysis and fund management. 'From MGT's point of view they are setting great store by a rationalisation of the Investment Management side more than anything else and whether we [Morgan Grenfell] participate or not they will certainly proceed to develop this side of their business as soon as possible'.[34]

Morgan Stanley, on the other hand, were more concerned with underwriting and thus with maintaining the position of MECI,[35] although the firm were not united in their approach to the negotiations. On the one hand, 'buoyed by its success in Paris, the firm felt understandably brash and confident and willing to go it alone abroad . . .' Yet not everyone was opposed. Sheppard Poor later said, 'The internationalists thought it would be beneficial to expand our ties overseas. The domestic people thought we would be giving away more than we were getting'. Worried about Morgan Stanley's limited capital [it was a partnership], Frank Petito felt strongly about his firm's need for Morgan Guaranty's deep pockets. But the chief executive, Bob Baldwin, was suspicious of foreign business, which he often saw as a waste of time and money, and failed to provide the necessary push.[36]

On a more personal note, the Morgan Guaranty people apparently had secret reservations about entering into a substantial joint venture with Morgan Stanley. 'As a former official at 23 Wall noted, "There was always a feeling at the bank that Wall Street [i.e., Morgan Stanley] was full of get-rich people." The salary differential had always been a sore point: ... in a good year ... even a junior partner [at Morgan Stanley] might earn more than Morgan Guaranty's chairman. Anyone who stayed at Morgan Guaranty had to believe it represented something superior'.[37]

For their part, Morgan Grenfell had a bundle of objections. If they were to become part of Morgan International, they believed that 'London was really the capital market of the EEC and that we regarded ourselves as an operation which should be used to lead the Morgan attack on business in this area'.[38] On the other hand, they would either be carved up, or at least lose their independence. The sentimental pull of the Morgan name meant more to the older directors, in particular to those with family connections with Morgan Grenfell, such as Harcourt [J.S. Morgan's grandson], Catto and Collins; they were drawn to the idea of a new House of Morgan, although not necessarily on the basis proposed. They were also the predominant non-institutional shareholders. The newer directors were more influenced by the pulling power of the Morgan name in gaining business, but they believed that in any case Morgan Grenfell were the lineal descendents of the first Morgan bank, and thus the Americans could not force them to give up the name (although an implicit threat was made). It is also significant that they were not shareholders, and thus would not gain from a share exchange, while losing control to the Americans. They also felt that Morgan Grenfell had begun to take off, particularly in banking and corporate finance, and indeed were considering their own plans for overseas expansion: they were thus loath to surrender the gains they had made and expected to make. All in all, it was clear to Morgan Grenfell that the next series of meetings between the three banks, to be held on 20–22 June 1973 at the Grotto Bay Hotel in Bermuda – usually a venue for honeymooners – would bring matters to a head.

By the time the meetings began, Stevens hardly knew what he wanted from the talks, if anything, but he thought that something might be salvaged. The opening statement by Morgan Stanley, however, made manifest what would become a fundamental reason for the failure of the talks: their refusal to put either their US issuing business or their Eurobond business into the Morgan International pot – what were they proposing to contribute? Stevens made an opening statement for Morgan Grenfell, and the two American firms

> were somewhat taken aback by our opening remarks in which we repeated that the Proposal was unacceptable, both to MG's Board and the Bank of England, that the concept of co-operation rather than union was far more practicable, and also outlined the areas of

> growth for MG which we saw as being likely over the next few years. In spite of the fact that the former had been communicated to them on several occasions in the past, this appeared to be the first time that they, and particularly Pat Patterson, appreciated the firmness of our views. It was necessary to reiterate that it would not be possible to increase the American involvement in MG both because we did not wish such a thing to happen and also because it was not possible if we wished to remain a member of the BBA (British Bankers' Association] and an Accepting House.[39]

Stevens then turned things over to Bendall. His argument was that since Britain was about to join the EEC, it would benefit all three houses if Morgan Grenfell had the flagship position in Europe, because they would have a better position compared with American banks. He added that Europeans did not like Anglo-Saxons, but they disliked the British less than the Americans. The meeting came to a rather rapid close after his statement, with the Americans asking for a recess; during this period the representatives of the two American banks plus Stevens – but not Bendall, by special American request – had a meeting, during which Stevens discovered just how badly the Americans had taken Bendall's remarks: the Americans' decision was that there was no need for further meetings. Apparently he had shocked them badly, since they had never, they said, found themselves unpopular in Europe. In general terms the Americans could be excused for being shocked: there is some reason to think that Stevens had not warned them that he had been unable to sell the concept of Triangle to his own colleagues, and therefore Morgan Grenfell's statement came, apparently, as a complete surprise.[40]

In an informal meeting between Stevens, Bendall and the two Morgan Guaranty men, Patterson and Preston, Preston 'reacted rather excitedly with a threat to sell out all MGT's shares in MG. [Patterson] was much calmer and suggested a further meeting on the following morning since lack of prior consultation had produced embarrassment to them and closer regular consultation should be established. We [Morgan Grenfell] raised again the fact that their present shareholding was not sacroscanct and they drew our attention to the problem of the name.'[41] However, Morgan Guaranty the following month underlined its desire to retain their one-third holding.

III

The whole enterprise had collapsed in a muddle of false expectations, resentment and embarrassment. In an attempt to salvage something from the fiasco, it was agreed that there would be quarterly summit meetings between Morgan Grenfell and the two American banks either in London or New York,[42] and these lasted until 1981. In addition, Morgan Grenfell and Morgan Guaranty made some effort to keep each other informed of their activities and to try and find specific areas of co-operation. At a meeting in September between directors of the two banks, they agreed that there should be a monthly meeting in London between one or two members of each group which would review the activities of the banks and discuss current problems and activities; this would be followed by the formal quarterly meetings. The first monthly meeting took place on 24 October 1973, at which it was further decided that representatives of Morgan Grenfell and Morgan Guaranty's London operation would attend certain of each other's departmental meetings. On the institutional level, discussions were held with both American banks, separately and in different years, about setting up a joint venture in the secondary eurobond market, but in each case Morgan Grenfell preferred to go it alone.[43]

In fact, each set of discussions with the American cousins seemed to intensify Morgan Grenfell's sense of being a *British* merchant bank more than being a Morgan bank. It was not that they necessarily wished to remain wholly separate and independent: even during the Triangle talks, merger discussions were in train with Robert Fleming & Co. in London, a merger/takeover with Brown Shipley & Co. was briefly mooted, and a substantial cross shareholding with Compagnie Financière de Suez – referred to as Triangle 2 – was being planned.[44] It was not that they did not appreciate the benefits flowing from being a Morgan bank, or from co-operation with their cousins. But what seems to have been the crux of the matter was control. While with a Fleming or Brown Shipley merger Morgan Grenfell would have expected to remain dominant, and while with a Suez cross-shareholding they would carve up or share areas but not try to run each other's businesses, with Triangle in particular dominance would clearly pass to the American banks. Objections took two forms: there was Bendall's and others' contentions that in the new EEC, a British bank would have to remain British to be accepted as a European bank; on a personal note, dominance by the two American banks would mean dominance by Americans in London, even if there was still an entity called Morgan Grenfell.

The overarching reason for Morgan Grenfell's desire to control their own destiny was clearly that by the early 1970s, they felt that they had a worthwhile destiny to control. The Triangle discussions intensified the growing feeling that the Morgan Guaranty one-third shareholding was beginning to constrain, and by July 1973 the directors believed that it should be reduced to 15 per cent. One very important constraint was that it was difficult, for legal and business reasons, for Morgan Grenfell to expand into the growing American market; the failure of Triangle triggered a decision to go ahead and in 1974 they sent a resident representative to New York, while in 1979 they opened their own branch there, which was incorporated as Morgan Grenfell Inc. in March 1980.[45]

Between 1973 and 1980, Morgan Guaranty continued to insist that they wanted to maintain their full shareholding in Morgan Grenfell, arguing that this formed an important part of their international strategy. However, the fact that they were not fully informed of Morgan Grenfell's plans nor allowed a seat on the board rankled, since a one-third shareholding meant that the Bank of England assumed that they stood behind Morgan Grenfell and expected the New York bank to share any losses.[46] By the late 1970s, in spite of the fact that they co-operated around the world, particularly in project finance, the two were clearly going their own ways.

The refusal of Morgan Grenfell to agree to a joint venture in Eurobonds, and particularly the decision to incorporate in New York, appear finally to have decided Morgan Guaranty to sell the shares as a block. But Morgan Grenfell wanted to retain their independence, and the purchase of 33 per cent of their shares would, because of the Takeover Code, necessarily have triggered off a full bid. Furthermore, it was feared that if Morgan Guaranty sold 100 per cent of their shareholding, it would be interpreted as a lack of confidence in Morgan Grenfell.[47] Therefore, a way was found both to give Morgan Guaranty their premium while allowing Morgan Grenfell's shares to find safe harbour: Morgan Guaranty's shareholding was converted into high-interest cumulative preference shares and placed with institutions.[48]

IV

And so ended the House of Morgan. Beginning as an American bank in London, it ended as two American banks and a London one. The emphasis on national identity is crucial. First of all, it meant that merger might bring geopolitical problems. Morgan Grenfell could and did arrange financing for Cuba and North Korea, while this was forbidden to the Americans.[49] What was of more substantial importance was that Morgan Grenfell were free to exploit the relationship Sir John Stevens had built up over the years with the Soviet Union, so that Morgan Grenfell became, and still remain, the London merchant bank with the closest links with the Soviet Union and Eastern Europe.[50] Cold War politics prevented the American banks from building up analogous links.

On the face of it, this very lack in the Americans' coverage might have been a strong reason for pushing for agreement with Morgan Grenfell, and perhaps it was. Banks in different hemispheres can bring together complementary strengths. But the reverse side of this can be cultural incompatibility, and certainly, cultural differences were very strong. This comes out most clearly between Morgan Grenfell and Morgan Stanley, since the Morgan Guaranty culture was closer to that of Morgan Grenfell in certain ways than to that of Morgan Stanley under its new leadership. Many in Morgan Grenfell simply could not stomach the blatantly go-getting nature of Morgan Stanley. There is a certain irony in the fact that a decade later, Morgan Grenfell would be exhibiting substantially the same approach, particularly in their corporate finance department.

In sum, Morgan Grenfell did not want to be run by Americans. Indeed, if such a merger between banks with a common tradition and continuing close links, but originating in and based in different countries, proved to be impossible, this underlines the difficulty of cross-cultural mergers. It also shows up the heavy-handed and conservative nature of Bank of England control at that time: certainly a lighter touch towards foreign control of banks would be required for London to consolidate its renewed position as a major international financial centre.[51] And there are little bits of evidence here and there that the resurgence of Morgan Grenfell and its desire to stand alone reflected their sense of this resurgence of London as a financial centre as it emerged from the shadow of New York.[52] In the end the banks' perceptions of their business priorities dominated and they finally separated, but it was a tribute to the power of the Morgan name and the sense of a shared history that it took them so long to do so.

NOTES

1. For details on the organisation of the various Morgan banks, and on their early histories in general, see K. Burk, *Morgan Grenfell, 1838–1988: The Biography of a Merchant Bank* (Oxford, 1989), Chs. 1–3; V.P. Carosso, *The Morgans: Private International Bankers, 1854–1913* (Cambridge, MA, 1987); and Morgan Guaranty Trust Co., Paris, H.O. Loderhose, 'History of Morgan, Harjes & Cie (Now Morgan & Cie), 1872–1932', April 1933.
2. Federal Reserve Committee on Branch, Group and Chain Banking, *225 Bank Suspensions: Case Histories from Examiners' Reports* (Washington, DC, 1932); H. van B. Cleveland and T.F. Huertas, *Citibank, 1812–1970* (Cambridge, MA, 1985), p.401, argue that the Federal Reserve study was incorrect in its conclusion and that the Depression, not banks' investments in bonds, caused the failures: 'The depression reduced the value of both loans and investments, reducing banks' net worth. It was merely easier to measure the depreciation in banks' bond accounts than in their loans, since bonds generally traded on a secondary market and could therefore be readily priced'.
3. Burk, *Morgan Grenfell*, pp.101–2.
4. R. Chernow, *The House of Morgan* (1990), pp.387–91.
5. Morgan Grenfell Group, London (hereafter MGG), the Secretariat, Chairman's Speech for 1949, given 29 June 1950, and for 1962, given 27 June 1963; Morgan Grenfell Holdings Minute Book 1971–80, board meeting, 21 Sept. 1977; Interview with Lord Catto, then the Chairman, 27 May 1987.

6. MGG, the Secretariat, Chairman's Speeches for 1952, 1953, 1955, 1956, 1959, 1960 and 1961, and Annual Review for 1967; interview with Lord Catto, 27 May 1987. For further details on the Australian and Canadian ventures, see Burk, *Morgan Grenfell*, pp. 226–8.
7. Chernow, *House of Morgan*, pp. 532–5.
8. Ibid., p. 541.
9. 'Regulation Q' derives from the Banking Act 1933 and subsequent amendments. The Act authorised the Board of Governors of the Federal Reserve System to issue regulations limiting the rate of interest payable on time deposits. The maximum rate for 3-month deposits was fixed at 2½ per cent until 1962.
10. MGG, MGP, Box P.667, File Morgan & Cie S.A., 1961 Formation etc., Allen to Collins, 7 Dec. 1960 and Catto to G. F. Verbeck, 30 Oct. 1960; Burk, *Morgan Grenfell*, p. 230.
11. MGG, MGP, Box P.667, File Morgan & Cie S.A., 1961 Formation etc., Catto to P. R. Legh, Bank of England, 30 Jan. 1962; Bank of England to Morgan Grenfell, 14 Feb. 1962; and Verbeck to Lord Harcourt of Morgan Grenfell, 23 Feb. 1962. The Secretariat, Annual Review for 1966. The two Dutch banks were Hope & Co. of Amsterdam and R. Mees & Zoonen of Rotterdam.
12. MGG, MGP, Box P.667, File Morgan et Cie S.A., 1961 Company Formation etc., Memos, A. M. Vagliano, 'Memorandum', Strictly Confidential, 30 Nov. 1961.
13. For details see Burk, *Morgan Grenfell*, pp. 231–2.
14. Chernow, *House of Morgan*, p. 549.
15. MGG, MGP, Box P.667, File Morgan & Cie S.A., Memos, 'Morgan et Cie: Proposed Participation of Morgan Stanley & Co.', 18 Sept. 1963; 'Morgan & Cie: Comments and questions on the numbered paragraphs of Morgan Stanley & Co. Memorandum of March 15, 1966', circulated in Morgan Grenfell 27 April 1966; 'Re: Morgan & Cie', 1 Nov. 1966; *New York Times*, 16 and 17 Aug. 1966; The Secretariat, *Annual Review for 1966*.
16. Chernow, *House of Morgan*, p. 549.
17. Ibid., pp. 582–8 and Burk, *Morgan Grenfell*, pp. 225–6.
18. Christopher Reeves Papers (private possession), File Triangle, 'Record of a meeting on 16/17 Jan. 1972'.
19. Reeves Papers, File Triangle, K. C. Barrington, 'Private and confidential memorandum to Holding Company Directors', 21 Jan. 1972. Sword added 'that in their view only the Rothschilds had an opportunity which was in any way comparable, but that they were too selfish to grasp it'.
20. Reeves Papers, File Triangle, Bank of England, 'Banking Mergers and Participations', November 1972. For analogous discussions on Bank of England restrictions on foreign ownership of banks see G. Jones, 'The British Government and Foreign Multinationals before 1970', in M. Chick (ed.), *Governments, Industries and Markets: Aspects of Government–Industry Relations in the UK, Japan, West Germany and the USA Since 1945* (Aldershot, 1990), pp. 204–5 and G. Jones, 'Competitive Advantages in British Multinational Banking Since 1890', in G. Jones (ed.), *Banks as Multinationals* (1990), p. 52.
21. Reeves Papers, File Triangle, Phillip Chappell, 'Secret Draft Memo', 27 Jan. 1972, circulated to Stevens, Barrington and Reeves.
22. Reeves Papers, File Triangle, Sir John Stevens, 'Visit to Morgan Stanley', ?11 Feb. 1972, secret memo sent to Lord Harcourt, Lord Catto and J. E. C. Collins of the Holdings Board.
23. The point about Bermuda was that all of this putative co-operation and combination had to take place outside the United States: any such agreement inside the USA would be illegal on anti-trust grounds and as contravening Glass-Steagall. The 1919 Edge Act, however, specifically permitted a commercial banker and a securities house to combine for business outside of the USA.
24. Reeves Papers, File Triangle, Sir John Stevens, 'Note on Morgan Stanley', 2 March 1972, Secret.
25. 'Visit of JMS and EPC to New York, 10 August 1972', Strictly Confidential, to all

Holdings and Bank Board Directors, 16 Aug. 1972, File Triangle, Reeves Papers. Preston had been head of Morgan Guaranty's London operation in the late 1960s.

26. 'Triangle Meeting at Morgan Guaranty, New York, Friday, 10th November 1972'; Bank of England, 'Banking Mergers and Participation', Nov. 1972; J.M.S., E.P.C., C.R.R., 'Triangle', 8 March 1973; J. Stevens, 'Note of conversation with the Governor of the Bank of England – 7th May 1973', 8 May 1973, all File Triangle, Reeves Papers. Interview with Sir George Blunden, 6 July 1987.
27. Reeves Papers, File Triangle, E.P.C., 'The Morgan Relationship', 1 Jan. 1973, circulated for discussion at the meeting on 17 Jan. 1973 of the Holdings Board.
28. Reeves Papers, File Triangle, JMS, 'Visit to MS', Secret Memo, 10/11 February 1972.
29. Reeves Papers, File Triangle.
30. Reeves Papers, File Triangle, Bendall to Reeves, copies to J.M.S., P.F. [P.F.P.], E.P.C., 4 May 1973. Peter Phillips pointed out that under the plan effective control of Morgan Grenfell would pass to the two American firms, which the Bank of England had already made clear would not be allowed, and therefore 'an overall Triangle operation' was necessarily put 'into abeyance for the time being'. P.F.P., 'Triangle: An Appraisal', 20 May 1973.
31. Reeves Papers, File Triangle, C.R.R., Record of a meeting on 6th May with Walter Page [of MGT]', attended by Harcourt, Stevens, Chappell and Reeves.
32. Quoted in Chernow, *House of Morgan*, p. 593.
33. Note from George Law to the author, 22 Sept. 1987.
34. Reeves Papers, File Triangle, C.R.R., Record of a meeting on 6th May with Walter Page (MGT's president].
35. Reeves Papers, File Triangle, C.R.R., 'Record of a meeting on 6th May with Walter Page'.
36. Chernow, *House of Morgan*, pp. 593–4.
37. Ibid., p. 593.
38. Interview with David Bendall, 2 June 1987.
39. Reeves Papers, File Relations with MGT after July 1973, Part 1, 'Triangle Talks in Bermuda on 20–22nd June with MGT and MI', 25 June 1973.
40. Ibid.
41. Ibid.
42. Reeves Papers, File Relations with MGT after July 1973, Part 1, E.P.C., 'Triangle', 31 July 1973. The Edge Act permitted both Morgan Stanley and Morgan Guaranty to meet Morgan Grenfell in Bermuda, since they were discussing non-US business; however, the summit meetings were intended to cover business throughout the world, and Morgan Grenfell therefore met either one or the other, but not the two together.
43. Reeves Papers, File Relations with MGT after July 1973, Part 2, 'Record of a Meeting in New York on 11th September 1973', and 'First Monthly Meeting between MG and MGT', 24 Oct. 1973. MGG, the Secretariat, Management Committee Minutes 1978. Burk, *Morgan Grenfell*, pp. 248–51.
44. Reeves Papers, File Triangle, P.F.P., 'Triangle: an Appraisal', 20 May 1973 and P.F.P., 'Triangle 2', 10 April 1973. Burk, *Morgan Grenfell*, pp. 202, 239.
45. Reeves Papers, File Relations with MGT after July 1973, Christopher Reeves, 'Triangle', 16 July 1973. Burk, *Morgan Grenfell*, pp. 246–50.
46. Reeves Papers, File Relations with MGT after July 1973, Part 1, Patterson to Harcourt and Stevens, 13 Aug. 1973.
47. Morgan Guaranty agreed to sell only 29.02 per cent in the first instance in May 1981; the remainder was quietly placed with friendly institutions in May 1982.
48. For details see Burk, *Morgan Grenfell*, pp. 253–5.
49. Chernow, *House of Morgan*, p. 592.
50. Burk, *Morgan Grenfell*, pp. 209, 214.
51. The situation is still problematical about the possibilities of foreign control of, or even substantial foreign investment in, clearing banks.
52. In 1976 Morgan Stanley International decided to build up a trading capability in the secondary Eurobond market and to site it in London rather than in Paris (Morgan Grenfell had already turned down tentative proposals to co-operate with them). G. W.

Mackworth-Young, the chief executive of MG, 'said that I welcomed their decision to move to London because it showed that foreigners still had confidence in the survival of London as a major international financial centre.' Reeves Papers, File Relations with MGT after July 1973, Part 1, GWM-Y, 'Memorandum', 26 May 1976.

INDEX